Selected Reading Lists and Course Outlines from American Colleges and Universities

World History

edited by
Kevin Reilly, World History Association

MARKUS WIENER PUBLISHING, INC.

Second Printing 1986
©1985 by World History Association

All rights reserved. No part of this book may be reproduced without prior permission from the copyright holder. For information, write to M. Wiener Publishing, Inc., 2901 Broadway, New York, NY 10025

ISBN 0-910129-23-1
Library of Congress Card No. 84-050565
Printed in America

TABLE OF CONTENTS

INTRODUCTION..7

I. World History Surveys and Introductory Courses

   A. One Year Sequence in 3 Quarters

      1. WILLIAM H. MCNEILL, University of Chicago
         "World History to A.D. 200"..........................9

      2. WILLIAM H. MCNEILL, University of Chicago
         "World History from A.D. 200 to 1750"...............12

      3. WILLIAM H. MCNEILL, University of Chicago
         "World History since 1750"..........................15

   B. One Year Sequence in 2 Semesters

      4. LYNDA SHAFFER, et al, Tufts University
         "Itinerary for a Tour of the Medieval World:
            History of Civilization before 1500"...........20

      5. LYNDA SHAFFER, et al, Tufts University
         "The Making of the Modern World"....................27

      6. ROSS DUNN, San Diego State University
         "World History to 1600".............................35

      7. ROSS DUNN, San Diego State University
         "World History after 1600"..........................40

      8. KEVIN REILLY, Somerset County College (N.J.)
         "World Civilization I" (to 1500)....................43

      9. KEVIN REILLY, Somerset County College (N.J.)
         "World Civilization II" (since 1500)................47

   C. One Term Survey

     10. GEORGE E. BROOKS, JR., Indiana University
         "World History".....................................54

     11. LOWELL J. SATRE, Youngstown State University
         "Introduction to World History".....................63

     12. TIM BRADSTOCK and MICHAEL GORDON, Denison Univ.
         "World History".....................................65

     13. AMY G. GORDON and DONALD G. SCHILLING, Denison Univ.
         "World History".....................................67

D. World History to 1500 in 1 Term

   14. WILLIAM DENNIS, AMY G. GORDON, and MICHAEL
       GORDON, Denison University

          "World History I: The World and the West"...........70

   15. AMY G. GORDON and KRISTEN B. NEUSCHEL,
       Denison University

          "The World and the West: The Civilization
              of Eurasia to 1500"...........................72

E. World History since 1500 in 1 Term

   16. CRAIG LOCKARD, University of Wisconsin at Green Bay
       "History of the Modern World"......................75

   17. ROBERT E. ROEDER, University of Denver
       "Historical Introduction to the Modern World".......86

   18. SARAH S. HUGHES, Hampton Institute
       "World Civilizations II"...........................94

   19. GEORGE HIGGINBOTTOM, Broome Community College (N.Y.)
       "The West and the World: Contemporary Problems
           in Historical Perspective"....................107

F. World History since 1500 in 2 Terms

   20. PHILIP D. CURTIN, The Johns Hopkins University
       "The World and the West" (1500-1800)...............110

   21. PHILIP D. CURTIN, The Johns Hopkins University
       "The World and the West: The Revolution of
           Modernization"...............................116

G. World History since 1900 in 1 Term

   22. CARTER FINDLEY and JOHN ROTHNEY, The Ohio State Univ.
       "Critical Issues of the Twentieth-Century World"...122

   23. MICHAEL ADAS, Rutgers University
       "The Twentieth Century"...........................127

II. Global, Comparative and Transregional History

H. Topical Global and Comparative History

24. RUDOLPH BELL, TRAIAN STOIANOVICH, and DONALD RODEN, Rutgers University
    "Global History: Love in History"...................130

25. RUDOLPH BELL, TRAIAN STOIANOVICH, and DONALD RODEN, Rutgers University
    "Global History: Death in Japan and Europe"........132

26. RICHARD D. FINK, Amherst College
    "Scarcity and Plenty in History"...................135

27. PETER KARSTEN, University of Pittsburgh
    "Comparative Military Systems".....................141

28. A.J.R. RUSSELL-WOOD, The Johns Hopkins University
    "Gold and Society in Colonial Brazil: A Comparative Approach" (Brazil, North America, Siberia, and South Africa)......................................150

I. Transregional History

29. LEE DANIEL SNYDER, New College of the University of South Florida
    "Ancient History Expanded, 1200 B.C.E. - 600 C.E.".157

30. ROSS DUNN, San Diego State University
    "Society and Culture in the Fourteenth Century: A Global Approach to a Medieval Age"..............158

31. WILLIAM R. ROFF and RICHARD W. BULLIET, Columbia Univ.
    "The Indian Ocean".................................162

J. Atlantic Global History

32. ARTHUR P. DUDDEN and PATRICK MANNING, Bryn Mawr College
    "History of Three Worlds - Africa, America, Europe"..................................167

33. JOHN GILLIS and ALEN HOWARD, Rutgers University
    "Global History: The Making of the Modern World, 1000-1984"................................174

K. Modernization

34. CYRIL E. BLACK, Princeton University
    "Comparative Modernization"........................182

35. JOHN BROOMFIELD, University of Michigan
    "Comparative Studies in Historical Cultures II: Progress or Decay? Conflicting Ideas on the Development of the Modern World"...................185

36. MICHAEL ZUCKERMAN, University of Pennsylvania
    "Tradition and Modernity"..........................193

L. Women in World History

   37. JOAN COCKS, ANNE EDMONDS, HAROLD GARRETT-GOODYEAR,
       EUGENIA HERBERT, and ANDREW LASS, Mount Holyoke College
       "Women, Spirituality and Power: Cross-Cultural
       Comparisons".......................................196

   38. BARBARA N. RAMUSACK, University of Cincinnati
       "Women in Asia: India, China, Japan"...............204

M. History of the Third World

   39. MICHAEL ADAS, Rutgers University
       "The Emergence of the Third World".................210

   40. CRAIG LOCKARD, University of Wisconsin at Green Bay
       "The Third World: Development or Despair?".........213

N. History of Global Events and Movements

   41. ROBIN W. WINKS, Yale University
       "The British Empire and Commonwealth: From the
       American Revolution to the "New Imperialism"".....222

   42. IVO BANAC, Yale University
       "History of the International Communist Movement"..225

O. History of Global Awareness and Influences

   43. TIM SHIN, Boise State University
       "Cross-Cultural History"...........................228

   44. AINSLIE EMBREE and ROBIN LEWIS, Columbia University
       "India in the Western Historical Imagination"......230

P. Interdisciplinary Comparative Social History

   45. SUSAN NAQUIN (History) and SUSAN WATKINS (Sociology),
       University of Pennsylvania
       "The Family in England and China: Continuity
       and Change"..233

   46. ISSER WOLOCH (History) and MYRON COHEN (Anthropology),
       Columbia University
       "Colloquium on Peasant Societies and their
       Transformation: France and China"..................240

About the Editor..244

   Documents have been reproduced from the originals submitted.

INTRODUCTION

The time for world history has arrived. Its teaching is becoming a matter of almost national concern. Already the variety of courses at Colleges and Universities is enormous. While more students are exposed to introductory survey courses, there is also a growing number of specialized, upper division, and graduate level courses in world history. This collection attempts to do justice to that diversity.

The first half of the volume concentrates on introductory and survey courses. These are courses which introduce students to the entire globe in some sense. They vary from cautious attempts to internationalize the "Western Civilization" course to boldly global visions that see Europe as a small peninsula. They vary in intention as well, from those that attempt to tell the story, or reveal the architectonic, or world history to those that employ the histories and experiences of the world's peoples to better understand historiographical, perennial, or current issues. And they vary in the breadth of time surveyed, from over ten millennia to under one hundred years.

The courses in the second half of the volume are organized to suggest some of the differing ways in which history courses have been (and can be) made "more global." While these courses do not generally attempt to survey the entire world, they suggest various strategies for internationalizing the history curriculum. These include topical and comparative approaches, studies of large geographical regions, modernization studies, concentration on large social or cultural units, investigations of global events

7

and movements, and even histories of cultural conceptions of the other and the foreign. All of these are ways to stimulate our students to think less parochially, and to prepare them for a far more integrated and far smaller world than existed in the first half of this century.

I would like to thank the National Council on Foreign Language and International Studies and Dr. David Wiley of Michigan State University for a grant under the "Project on International Education in Undergraduate Disciplines" that aided the collection of these syllabi. I am also grateful to Samuel R. Gammon and Jamil S. Zainaldin of the American Historical Association for their assistance in aiding our call. Without the officers and members of the World History Association, however, the task would have been impossible. Ross Dunn laid the groundwork with his "Sampler" of world history syllabi duplicated at San Diego State University. Drexel University, through the support of the World History Bulletin, has furnished a medium for our call and a continuing forum. Lynda Shaffer, Arnold Schrier, and other members of the Association provided invaluable help in gathering syllabi. This collection belongs literally to them, to the World History Association, to the contributors who generously consented to the publication of their efforts, and to all those who contributed course outlines that could not be included despite their quality and interest.

New York
November 1984

Kevin Reilly

University of Chicago

HISTORY 141 — Autumn 1982 — Instructor: Wm. H. McNeill
World History — Harper 130 — 962-8399 SS 513
2:30 M.W.F. — Assistant: James Grubb
— 324-4961

PROCEDURE

On Mondays the instructor will lecture, centering his remarks around slides. On Wednesdays he will attempt an explication of texts assigned for reading each week. On Fridays, you are invited to raise questions about any aspect of the week's work, with special attention to anything unclear in the assigned chapter of the textbook.

REQUIREMENTS

1. Students will write a short essay (not more than two pages) based on the primary readings assigned each week, except the last. Papers will be due at the beginning of the class hour on Mondays. Late papers NOT accepted.

   Note: Questions to be addressed each week are listed in the schedule. The effort is to make each of you a _real_ historian in the sense that you will be asked to answer a question _on the basis of primary source material_, i.e., the assigned readings. This means that taking others' ideas from the introductions, the textbook, and other secondary authorities is _not_ appropriate. Your intelligence, grappling with the data provided by the week's reading, is what ought to be at work. Additional background reading is, of course, permissible; but in general you are expected to work from what has been assigned.

   A satisfactory performance is one that connects your conclusion with the texts you have read directly and unambiguously. Judicious quotes, with page references, is a good way to do this. Page and line references without quotes often suffice. But some form of reference to the sources is vital for the instructor to be able to appraise your skill as an historian.

2. Students will be required to take two quizzes, administered in class on October 22 and December 3. Time: 30 minutes each. These quizzes are factual: will take the form of a list of names and technical terms mentioned in the textbook which you will be asked to identify. Brevity, accuracy, and the number of items answered will determine the score. Precise locations in space and time are particularly important for maximum scores. Part of the quiz will be geographical, asking you to locate cities and natural features on a map.

3. A final exam will be based on slides, which you will treat as historical source material in brief essays.

GRADES will be assigned on the basis of your six best essay grades (50%); the two quizzes (25%); and the final exam (25%). This means that two of the essays will not count. BUT essays will NOT be accepted late. If you fail to get your essay handed in when it is due, skip it, and start the next week with a clean slate. Missing more than two essays will mean commuting an F into your grade for those weeks you miss, unless sickness or some other special emergency requires you to interrupt your schoolwork. In such a case, special arrangements with the instructor must be made.

History 141   Wm. H. McNeill p. 2
SCHEDULE

Oct. 1   Slide lecture: Human Origins and the Neolithic Revolution.
            Reading: World History, Ch. I

Oct. 4-8   Rise of Civilization in Mesopotamia and Egypt.
                        Readings: World History, Ch. II
                        Oxford Readings in World History I
                            Enuma Elish, pp. 5-28;
                            Theology of Memphis, pp. 29-34;
                            Gilgamesh, pp. 82-152;
                            Si-nuhe, pp. 176-87.
            Essay topic: Can you see any connection between the religious
                        ideas of Mesopotamia and Egypt and the political
                        systems of the two lands, as sampled in our
                        readings? Due date: Oct. 11

Oct. 11-15 Rise of Empire in the Ancient Near East.
                        Readings: World History, Ch. III.
                        Oxford Readings in World History I
                            Sargon, pp. 52-56.
                        Oxford Readings in World History II
                            Hattusilis, pp. 31-42;
                            Biblical extracts, pp. 57-96;
                            Darius, pp. 117-134.
            Essay topic: All the rulers in our readings were usurpers.
                        How did they justify their power? Do you notice
                        any development across the centuries? Due: Oct. 18

Oct. 18-22 Rise of Monotheism in the Ancient Near East
                        Readings: Oxford Readings in World History II
                            Hymn to Aton, pp. 215-20;
                            Tutankhamen, pp. 221-25;
                            Biblical extracts, pp. 230-39;
                            Gathas, pp. 245-61.
            Essay topic: Are any of these texts clearly and unambiguously
                        monotheistic? How do they depart from the older
                        polytheism of Sumer as shown by Enuma Elish?
                        Due: Oct. 25

Oct. 22 --- First Quiz in Class, on Chapters I-III of World History.

Detailed weekly assignments for the balance of the quarter will be distributed as soon as possible. Topics, week-by-week, will be as follows:

    Oct. 25-29   Definition of Indian Civilization
    Nov. 1-5   Definition of Greek Civilization
    Nov. 8-12   Definition of Chinese Civilization
    Nov. 15-19   Flowering of Hellenism to 300 B.C.
    Nov. 22-25   Expansion of Hellenism, east and west, to 200 A.D.
    Nov. 29 - Dec. 3   Developments in the rest of the world to 200 A.D.
            Second quiz in class, Dec. 3. Based on World History, Chs. 4-7.
    Dec. 6-10   Final exam to be arranged.

Continuation - HISTORY 141, FALL 1982

Oct 25-29   Definition of Indian Civilization
             Readings: World History, Ch 4
                       Readings in World History IV
                          Arthashastra, pp. 19-36
                          Edicts of Ashoka, pp. 103-12
                          Vedic hymns, pp. 181-86
                          Upanishads, pp. 188-96
                          Buddhist stories, pp. 221-241
             Essay question: What changes in Indian religious idea
                do our texts indicate? Due Nov. 1

Nov 1-5   Definition of Greek Civilization
             Readings: World History, Ch 5
                       Readings in World History, III
                          Tyrtaeus, pp. 4-7
                          Anaxagoras, pp 14-18
                          Aeschylus, pp 21-37
                          Herodotus, pp. 38-44
             Essay question: How did Greek ideals differ from
                those of the Middle East according to
                our readings? Due Nov. 8

Nov 8-12   Definition of Chinese Civilization
             Readings: World History, Ch 6
                       Readings in World History V
                          Numerous Regions, pp. 115-19
                          Poems, pp. 244-63
                          Confucius, pp. 7-20, 55-58, 172-74
                          Ssu-ma Chi'en, pp. 142-52
             Essay question: What does Confucius share with
                the other three readings? Due Nov. 15

Nov 15-19   Flowering of Hellenism
             Readings: World History, Ch 8
                       Readings in World History III
                          Thucydides, pp. 46-68
                          Plato, pp. 72-100
             Essay question: How do our two authors regard the
                Anthenian polis?

Nov 22-25   Impace of Hellenism, east and west
             Readings: World History, Ch 9
                       Readings in World History III
                          Rosetta decree, pp. 104-13
                          Philo Judaeus, pp. 130-40
                          Extracts from the New Testament,
                             pp. 164-75
                          Juvenal, pp. 269-72
                          Marcus Aurelius, pp. 273-81
             Essay question: Compare Jewish to Roman interaction
                with Greek culture as reflected in our
                readings. Due Nov 29

Nov 29-Dec 3 Developments in the rest of the world to 200 A.D.
             Readings: World History, Chas 7, 10
             Second quiz in class DEC 3 based on World History
                Chs 4-10

Final exam   To be arranged   11

University of Chicago
History 142: World History 200-1750   W.H. McNeill, Instructor
                                                Office - SS-513
                                                Wednesday 3:30-5:00
                                                James Grubb, Assistant

Format of the course will be the same as last quarter. Weekly 2 page essays due each Monday; two quizzes as listed on the schedule; final exam based on slides.

Late papers will not be accepted. Grades will be assigned on the basis of your six best essays (50%); two quizzes (25%) and the final (25%).

Papers should answer the question <u>on the basis of the assigned readings</u>. Say only what the sources allow you to infer. The idea is to make you try to be real historians: answering a question from authentic source materials.

<u>Books to Buy</u>
   W. H. McNeill, <u>A World History</u>
   W. H. McNeill, <u>Readings in World History</u>, vols. 3, 4, 5,8 & 10
   Note: Vols 6 and 9 of <u>Readings in World</u> History are out of prints. Xerox selections from them will be available at the Seminary Bookstore, 58th and University for sale. These are marked with * in the assignments below. In addition, a few copies of the original books are on reserve in Harper but not enough to allow everyone to have easy access to the readings in the week when the essay is due, alas.

Jan 3-7   Flowering of Indian Civilization
              Readings: <u>World History</u>, Ch 11
                        <u>Readings in World History</u> Vol 4
                           Shakuntala pp. 72-81
                           Laws of Manu pp. 139-74
                           Bhagavad Gita pp. 88-100, 202-162

           Essay question: What do our readings tell us about caste in India?

Jan 10-14 Expansion of Indian civilization
              Readings: <u>A World History</u>, Ch. 12
                        <u>Readings in World History</u> Vol 3
                           Plotinos, pp. 197-204
                           Augustine, pp. 284-300
                        <u>Readings in World History</u> Vol 5
                           Mou Tzu, pp. 218-30
                           Liu I-min and Sung Chao, pp. 232-33
                        Xerox: <u>Chronicles of Japan</u>, extract

           Essay question: Compare Far Eastern reaction to Indian ideas with the outlook of Plotinos and Augustine.

Jan 17-21 Rise of Islam to 1000
              Readings: <u>A World History</u>, Ch 13
                        <u>Koran</u>, suras 3, 4, 6, 19, 24, 65, 73, 75, 76, 81, 82, 84
                        <u>Readings in World History</u> Vol 6
                           *Ibn Ishaq, pp. 16-22
                           *Al Tabari, pp. 75-81
                           *Shafi'i, pp. 136-42

           Essay question: What was the relation of Islam to Christianity and Judaism according to these readings?

12

Jan 24-28   Far East-Far West to 1000
            Readings: A World History, Ch 14
                      Readings in World History, Vol 7
                          Decrees, pp. 5-13
                          Wang An shih, pp. 36-45
                          Prince Shotoku, pp. 208-12
                          Taika reforms, pp. 214-18
                      Readings in World History, Vol 8
                          Beowulf, pp. 5-18
                          Rule of Benedict, pp. 22-33

    Essay question: Compare Chinese, Japanese and west European
    ideals of government as expressed in the readings.

Jan 31-Feb 4   Turks and Mongols.: Cross Cultural Contacts 1000-1500
            Readings: A World History, Ch 15
                      Readings in World History, Vol 6
                          *Ibn Al-Athar and Juvaini, pp. 248-62
                          *Rumi, pp. 241-43
                      Readings in World History, Vol 7
                          Firuz shah, pp. 147-60
                          Shankara, Kabir, Nanak, pp. 173-83
                      Readings in World History, Vol 8
                          William of Rubrick, pp. 270-81

    Essay question: Compare Moslem-Christian reactions to the
    Mongols with Moslem reactions to Hindus as attested in our
    readings.

Feb 7-11   Far East-Far West, 1000-1500
            Readings: A World History, Chs. 16, 17
                      Readings in World History, Vol 7
                          Shinto texts, pp. 243-254
                          Buddhist texts, pp. 256-71
                      Readings in World History, Vol 8
                          Christian texts, pp. 227-50

    Essay question: Compare religious ideas and observances in
    medieval Europe and Japan.

    First Quiz: In Class; Friday, Feb 11 on A World History, Chs 11-17 +
    geography.

Feb 14-18   Europe's Self Transformation I: Renaissance and Reformation
            Readings: A World History, Chs. 18, 19, 20
                      Readings in World History, Vol 10
                          Machiavelli, pp. 15-26
                          Luther, pp. 27-39
                          Loyola, pp. 45-52

    Essay question: Compare Machiavelli's outlook with that of our
    other authors.

Feb 21-26   Asian and African Responses down to 1700
            Readings: A World History, Chs 21, 22
                      Readings in World History, Vol 9
                          *Afonso, pp. 44-53
                          *Xavier, pp. 4-28
                          *Bungo, pp. 29-30
                      Readings in World History, Vol, 10
                          Berna Diaz. pp. 60-86

    Essay question: What assisted and what hindered European missionary
    efforts according to our readings?

Feb 28-Mar 4   Europe's Self Transformation, II: The Old Regime
       Readings: A World History, Chs. 23, 24
                  Readings in World History, Vol 10
                     Galileo pp. 88-98
                     Descartes, pp. 99-114
                     Bossuet, pp. 118-26
                     Locke, pp. 127-37
       Essay question: How do Christian faith and human reason get along
       with one another in our readings?

Mar 7-11   Asian and African Responses to 1850
            Readings: A World History, Ch 25
                       Readings in World History, Vol 9
                          *Equiano, pp. 75-89
                          *Sugita Gempaku, pp. 137-40
                          *Ram Mohun Roy, pp. 91-110
                          *Liu, pp. 111-118
            Essay question: How do you account for these diverse responses to
            Europeans and their ideas?
            Q   in class March 11, A World History, Chs 18-25 plus geography

Mar 14-18 FINAL EXAM: To be arranged

University of Chicago

HISTORY 143 W. H. McNeill, Instructor
Spring 1980

CLASS SCHEDULE

Procedure:
As before, on Mondays the instructor will lecture on the basis of slides; on Wednesdays he will use the texts assigned for the week as the basis for his remarks; and on Fridays you will ask questions about matters touched on in the readings, the lectures, and the assigned portion of the textbook.

Requirements:

1. A grade on five weekly essays (2 pp. maximum please).

2. A paper of 8-10 pages in length dealing with a topic that affects at least two of the world's civilizations in the period after 1789. This is due on May 30.

3. Two quizzes based on the textbook, on May 9, June 6..

4. A final examination based on slides, week of June 9-13.

Course grade will be assigned on the basis of an average of your grades in each of these exercises, 25% weight given to each of the four.

* * * * * *

The longer paper will allow you to try your hand at larger-scale historical writing than hitherto in this course. You are free to choose any topic that attracts you, and may read beyond the assigned course readings if you have time and wish to do so. On the other hand, papers may be written on the basis of the assigned readings only. Possible topics include:

a. Comparison of Japanese and Chinese reactions to western civilization since 1839, as illustrated in our readings.

b. Comparison of Hindu and Islamic reactions to western civilization since 1789, as illustrated in our readings.

HISTORY 143   page 2

      c. Industrialism and democracy in Europe and their impact on some other civilization, as illustrated in our readings.

      d. Military organization of two rival civilizations since 1789. (Not illustrated in our readings, so requiring outside work.)

      e. The frontier in European and American history. (Not illustrated in our readings and requiring outside work.)

These are merely illustrative suggestions; if in doubt about what to write on, consult your instructor, who will have recommendations about what you can best do.

      Clarity, conciseness and <u>accurate citation of your sources</u> are the qualities on which the papers will be judged—short and long. Awareness of time and place and of the possibility that things change both in time and space will be especially appreciated.

      * * * * * *

Books Required:

    McNeill, <u>A World History</u>. (As before, those who prefer may read <u>The Rise of the West</u> instead.)

    <u>Oxford Readings in World History</u>, vols. VI, IX, and X. A limited number of these texts are on reserve in Harper.

SCHEDULE:

Week of
31 Mar.- 4 Apr.   Islam in Opposition to Expanding Europe

        <u>World History</u>, Ch. 21
        <u>Readings in World History</u>, VI
            Kritovoulos, pp. 312-36
            Selim and Ismail, pp. 338-44
            Portraits of Three Monarchs, pp. 344-91

        Question: How do you account for Islam's continued expansion? Essay due 7 April.

HISTORY 143

Week of
7-11 April

Europe's Self Transformation I:
Renaissance and Reformation

World History, Chs. 19, 20
Readings in World History, X
    Vasari, pp. 3-14
    Machiavelli, pp. 15-26
    Luther, pp. 27-39
    Loyola, pp. 43-52
    Harrison, pp. 53-58

Question: Compare Europe's Renaissance and Reformation, as sampled here, with changes in the world of Islam, as studied last week.
Essay due 14 April.

Week of
14-18 April

European Oceanic Discoveries

World History, Ch. 18
Readings in World History, X
    Bernal Diaz, pp. 62-86
Readings in World History, IX
    Xavier, pp. 4-28

Question: Compare the Europeans' reactions to their encounter with Mexicans, Indians, and Japanese as recorded in these readings.
Essay due 21 April.

Week of
21-25 April

Asian and African Responses to 1700

World History, Ch. 22
Readings in World History, IX
    Bungo, pp. 29-30
    Hsu Kwang-ch'i, pp. 31-42
    Alfonso I, pp. 44-71

Question: Compare the three reactions to encounter with Europeans recorded in our readings. How do the three authors reflect their respective societies' circumstances?
Essay due 28 April.

HISTORY 143 page 4

Week of
28 Apr.- 2 May   Europe's Self Transformation II:
                 Old Regime

                 World History, Chs. 23, 24.
                 Readings in World History, X
                     Galileo, pp. 87-98
                     Descartes, pp. 98-114
                     Bossuet, pp. 117-26
                     Voltaire, pp. 139-42

                 Question: Compare the outlook of our four
                 authors of this week with the ideas of
                 those read in the week of April 7-11.
                 Essay due 5 May.

Week of
5-9 May   Asian and African Responses to 1850

                 World History, Ch. 25
                 Readings in World History, IX
                     Equiano, pp. 75-89
                     Ram Mohun Roy, pp. 91-110
                     Lin, pp. 111-18
                     Sugita Gempaku, pp. 137-40

                 First Quiz, on Chapters 18-25, in class
                 May 9,   30 minutes.

Week of
12-16 May   Europe's Self Transformation III:
                 Industrial and Democratic Revolutions
                 to 1914

                 World History, Ch. 26.
                 Readings in World History, X
                     Locke, pp. 127-37
                     Declaration of Rights, pp. 166-69
                     Robespierre, pp. 170-74
                     Owen, pp. 178-90
                     Marx and Engels, pp. 191-215
                     Bismarck, pp. 217-25

                 TITLE of your longer paper due May 12. In case
                 of doubt -- CONSULT!

HISTORY 143   page 5

Week of
19-23 May   Asian and African Responses to 1914

             World History, Chs. 27, 28
             Readings in World History IX
                 Kume Kunitake, pp. 141-43
                 Iwasake Yataro, pp. 144-46
                 Fukuzawa Yukichi, pp. 149-66
                 Vivekananda, pp. 170-83
                 Hu Shih, pp. 185-93
             Readings in World History VI
                 The Mahdi, pp. 463-68

             OUTLINE of your paper due May 19. Not more than
             a page.

Week of
26-30 May   Europe's Self Transformation IV:
             World Wars I and II

             World History, Ch. 29
             Readings in World History, X
                 Owen, pp. 229-33
                 Bolshevik Peace Proclamation, pp. 235-39
                 Wilson, pp. 241-47
                 Mussolini, pp. 249-62
                 Hitler, pp. 263-79
                 Roosevelt, pp. 280-85

             FINISHED PAPER DUE, 8-10 pages
             MAY 30.

Week of
2 - 6 June   Asian and African Responses

             World History, Ch. 30
             Readings in World History, IX
                 Nehru, pp. 222-31
                 Mao Tse-tung, pp. 240-51
                 Senghor, pp. 265-85
             Readings in World History, VI
                 Afghani, pp. 423-31

             Second Quiz, 6 June, on Chapters 26-30

FINAL EXAM: To be Arranged, Week of June 9-13.

Tufts University   ITINERARY FOR A TOUR OF THE MEDIEVAL WORLD   May 1984 **1.**
                  History 7, COMPARATIVE HISTORY OF CIVILIZATIONS BEFORE 1500.

The Guides, in order of appearance:

   Lynda Shaffer, History   Madeline Fletcher, Romance Languages   Peter Winn, History
   Steven Hirsch, Classics   Randall Packard, History   Dane Morrison, History
   Sugata Bose, History   George Marcopoulos, History   Howard Malchow, History*
   Leila Fawaz, History   Steven Marrone, History   Gerald Gill, History*
                                                                                          *Spring Semester Only
Arrival and Departure Times: In the 8-7 Block; M. W. Th 2:30-3:30

                                          THE SCHEDULE

Sept. 7   i. DATE OF EMBARCATION. Introductions.
Wed.

          ii. ROME AND THE ROMAN EMPIRE
              Local Guide: Steven Hirsch
              Empire and Transcontinental Trade

    The Roman demand for African and Arabian incense, African and Indian ivory, Indian
cottons, spices and gems and Chinese silk stimulated a further development of hemispheric
trade routes, including an Indian Ocean trade route that stretched from Africa to the
South China Sea. Since Rome and China were at opposite ends of the Eastern Hemisphere and
the Roman Empire extended onto the African continent, these two great empires and their
wants tended to draw the entire hemisphere together. India, strategically situated between
the two, at the center of the Indian Ocean, was in a position to facilitate this trade.
Emphasis in this section is placed upon those urban classes in Rome who came to enjoy a
life style that defined foreign products as necessities as well as luxuries, and the
merchant-travelers who made this possible. (The first official record of merchants from
the Roman Empire reaching China via a direct sea route is from 166 A.D.)

              Required Reading:

Sept. 8   Chester Starr, The Emergence of Rome as Ruler of the Western World, 2nd
Thur.   edition (Ithaca, N.Y.: Cornell University Press 1953) (paperback)
              Read the entire book. TO BE PURCHASED.

Sept. 12   William Arrowsmith (trans.), Petronius: The Satyricon, (New York: New
Mon.   American Library, 1959) pp. 38-84 ON RESERVE (Students may wish to purchase
              this book. 'It's not expensive.)

Sept. 14   G.W.B. Huntingford, The Periplus of the Erythraean Sea, (London: The
Wed.   Hakluyt Society, 1980) pp. 1-8, chapters 1, 19-31, 41-49, 54-66 (= pp. 19,
              31-38, 43-48, 50-57). In conjunction with reading, students should also
              consult map between pp. 76 and 77. ON RESERVE.

              Recommended Reading:

              M.P. Charlesworth, Trade Routes and Commerce of the Roman Empire (Cambridge,
              Eng., 1924) pp. 58-73, 98-111 ON RESERVE.

Sept. 15 iii. ROME'S TRADING PARTNERS: INDIA AND CHINA
Thur.   Local Guide: Lynda Shaffer

              Required Reading:

              Kenneth Hall, "Maritime Trade and Statecraft in
              Early S.E. Asia " MANUSCRIPT ON RESERVE, Chap. II, pp. 39-79.

SOUTH AND SOUTHEAST ASIA

I. A. GUPTA INDIA, ca. 320 A.D. to 535 A.D.
Local Guide: Sugata Bose
Capital at Pataliputra

Sept. 19 Mon.
Sept. 21 Wed.
Sept. 22 Thur.

After the Roman and Chinese Empires declined in the 3rd century AD, the land route across the Eurasian continent became more treacherous than usual. The maritime route gained importance, and India was the important pivot between Africa, Western Asia, and the Mediterranean on the one side and Southeast Asia and China on the other. Goods originating to the west were unloaded on India's Arabian Sea coast and trekked across the subcontinent to be put onto ships going through Southeast Asia to China. India became the place for East Asians to buy western goods, and those to the west to buy Chinese goods brought to India both by sea and by overland caravan. In northern India the Guptas assumed a key role in the development of this commercial contact and prospered from it.

Traces of Gupta influence and Gupta presence can be found from Africa to Japan. (It is most apparent in Southeast Asia.) Theirs was an impressive civilization with an advanced agriculture, great popular literature and art, and a booming sophisticated commercial sector. The Indians of the Gupta period are responsible for laying the foundations of modern mathematics: they conceived the zero, our "Arabic" numbers, and the decimal system that democratized mathematics. India during those centuries was also seen by its contemporaries as the center of learning and the center of the Buddhist faith. Students came from all over Asia to study there. In part, we will examine India through the eyes of one Chinese pilgrim-student, Fa Xian, who spent almost a decade on the Indian subcontinent.

Required Reading:
Romila Thapur. A History of India, Volume I. pp. 15-27, 109-193 ON RESERVE

Sept. 26 Mon.
Sept. 28 Wed.

I. B. JAVA (ca. 570-1500)
Local Guide: Sugata Bose
Borobudor built ca. 772 A.D.

The treatment of Java will be divided into two parts: an initial phase in which Javanese elites localized elements of Indian civilization, for their own reasons, and a second phase of "cultural independence" and flourishing that began at the turn of the 11th century. During the first phase the focus will be on the realm of the early Mataram monarchs of central Java and the temple at Borobudor (ca. 722 AD). The second phase begins with King Airlangga (1019-1049) and the shift in power to Eastern Java. This section will end with a study of the Majapahit kings, after the 13th century, and the entrepreneurs of this realm who promoted the production of spices for the world market. This unit on Java lays a foundation for the importance of Spice Islands in the second semester. (The Malay maritime state of Srivijaya and the mainland kingdoms such as Angkor will be covered in the process of describing Java's world. Comparisons among the various centers of Southeast Asia will be made.)

Required Reading:
Kenneth Hall, "Maritime Trade and State Development in Early Southeast Asia." Manuscript. ON RESERVE
Chapter I "Trade and Statecraft in Early Southeast Asia: An Historical Introduction" pp. 1-27, notes 28-38.
Chapter IV "Trade and Statecraft in Early Srivijaya" pp. 138-171, notes 172-185
Chapter V "The Sailendra Era in Javanese History" pp. 186-234, notes 235-258
Chapter VIII "Transitions in the Southeast Asian Commercial and Political Realm: 1000-1300 A.D." pp. 372-378, 394-412, notes 413-431

EAST ASIA

II. A. SONG CHINA, 960-1279 AD
Local Guide: Lynda Shaffer

Sept. 29 Thur.,
Oct. 3 Mon.
Oct. 5 Wed.

Capital at Kaifeng 960-1127, at Hangzhou 1127-1279

This unit focuses on the political, social, and commercial revolution of Song China: the end of aristocratic power, the triumph of the examination system, the peak of China's iron and steel industry, and the rise of a powerful commercial class. The invention of the printing press during Tang times had by the Song caused major social and political changes as exemplified by the regular selection of officials by exam. For the first time, the compass was used for navigation, and gunpowder was a factor in warfare. China's navy would remain the world's most powerful until the 15th century. We also examine the role that Confucianism and Buddhism played in these developments.

Required Reading:
Jacques Gernet. Daily Life in China on the Eve of the Mongol Invasion. (Original French edition, 1959. Stanford paperback, 1970) Required reading: pp. 13-112, 219-249 TO BE PURCHASED
Teng, Ssu-yu (Deng Siyu). "Chinese Influence on the Western Examination System." Harvard Journal of Asiatic Studies, Vol. 7, (1942-43) pp. 267-312. Required reading pp. 301-312. ON RESERVE
Joseph Needham. "Science and China's Influence on the World." In Raymond Dawson ed., The Legacy of China. (Oxford University Press, First edition, 1964. Paperback, 1971) pp. 234-308. Required reading: 234-252, 256-258, 290-294, 299-308 ON RESERVE Pages on water-mill
Robert Hartwell. "A Revolution in the Chinese Iron and Coal Industries during the Northern Sung (Song), 960-1126 A.D." Journal of Asian Studies, Vol. XXI, Number 2, (1962), pp. 153-162. ON RESERVE
Lo, Jung-pang (Luo Rongbang). "The Emergence of China as a Sea Power during the Late Sung (Song) and Early Yuan Periods." Far Eastern Quarterly, Vol 14, Number 4 (1955) pp. 489-503. Required Reading, pp. 489-503. ON RESERVE

II. B. JAPAN, 552-1467

Oct. 6 Thur.
Oct. 11 Tues.
(Mon. schedule)

Local Guide: Lynda Shaffer
Capital at Heijo (Nara) 710-784, at Heian (Kyoto) 794-1867

As in the case of Java, the focus on Japan has two parts. In the first section we emphasize that period when Japanese rulers borrowed from the continent. Buddhism brought clerks and literacy; Chinese statecraft brought centralization; Buddhist monasteries introduced new agricultural technologies; and urban centers developed for the first time. We then move on to the time of "cultural independence" when all the borrowings have become so Japanese that the Japanese themselves no longer think of them as foreign. The focus is on the world's first great novel, Lady Murasaki's Tale of Genji, and the society that produced it. We leave Japan just as the northern part of the country is beginning to figure in Japanese politics, and this feudal north is swamping the urban, aristocratic south.

Required Reading:
Varley, Paul H. Japanese Culture: A Short History, Praeger, 1973. pp. 3-94. ON RESERVE

ISLAMIC WORLD

III. A. ABBASID IRAQ CA. 750-1278
Local Guide: Leila Fawaz
Damascus, capital of Umayyad Caliphate 661-750

Oct. 12 Wed.
Oct. 13 Thur.
Oct. 17 Mon.

Baghdad, capital of Abbasid Caliphate 750-1258 Goldern Age, 850-1100
In this unit we examine the rise of Islam and the role that it played in creating what we now perceive of as the Middle East. In particular we examine the capital of the Abbasid caliphate, Baghdad. It, too, became a center of the arts and sciences, as well as a center of international trade and industry.

Required Reading:
S.N. Eisenstadt, The Political Systems of the Empires (N.Y.: 1963) pp. 3-32. ON RESERVE
"Baghdad," Encyclopedia of Islam, new ed. (Reference Desk)
J.J. Saunders, A History of Medieval Islam (Routeledge & Kegan, 1978) TO BE PURCHASED $8.95.

III. B. ISLAMIC SPAIN 710-1492
Local Guide: Madeleine Fletcher

Oct. 19 Wed.
Oct. 20 Thur.

Capital at Cordoba
As in the case of Java and Japan, we separate our treatment of Spain into a period of intensive Islamization and its cultural impact, and a period of "cultural independence" when Islamisized Spaniards challenged the old centers of culture and power. Spain (and Morocco) are seen as a crucial meeting place of products and peoples from Europe, the Middle East and Africa. Its architectural achievements are emphasized as well as its literature.

Required Reading:
Duncan Townson, Muslim Spain. (New York: Cambridge U. Press, 1973) 48 pages. ON RESERVE
James T. Monroe. The Shu'ubiyya in Al-Andalus: the Risala of Ibn Garcia and Five Refutations. (U. of California Press, 1970.) Read pp. 1-62 ON RESERVE

Oct. 24 Mon.
iv. ****DISCUSSION DAY****

Oct. 26 Wed.
v. ****MIDTERM****

SUDANIC EMPIRES OF WEST AFRICA 5.

	IV. A. GHANA (ca. 750-1203), peak 9th-11th C
	Local Guide: Randall Packard
Oct. 27	Capital at Kumbi-Saleh (aka Wagadou) now in S.E. Mauritania
Thur.	
Oct. 31	We examine the roots of empire on the West African savannah with reference
Mon.	to climate and geography, agriculture, trade and international commerce,
Nov. 2	traditional kingship, and the role of Islamic scribes. The Soninke kings of
Wed.	Ghana reigned over a realm that extended from the Senegal River on the west to the Niger River on the East (more than 600 miles), and from the Sahara in the north to the Bambuk gold fields in the south (about 400 miles). Ghana's wealth was legendary, and came in part from the salt and gold trade, but it also had a more mundane foundation based on local trade between the various climatic zones. (Kola nuts, the essence of which we now imbibe in cola drinks, were already a popular product of the West African rain forest in the medieval period.)

Required Reading:
Robert July. A History of the African Peoples. (New York: Charles Scribner's Sons, Third Edition, 1980) pp. 3-31, 122-145, 151-182, 57-79. TO BE PURCHASED.

	IV. B. MALI (ca. 1213-1473) peak in 14th C
	Local Guide: Randall Packard
Nov. 3	Cities: Boure-Niani (now in Guinea, one km from Guinea-Mali border),
Thur.	Jenne-Jeno and Timbuktu (both in contemporary Mali)
Nov. 7	
Mon.	After the demise of Ghana, the political center of gravity in West Africa shifted south and east to the western portion of the Niger River, from Mali's first capital, Boure-Niani (on the Sankarani tributary), to Jenne-Jeno, a commercial center on the rice-growing Inland Delta; to the Saharan "port" city of the Niger Bend, Timbuktu. Sundiata, a Malinke prince of what had been the Mandingo state, had founded the empire of Mali by 1240. In another hundred years the kings of Mali would reign over a land as large as Western Europe. During Mansa Musa's reign (1312-1337) Islam became well established at the court, and in 1324 he made an unforgettable pilgrimage to Mecca. (Among other things, he brought so much gold with him that its price in Egypt fell.) We examine the role of traditional religions and Islam, domestic and international commerce, the cities of the empire, and the structure of politics, as well as the demise of Mali and the rise of Songhay whose forces captured Jenne-Jeno in 1473.

Required Reading:
July, pp. 79-86
Susan and Roderick McIntosh. "Finding West Africa's Oldest City," National Geographic, Vol. 162, No. 3 (September, 1982) pp. 396-418. ON RESERVE.
D.T. Niane, ed., Sundiata: An Epic of Old Mali. (Essex, England: Longman Drumbeat, Third Impression, 1982) (US Distributor: Humanities Press, Atlantic Highlands, N.J.) pp. vii-viii, 1-96. TO BE PURCHASED.

CHRISTIAN WORLD

V. A. BYZANTIUM c. 330-1453
       Local Guide: George Marcopoulos
Nov. 10   Capital at Constantinople
Thur.   Focus on Macedonian Period, 9th to 11th centuries
Nov. 14
Mon.   Constantinople, the second Rome, was for many centuries the center of
Nov. 16   European commerce and industry. It was also under the aegis of the
Wed.   Byzantines that Christianity spread to many parts of Europe. In this
section we will examine the history of Christianity, including the origins
of its monastic movements. Byzantium's codification of Roman law,
architectural masterpieces, its hospitals and medical school, and its
silk industry all deserve some attention. We will spend time with Anna
Comnena, a historian and one of the leading political and intellectual
personages of her day. Byzantium's trading networks, which stretched from
northwestern Europe to India will be highlighted as well, with special
attention going to Kiev and the Varangians.

Require Reading:
Steven Runciman, Byzantine Civilization (Meridian Books, 1965)
    Chapters I, "Foundations of Constantinople," pp. 9-24; II, "Historical
    Outline," pp. 25-50; V, "Religion and the Church," pp. 87-108;
    VII, "Commerce," pp. 130-142; and XII, "Byzantium and the Neighboring
    World," pp. 222-240. ON RESERVE.

V. B. WESTERN EUROPE: THE PAPACY AND VENICE 381-1500
       Local Guide: Steve Marrone
Nov. 17
Thur.   In the first section we will examine the decline of Roman power and the
Nov. 21   Byzantine impact on Italy (including its cultural, religious, political, and
Mon.   commercial ramifications). The second section will once again focus on
"cultural independence," wherein we will examine the emergence of the papacy,
its efforts to Christianize Western Europe, the crowning of Charlemagne, and
ultimately, the break between the Roman Catholics and the Orthodox East,
which just happened to come at the same time that Venice managed to slip out
from under Byzantine commercial control. The third section will focus on
Venice, its commercial network, its politics, its challenge to Byzantium,
and the Renaissance.

Required Reading:
Robert S. Lopez. The Commercial Revolution of the Middle Ages, 950-1350.
    (Cambridge University Press, paperback 1976)
    Pages 1-70, 79-102, 106-119, TO BE PURCHASED.
Geoffrey Barraclough. The Medieval Papacy. (New York: Norton, 1979)
    Pages 27-52. (Chapters on "The Emancipation of the Papacy,"
    "The Papacy and the Franks," and "The Western Peoples and Rome."
    ON RESERVE.

Recommended Reading:
William H. McNeill. Venice, The Hinge of Europe, 1081-1797.
    (University of Chicago Press, 1974) Pages 1-89 (Chapters 1 & 2).
    ON RESERVE.

Nov. 23   ****DISCUSSION DAY****
Wed.

WESTERN HEMISPHERE

VI. A. MEXICO CA. 1 A.D.-1515 (AZTECS 1253-1515)

Local Guide: Peter Winn

Nov. 28 Mon. Aztec capital at Technochtitlan

Nov. 30 Wed.
Dec. 1 Thur.
Civilization, based on the cultivation of maize, beans, and squash, emerged in the Western Hemisphere, in Mexico and Peru, around 1000 B.C. This unit will focus on the Aztecs, after a discussion of the legacy of earlier Mexican civilizations: the Olmec, Teotihuacan, Mayan, and Toltec. This legacy was exceedingly rich. The Olmecs had domesticated cotton, and the Mayans had a writing system, calendars, astronomy and mathematics. Mayan mathematics had an uncanny resemblance to that of the Gupta Indians: a place system and a zero. The legacy of the Teotihuacan was one of empire, of commerce and cities, of chinampa agriculture (floating beds in lakes), and of monuments such as the pyramids near Mexico City. We will analyze the transformation of the Aztec peoples from wandering mercenaries to rulers of an empire. Of special interest are the commercial networks which linked the central plateau both with the northern frontiers and with the tropical lowlands to the east, west, and south, and the development of imperial religion.

Required Reading:
Jacques Soustelle. Daily Life of the Aztecs on the Eve of the Spanish Conquest. Stanford UP, pb., 1961. $4.95 pp. 120-162, pp. 163-203. TO BE PURCHASED.
R.C. Padden. The Hummingbird and the Hawk. Harper & Row pb., 1970 $4.95 pp. 2-99. TO BE PURCHASED.

VI. B. THE ANASAZI OF THE COLORADO PLATEAU
Local Guide: Dane Morrison

Dec. 5 Mon.
Dec. 7 Wed.
The focus here will be on the peoples of the Chaco Canyon in what is now New Mexico, U.S.A. By 1000 A.D. they lived in urban centers, possessed a sophisticated agriculture, a ritual calendar, and an artistic tradition (most evident in their pottery). We will be comparing the ideas of those scholars who see this development as completely locally generated with the ideas of Charles C. Diposos, who believes that long-distance traders from what is now called the Valley of Mexico stimulated this development.

Required Reading:
Edward Dozier. Pueblo Indians of North America, pp. 1-5, 31-43. ON RESERVE.
Thomas Y. Canby. "The Anasazi: Riddles in the Ruins." National Geographic, Vol. 162, No. 5 (November, 1982), pp. 562-592. ON RESERVE.

Dec. 8 Thur   ****DISCUSSION****

Dec. 21 12 Noon   ****FINAL EXAM****

Tufts University   WORLD HISTORY II   May 1984

                  History 08, THE MAKING OF THE MODERN WORLD

The Cast:

    Leila Fawaz, Middle East   Dane Morrison, North America
    Sugata Bose, South and Southeast Asia   Randall Packard, Africa
    Gerald Gill, North America   Lynda Shaffer, East Asia
    Howard Malchow, British Isles   Peter Winn, Latin America

In Six Acts:

        A Prologue: Patterns of the Past and Questions of the Present

   I.   The Established Centers of the Eastern Hemisphere, 1453-1620

  II.   The Globe Encompassed: Iberian Transoceanic Routes and the New World, 1415-1620

 III.   The North Atlantic Newcomers: Dutch, French, and English, 1600-1776

  IV.   Facing the Demands of the Industrial Revolution, 1776-1870

   V.   Competition and Partition: "Melon-slicing," 1870-1945

  VI.   International Systems and Decolonization: 1914-Present

        Epilogue: The Challenge of the South

Curtain Time: The 8-block. M.W.Th., 2:30-3:20

Books referred to on the syllabus:

    John J. Saunders (ed.), The Muslim World on the Eve of Europe's Expansion
    Norman Itzkowitz, Ottoman Empire and Islamic Tradition
    John H. Parry, The Establishment of European Hegemony, 1415-1715: Trade and
                Exploration in the Age of the Renaissance
    Alfred Crosby, The Columbian Exchange: Biological and Cultural Consequences of 1492
    Francis Jennings, The Invasion of America: Indians, Colonialism and the Cant
              of Conquest
    Gary Nash, Red White and Black: The Peoples of Early America
    Walter Rodney, How Europe Underdeveloped Africa
    Daniel Headrick, Tools of Empire: Technology and European Imperialism
    Tony Smith, The End of the European Empire: Decolonization after World War II

Jan 19　Prologue: Patterns of the Past and Questions of the Present　　　　Shaffer
Thur.

I. THE SETTING: THE ESTABLISHED CENTERS OF THE EASTERN HEMISPHERE, 1453-1620

UNIT THEMES. Unit 1 is an examination of the international "establishment" from roughly 1453 to 1620, from the Ottoman conquest of Constantinople to the end of the "golden ages" of the Turkish empires. Once one understands the international establishment of the hemisphere, one is in a better position understand both Iberia's motivation for sponsoring voyagers and the difficulties that confronted them. They were not sailing off into a vacuum. The routes they pioneered around Africa and across the oceans were new, but once they arrived at their destination, the old routes of the Indian Ocean and the seas of Asia, they were simply the new kids on a very old and established block.
　　The basic theme is that prior to the Iberian-sponsored voyages and for roughly a century or more thereafter, (from roughly 1450 to 1620) the entire Eastern Hemisphere could not escape the implications of its dynamic Turkish center. All across the Eurasian continent, from Spain to Ming China there was concern due to the expansion of these recently Islamisized steppe peoples. Furthermore, Islamic traders of many nationalities predominated on the hemisphere's international trade routes from the empire of Songhai in West Africa to the realm of Mataram in Southeast Asia, and "from Ghana to Ferghana," as the Arabs sometimes put it. In order to understand the non-Islamic edges, (Russia, Western Europe, Ethiopia, southern Africa, southern India, and East Asia) it is necessary first to understand this new Islamic power at the center, for it was new. Turkish peoples from the steppes of Asia had conquered the old Islamic centers and were expanding from them. To understand these territorial empires, both their strengths and their vulnerabilities, one must understand their origins and the structures, political, economic, and social, that held them together.
　　It is also necessary to understand the dynamic of the relationship between these Islamic powers and two non-Islamic powers, Venice and Ming China. Although not Islamic, they were a part of this same international establishment. Venice had for several hundred years acted as the Western European distributor for the Islamic center, and its fortunes rose and fell in tandem with these Asian powers, and it should be considered along with them. Ming China, at the opposite end of the Eurasian continent, was a major supplier of the international trade routes, and a consumer of its products, as well. Like Venice, it was a part of the system. Yet, Ming China feared the peoples of the steppes, especially the Islamisized Turks, and it was concerned about stability on the international routes, overland and oversea. In the early 1400s its navy was the most powerful in the world, and its ships were voyaging all the way to East Africa at the same time that the Portuguese were exploring a new maritime route down the West African coast. Understanding why the Chinese did not bother to round the Cape of Good Hope in order to find a sea route to western Europe helps to illuminate why the Portuguese did in order to find a new maritime route to Asia. In short, China was a part of the old establishment, Portugal was not.

　　　　　　　A. An Islamic Turkish Center

Jan. 23　　　1. The Ottoman Empire (1453-1923) (Peak 1522-1640)　　Fawaz
Mon.　　　　　Itzkowitz, xi-61
　　　　　　　Saunders, 1-30 49-55 129-136

Jan. 25　　　2. The Safavids of Iran (1501-1747) (Peak 1588-1629)　　Fawaz
Wed.　　　　　Saunders 31-47
　　　　　　　Roger M. Savory, "Land of the Lion and the Sun,"
　　　　　　　　in Bernard Lewis, Islam and the Arab World, 245-
　　　　　　　　254 and photos (ON RESERVE)

Jan. 26 Thur.		3. The Moguls of India (1526-1739, nom. to 1857) (Peak 1556-1605) Saunders, 69-82 S.A.A. Rizvi, "Muslim India," in Bernard Lewis, Islam and the Arab World, 301-310 and photos, (ON RESERVE)	Bose
Jan. 30 Mon.	B.	Outside Islam: The Opposite Ends of a Continent	Shaffer

    1. Ming China (1368-1644)(Manchus to 1912): Sea Voyages and Land Battles
       Wm. Willets, "The Maritime Adventures of Grand Eunuch Ho," in Journal of Southeast Asian History, Vol. V, No. 2 (September 1964) pp. 25-42 (ON RESERVE)

       Jung-pang Lo, "The Termination of the Early Ming Naval Expeditions," in James B. Parsons, (ed.) Papers in Honor of Professor Woodbridge Bingham: A Festschrift for his Seventy-fifth Brithday. (San Francisco: Chinese Materials Center, 1976) pp 127-140. (ON RESERVE)

    2. Venice and Europe (687-1797) (Peak 13th C to 1602)
       G.V. Scammel, The World Encompassed: "The Venetian Republic," 86-132 (ON RESERVE)

II. THE GLOBE ENCOMPASSED (ca. 1415-1620)
IBERIAN TRANSOCEANIC ROUTES AND THE NEW WORLD

THEMES FOR UNIT II. The periodization of this unit is based upon the linkages created between the eastern and western hemispheres by the Iberians. The 183 years from 1415 when Prince Henry the Navigator of Portugal captured the Moroccan port of Ceuta until 1622 when the Portuguese lost their fort at Hormuz, could be called "The Iberian Age." This label is appropriate not because Spain and Portugal dominated the globe. They certainly did not. Spain did capture the Pre-Columbian empires of the western hemisphere, but in the eastern hemisphere the Iberian impact was limited. At one end Songhai declined in part because of Portugal's new maritime routes and at the other, the Spanish had what was essentially a Mexican outpost at Manila, but in general the direct impact of the Iberians was felt only upon the sea lanes. Even in those areas where Portugal was able to capture coastal cities and trading entrepots, local traders generally managed to redirect their trade to alternative depots, which the Portuguese did not control. What was new and different, what was accomplished by the Iberians, was the circumnavigation of Africa and the creation of a totally unprecedented and earth-shaking linkage between the eastern and western hemispheres. For the first time two very separate worlds, two different biospheres, met and mingled. The globe had been encompassed. Not right away, but ultimately, the impact of this encircling, not just upon Europe, but upon the entire eastern hemisphere, would change the entire globe fundamentally. (American bullion and American food crops were introduced into Asia as well as Europe.) Some might argue that the European possession of the New World would become the most fundamental factor in explaining the 18th-century rise of the West.

Feb. 1 Wed.	A.	Meeting the Iberians: Where were they coming from? Parry 7-25	Winn
Feb. 2 Thurs.	B.	New Depots in West Africa and the Fate of Songhai Saunders 89-94 Parry 25-32 Rodney xi-xxiv 31-48 53-61 68-91 109 (3rd para)-113	Packard
Feb. 6 Mon.	C.	Destination: Spice Islands Parry 32-38 Saunders 83-87 John Villiers, "Trade and Society in the Banda Islands in the Sixteenth Century," in Modern Asian Studies, 15, 4 (1981) pp. 723-750 (ON RESERVE) Anthony Reid. "Trade and the Problem of Royal Power in Aceh: Three States: c. 1550-1700," pp. 45-49 (ON RESERVE)	Bose
Feb. 8 Wed.	D.	Old Depots and the Iberians: East Africa to Japan Parry 80-86 Rodney 48-52 Saunders 95-128 Itzkowitz 63-73	Bose
Feb. 9 Thur.	E.	Conquest and Coercive Labor in Spanish Territories: America and the Philippines to 1620 Parry 39-79	Winn
Feb. 13 Mon.	F.	Sugar, Slaves, and Plantations under the Portuguese Parry 114-116 Nash 156-161	Gill
	G.	Global Dispersions	
Feb. 15 Wed.		1. Crops, Animals, and Diseases Crosby xi-122	Packard
Feb. 16 Thur.		2. Bullion and Textile Flows Crosby 122-221	Winn

---

III. MEETING THE NORTH ATLANTIC PEOPLES, 1600-1776
DUTCH, FRENCH, AND BRITISH

THEMES IN UNIT III. It is in this unit that one sees the planting of British hegemony, but not the blossom. At the beginning of this epoch the Asian powers are still formidable, even though they must contend with the Portuguese on the sea routes. The Dutch and the English manage to take over the limited Portuguese position in Asia, with much Asian help. In fact, it might be more accurate to say that the Asians expelled the Portuguese with some help from the Protestant Europeans. Indeed, in East Asian waters Europeans were completely at the mercy of China and Japan, even on the seas. And, on the East African coast, where the North Atlantic nations were not involved, an alliance of Omani Arabs and Africans managed to roll back the Portuguese all the way to Mozambique, without any European assistance. With the exception of the Dutch position in the Moluccas and the Bandas (where they seized the spice islands), and on the southern tip of Africa (where they had a provisioning station), the northern European nations were still in a subordinate position. By the end of this epoch (with the exception of East Asia which had witnessed the rise of new and vigorous powers at the beginning of the epoch--the Qing Dynasty in 1644 and the Tokugawa in 1603) the Asian powers were in serious trouble, but the causes for their decline cannot be related to Dutch, French, or English power, per se. The causes were many and varied, and insofar as they related to the European maritime powers, they were indirect: inflation and other fiscal problems caused by New World bullion; population growth caused by the introduction of New World food crops, and trade route shifts initiated by the Europeans (from which Venice also suffered). However, the English were by 1750 well placed to benefit from the demise of the Safavids and the decline of the Moguls, their old sponsors.

In the Atlantic realm the story is similar. The North Atlantic nations started with the leftovers, those parts of the New World that the Iberians were not interested in. However, in the long run, these parts became exceedingly valuable additions to their mercantile realm. In the Americas, as in Asia, the Dutch were the leaders and France and Britain trailed behind. But, again, in the end, it was Britain that ended up with the strongest position. (This was in part due to their defeat of the Dutch in the Dutch-English wars.) In the Atlantic realm, as in Asia, we look at this process from the inside out, from the perspective of the Africans and Native-Americans as well as from the European side.

Feb. 21 Mon. Sched.	A.	Where were they coming from? Parry 93-133 149-169	Malchow
Feb. 22 Wed	B.	Old Depots, Old Powers and More New Customers Itzkowitz, 74-109 Iwao, Seiichi, "Japanese Foreign Trade in the 16th and 17th Centuries," ACTA ASIAT 30 (1972) 1-18 (ON RESERVE) Goodman, Grant Kohn, The Dutch Impact on Japan, pp. 8-34 (ON RESERVE) Leonard Karen, "The 'Great Firm' Theory of the Decline of the Mughal Empire," 151-167 (ON RESERVE) Parry, 143-148	Shaffer
	C.	Areas of Major European-Related Changes	
Feb. 23 Thur.	1.	The Javanese Realm and the Dutch Parry 93-133 149-169 Reid, pp. 49-55	Bose
Feb. 27 Mon.	2.	Native Americans, South Africans, and European Settlers Jennings 3-42 58-84 105-145 Nash 1-140 223-246	Morrison
Feb. 29 Wed.	3.	Slavery and Africa Rodney 92-109, 113-135	Packard
Mar. 1 Thur.	4.	Africans Abroad Nash 141-197	Gill
Mar. 5 Mon.	5.	New World Export Economies Jennings 85-104	Gill

Mar. 7 Wed.	6. India Partitioned Bingham, Conroy, and Ikle, A History of Asia, pp. 68-81 (ON RESERVE)	Bose

IV. FACING THE DEMANDS OF THE INDUSTRIAL REVOLUTION, 1776-1870

UNIT THEMES. This unit investigates an epoch in which the entire world faced a very new reality. Historians often point to the American revolution, to the political and intellectual revolution emanating from France, to the industrial revolution in England, and to the independence movements of Latin America. But there was another revolution, a revolution in the balance of world power, for this is the epoch in which European hegemony becomes real in the eastern hemisphere, in the old established world. For the first time, a European power can truly claim a global hegemony. But it was by no means an age of colonization, even though the takeover of India by the British East India company proceded apace, and France after 1830 was intent on seizing Algeria. Rather it was an era of decolonization in the New World and of a free trade revolution carried out by treaties, what the Chinese were to call "unequal treaties." The year 1776 was not only the year of the American Declaration of Independence, the first significant break in the mercantilist thrust emanating from Europe, it was also the year that Adam Smith published The Wealth of Nations, an argument for free enterprise and free trade. Both the enlightenment and the industrial revolution would set in motion forces that would bring an end to plantation slavery in the Atlantic realm. At the same time, it was an epoch in which European-Americans, drawn west by their thirst for land and enabled by their new technologies, would dispossess and finally defeat the Native-Americans of North America. In the U.S.A. it was the age of settlers, of cowboys and of Indians. We emphasize the global context for the generation of the industrial revolution in England, and the global impact that revolution had.

Mar. 8 Thurs.	A. Crisis in the System: American Independence Movements Nash 199-222 247-298	Morrison
	B. The Industrial Revolution at Home	
Mar. 12 Mon.	1. Industrialization in Britain	Malchow
Mar. 14 Wed. EXAM!	**** MIDTERM EXAM ON UNITS I-III	Mar 12 EXAM! Wednesday
Mar. 15 Thurs.	2. Free Trade in Britain	Malchow
	C. The Impact of the Industrial Revolution Abroad	
	Readings: Headrick, 3-95, 127-149, 180-191 Immanuel Hsü, The Rise of Modern China 183-269 (ON RESERVE)	
Mar. 26 Mon.	1. The Atlantic Realm	Winn
Mar. 28 Wed.	2. Native Americans and the Loss of a Continent	Morrison
Mar. 29 Thur.	3. Ottomans and the Mediterranean	Fawaz

Apr. 2 Mon.	4.	The Indian Ocean Realm	Bose
Apr. 4 Wed.	5.	Traditional Powers and Free Trade	Shaffer

V. COMPETITION AND PARTITION: "Melon-Slicing" 1870-1945

UNIT THEMES. The epoch from 1870 to 1945 is the age of colonies, an age that began with the Europeans carving up Africa and mainland Southeast Asia. The old rhetoric of free trade was largely abandoned and the European powers sought to mark off pieces of the world as their own. Even in those areas that were not formally colonized, such as Latin America and East Asia, "spheres of influence" served much the same purpose as colonies. Britain was no longer the paramount, unchallenged industrial power. New powers such as the United States, Japan, Germany, Russia, Belgium, and Italy could compete with Britain as a result of their own growing industrial sectors. New technologies developed in those industrial nations widened the gap in power between the West and the rest of the world at the same time that the Europeans discovered an old Asian remedy for malaria, quinine, which made it possible for them to survive in tropical regions. These new technologies allowed the Western powers to increase and intensify their presence around the globe. It allowed them to colonize. The process of carving and recarving continued through the settlements of World War I and World War II. Although colonies continued to exist, and indeed the colonial powers often intensified their control over the colonial areas after WWII, the system was already on the defensive after 1917, especially after the Leninist call went out against imperialism and Woodrow Wilson in his Fourteen Points proclaimed the principle of national self-determination. Thus this unit focuses on the years from 1870 to 1914.

Readings: Headrick, 96-126 150-179 192-210
Rodney, 135-281

Apr. 5 Thur.	A.	New (US, Japan, Germany, Russia, Belgium, Italy) and Old Powers in the Age of Steel and Gold	Malchow
Apr. 9 Mon.	B.	Changing Informal Spheres of Influence" in the "Independent" World, 1870-1930	Winn
Apr. 11 Wed.	C.	Formal Colonization in Africa and Asia	Packard
Apr. 12 Thur.	D.	Comparative Responses to Partition: Formal and Informal	PANEL
Apr. 15 Wed.	E.	Life in the Colonial World, to 1939	Packard

VI. INTERNATIONAL SYSTEMS AND DECOLONIZATION: 1914 TO THE PRESENT

UNIT THEMES. The thirty-one years from 1914 to 1945 were characterized by two opposing trends: the continued expansion of the colonial system and the power of the industrialized nations and increasing opposition to that power. From 1914 on, the European colonial powers were on the defensive, challenged by their neighbors in Europe, by the growing power of the U.S.A. and Japan, by those people within the "spheres of influence" and the colonized areas, and by the collapse of their own economies during the depression. World War I exposed the vulnerabilities of the colonial powers and stimulated the Bolshevik Revolution in Russia. The settlements that came out of that war were even more disruptive of the system, especially in East Asia and the Middle East (for example, the March

First Movement in Korea, the May Fourth
Movement in China, and the Arab Nationalist Movement in Saudi Arabia). In Latin America, especially, the effects of the depression stimulated profound disillusionment with the international economic order. It also had a profound impact on Japan and was in large part responsible for the paralysis of Japanese liberalism,and it served to increase the prestige and the significance of the U.S.S.R. In World War II, the allies had to rely on millions of soldiers from the colonies, as they had to a lesser extent in WWI, and they had to make promises to get the cooperation of the colonized. This, combined with the actions of both the United States and Japan during WWII (especially in the Southeast Asian theater where many Africans fought) and the growth of nationalist movements during the war, broke the back of the colonial system.

The years from 1945 to the present have witnessed the almost complete decolonization of the world. And yet, for the most part, the gap between rich nations and poor nations has not diminished. Many leaders of "southern" nations claim that colonialism has simply been replaced by neo-colonialism. Whether or not the problems of the South are caused by neo-colonialism, by the legacy of the colonial epoch, or by some other factors, the problems are real. Nor can we isolate ourselves from them. The year 1945 also marks the beginning of the age of nuclear weapons technology and the Cold War between the U.S.A. and the U.S.S.R. This hostility between the superpowers has created opportunities for the "south," but it has also involved various nations in Asia, Africa, and Latin America in international power struggles.

Readings: Smith vii-256

Apr. 19 Thur.	A. World War I as Destabilizer	Shaffer
Apr. 23 Mon.	B. Depression and its Meaning	PANEL
Apr. 25 Wed.	C. World War II and Decolonization	PANEL
Apr. 26 Thur.	D. The International Economic System: Neo-colonialism or interdependency?	Panel

Apr. 30 Mon.	****EPILOGUE: The Challenge of the South	Shaffer

May 10 Thur. EXAM!	****FINAL EXAM, 3:00 p.m.	May 10 Thur. EXAM!

San Diego State University
SYLLABUS

World History   Fall 1984
History 100   R. Dunn

<u>Course Description</u>: This is a course in the history of the human community from 500 B.C. to 1600 A.D. It differs from the traditional Western Civilization course (or the high school course inaccurately called "World History") in that it takes the entire globe as its field of historical study. Two ideas underlie the course. One is that the interdependence of mankind has deep roots in the past. This fact is not simply a consequence of twentieth century communications. No civilization or nation, no matter how far back in time, ever arose in isolation, but always as a consequence of its interrelations with neighboring and sometimes distant peoples and cultures. The second basic idea is that in order to understand the significance of man's interdependence in our own time, we must try to make sense of the history of the human race taken as a whole. We must try to make intelligible human history as if from a vantage point in outer space.

This course is not, however, a world survey of civilizations, countries, and dynasties. The history of mankind is more than the sum of the histories of particular nations or empires. The most important developments in history have not taken place merely within the boundaries of nations. Rather, their geographical and social range has almost always been greater than that, drawing peoples of different languages and cultures into a common historical experience. This course, then, will develop a number of themes stressing the interrelations of societies and cultures and comparing the experience of peoples and civilizations with one another. We will, however, also be concerned with the origins, development, and achievements of the major civilizations.

<u>Examinations</u>: We will have two examinations during the semester, plus a final exam during the testing period in December. All exams will consist of essay questions.

During the third week of classes, we will have a map quiz. Students must achieve a score of 72 out of 100 on the quiz or repeat it until they do. The map quiz does not count significantly toward the final grade, but all students must pass it in order to complete the course.

Study guides will be provided for the exams and the map quiz. Never miss an exam. Make-up tests will be given only if you supply documentation supporting your reasons for absence.

Participation: Assignments are given for each day of class. You should read the assignment carefully for each meeting. Participation in discussion and oral evidence of having read and understood the assignments will count toward your final grade.

Attendance: I will take attendance often and consider your record in arriving at your final grade. The lectures are like episodes in a continuing story. When you miss one, you lose some of the threads. Plan to come to class every time.

Weighting of Grades: Since we will not have objective examinations, the following proportionment of grades is only an approximation:

first hour examination	20%
second hour examination	30%
final examination	40%
participation and attendance	10%

Plus and minus grades will be awarded.

Office: AH 4123 (Tel. 265-6391)
  Office Hours: MWF 11-12 and by appointment

Required Readings:

L.S. Stavrianos, A Global History: The Human Heritage, 3rd edition
P. Bohannan and P. Curtin, Africa and Africana
A. Crosby, The Columbian Exchange
P. Curtin, Cross-Cultural Trade in World History
J. Gernet, Daily Life in China on the Eve of the Mongol Invasion
H. Smith, The Religions of Man

Week 1
Sept. 5   Introduction

Sept. 7   The Geography of Global History
          Stavrianos, Preface and chs. 1 and 2

Week 2
Sept. 10 Film/The Meaning of Civilization
          Stavrianos, ch. 3 (to 31)
Sept. 12 The Meaning of Civilization (cont.)
          Stavrianos, ch. 3 (31-45)
Sept. 14 The Meaning of Civilization (cont.)
          Curtin, Trade, 1-14, 60-75

Week 3
Sept. 17 Film/Mediterranean Civilization under Greek Leadership
          Stavrianos, ch. 5 (to 69)
Sept. 19 Mediterranean Civilization (cont.)
          Curtin, Trade, 75-81
Sept. 21 Map Quiz

Week 4
Sept. 24 The Hellenistic World
          Stavrianos, ch. 5 (69-71)
Sept. 26 Rome and the Unification of the Mediterranean
          Stavrianos, ch. 5 (71-81)
Sept. 28 Rome (cont.)
          Curtin, Trade, 90-101

Week 5
Oct. 1   Han China and the Unification of East Asia
          Stavrianos, ch. 7
Oct. 3   Han China (cont.)
          Smith, Religions, ch. 4
Oct. 5   Examination

Week 6
Oct. 8   Film/Hindu Civilization in India
          Stavrianos, ch. 6
Oct. 10   Hindu Civilization (cont.)
          Smith, Religions, ch. 2 (14-80)
Oct. 12   Expansion of Buddhism
          Stavrianos, ch. 4, Smith, Religions
          ch. 3 (90-139)

Week 7
Oct. 15   Sub-Saharan Africa and Its Links to the
          Intercommunicating zone
          Stavrianos, ch. 16 (to 206), Curtin and
                    Bohannan, chs. 2, 11, 12, 13,
                    (to 233)
Oct. 17   Invasions from the Steppe Lands
          Stavrianos, ch. 8 (to 111)

Oct. 19   Film/The Rise of Islam
          Stavrianos chs. 10 (to 137) and 12
          (to 156)

Week 8
Oct. 22   The Rise of Islam (cont.)
          Smith, Religions, ch. 6
Oct. 24   Civilization of the Abbasid Caliphate
          Stavrianos, ch. 10 (137-142)
Oct. 26   Abbasid Caliphate
          Curtin, Trade, 103-108

Week 9
Oct. 29   Film/The Emergence of Civilization in Europe
            Stavrianos, chs. 8 (111-114) and
            12 (156-160)
Oct. 31   Civilization in Europe (cont.)
            Stavrianos, ch. 14 (to 183)
Nov. 2   Film/The Economic Miracle of Sung China
            Stavrianos, ch. 13 (to 169)
            Gernet, chs. 1, 2, 7

Week 10
Nov. 5   Sung China (cont.)
            Curtin, Trade, 109-119
Nov. 7   Film/The Turko-Mongol Invasions
            Stavrianos, ch. 11
Nov. 9   Turko-Mongol Invasions (cont.)
            Stavrianos, ch. 13 (169-170)

Week 11
Nov. 12   Turko-Mongol Invasions (cont.)
            Curtin, Trade, 119-127
Nov. 14   Islamic Dominance of the Intercommunicating
            Zone
            Stavrianos, ch. 9
Nov. 16   Examination

Week 12
Nov. 19   Film/Africa and Islamic Expansion
            Stavrianos, ch. 16
Nov. 21   Africa (cont.)
            Bohannan and Curtin, chs. 13 (233-241)
            and 14 (to 252)
Nov. 23   Thanksgiving Vacation

Week 13
Nov. 26   Film/Civilization of Medieval Europe
            Stavrianos, ch. 14 (183-186)
Nov. 28   Medieval Europe (cont.)
            No assignment
Nov. 30   Civilization of Japan
            Stavrianos, ch. 13 (170-178)

Week 14
Dec. 3   Film/America before Columbus
            Stavrianos, ch. 17 (to 219), Curtin,
            Trade, 81-89
Dec. 5   Europe's World-wide Maritime Expansion
            Stavrianos, chs. 15 (to 195) and
            17 (219-221)
Dec. 7   Collapse of Civilizations in America
            Stavrianos, ch. 18, Crosby, chs. 1 and 2

Week 15
Dec. 10   Europe's Encounters with Asia and Africa
              Bohannan and Curtin, ch. 14 (252-260),
              Curtin, *Trade*, 127-260
Dec. 12   The Continuing Expansion of Islam
              Stavrianos, ch. 12 (160-163)
Dec. 14   Beginnings of the Modern World
              Crosby, chs. 3 and 5

SAN DIEGO STATE UNIVERSITY

SYLLABUS

World History   Spring 1984
History 101   R. Dunn

This is a course in the history of the human community from approximately
1600 to the present. This course differs from Western Civ. (or what is
misleadingly called "world history" in high school curricula) in that
the entire world rather than Europe is the focus of study. The central
question the course will ask is this: what is modernity (or the modern
world) and how have peoples and societies of the globe changed during
the past 300-400 years because of it? We will be particularly concerned with explaining the rise of Western Civilization to world
dominance during the past two centuries and the effect this has had on
peoples of Africa, Asia, and the Americas.

Required texts: L.S. Stavrianos, *A Global History: The Human Heritage*,
                     3rd edition
                  Chinua Achebe, *Things Fall Apart*
                  Donald Keys, *Earth at Omega*

Examinations: We will have two mid-term examinations and a final exam.
All exams will be essay type. Study guides will be provided for all
three exams.

Map Quiz: During the third week of classes we will have a fifteen
minute map quiz. A study guide will be provided. You must achieve
a score of 72 out of 100 in order to pass this test. The map quiz
will not count significantly in arriving at final course grades, but
you must repeat the test until you pass it in order to receive a final
grade.

Participation: Some time will be devoted to discussion during most
class periods. When class meets on Tuesday of each week, you should
have read carefully the assignments for that week and be prepared to
discuss or answer questions about them. Participation in discussion
and evidence of having read and understood the weekly assignments will
count toward your final grade.

Attendance: The class lectures are like episodes in a continuing
story. When you miss one, you lose some of the threads. Plan to
attend clsss every time.

Weighting of Grades: first mid-term   20%
                       second mid-term   30
                       final   30
                       participation   20
                       Plus and minus grades will be awarded.

Office: AH 4123 (tel. 265-6391)
         Office Hours: Tuesday and Thursday 1-3 p.m. or by appointment

World History   page 2

1. Jan. 24   Oblectives and Organization of the Course
       26   Phases of World History: 1500 to the Present

             Stavrianos, Preface xiii-xiv

2. Jan. 31   The World in the Sixteenth Century
   Feb. 2   Sources of Western Power: Political and Economic

             Stavrianos, chapter 21
             Daniel R. Smith, "Geography as a Tool to Understanding
                World History"

3. Feb. 7   Sources of Western Power: Scientific and Intellectual
   Feb. 9   Map Quiz and Discussion

             Stavrianos, chapters 14, 15, 22 (315-320)

4. Feb. 14   Rise of the Atlantic World: The Dominance of Europeans
   Feb. 16   The Atlantic Economic System and the Role of Africa

             Stavrianos, chapters 18, 19 (277-281), and 28 (to 411)
             Curtin and Bohannan, "The End of Isolation" and "The
                Era of the Slave Trade"

5. Feb. 21   The Russian Frontier of Settlement
   Feb. 23   Mid-Term Examination

             Stavrianos, chapters 20 and 24 (to 362)

6. Feb. 28   The Islamic World and the Forces of Modernity
   Mar. 1   China and the Forces of Modernity

             Stavrianos, chapters 10 (recommended only), 13 (170-
             174), 26 (to 388)

7. Mar. 6   The Atlantic World in Revolution: The Americas
   Mar. 8   The Atlantic World in Revolution: Europe

             Stavrianos, chapters 19 (281-287) and 23 (to 350)
             "The Declaration of Independence"

8. Mar. 13   Industrial Capitalism in Europe
   Mar. 15   Nineteenth century Frontiers of European Settlement

             Stavrianos, chapters 22 (321-334), 23 (350-356), and
                29
             Frank Thistlethwaite, "Migration from Europe Overseas in
                the Nineteenth and Twentieth Centuries"

9. Mar. 20   Africa and the World Economy
   Mar. 22   The Islamic Region and the World Economy

             Stavrianos, chapters 25 and 26(388-394)
             Curtin and Bohannan, "The Secondary Empires of the Pre-
                Colonial Century"

World History

10.	Mar. 27	China, Japan, and the World Economy
	Mar. 29	Mid-Term Examination

   Stavrianos, chapter 27

11.	Apr. 3	Europe's "New Imperialism"
	Apr. 5	African and Asian Responses to the New Imperialism

   Stavrianos, chapter 28 (412-420)
   Achebe, Things Fall Apart

12.	Apr. 10	World War I
	Apr. 12	Global Aftermath of World War I

   Stavrianos, chapters 24 (362-372), 33

13. Spring Recess

14.	Apr. 24	Global Aftermath of World War I (continued)
	Apr. 26	Origins of World War II

   Stavrianos, chapters 32, 34, 35

15.	May 1	Patterns of World Power after 1945
	May 3	Nationalism and Social Change in Africa and Asia

   Stavrianos, chapters 36, 37, 38

16.	May 8	Development and Dependency in the Third World
	May 10	Hopes and Fears of the Nuclear Age

   Stavrianos, chapter 39
   Keys, Earth at Omega

World Civilization I
Fall, 1984   Somerset County College

Instructors:

                Bud McKinley, room S-345, ext. 307 -- MWF classes
                Kevin Reilly, room S-338, ext. 299 -- TRF classes

Reading:

                Kevin Reilly, *The West and the World*, vol. 1 or
                    combined vol. (abbreviated as "WW" below)

                The Epic of Gilgamesh

                H. Hesse, *Siddhartha*

                The Bible

                Alfred W. Crosby, Jr., *The Columbian Exchange:
                    Biological and Cultural Consequences of 1492*

                Robert Goldston, *The Sword and the Prophet*

                Kakuzo Okakura, *The Book of Tea*

Classes and Assignments:

I. MEN AND WOMEN

    Aug. 27/28   Introduction to course;
                    *Video: *The World*: 1. Human Origins

    Aug. 29/30   Discussion of WW pp. 5-9: Human nature vs.
                        human history

    Aug. 31   Discussion of WW pp. 9-20: Cave men and women.
                    Video: *The World*: 2. The Agricultural Revolution

    Sept. 5/6   Discussion of WW, chap. 2: Was there a neolithic
                        matriarchy? How old is the patriarchy?

*Note to World History Association edition of syllabus:

"Video: The World" refers to "The World: A Television History"
based on *The Times Atlas of World History*, previewed for course
use during this semester. The full series should be available
for broadcast and distribution in 1985 or 1986.

World Civilization I
Fall, 1984/Page 2   Somerset County College

Classes and Assignments (continued):

II. CITIES AND CIVILIZATION

    Sept. 7   Video: The World: 3. The Birth of Civilization
                       Film : The Ancient Egyptians

    Sept. 10/11   Discussion of WW, chap. 3: What is civilization?
                       What does it have to do with city life?

    Sept. 12/13   Discussion of The Epic of Gilgamesh, pp. 61-119.
                       What does The Epic tell us about ancient city
                       life?

    Sept. 14   Video: The World: 4. The age of Iron
                                   5. Greece and Rome

    Sept. 17/18   Discussion of WW, chap. 4: Where would you
                       rather live? Athens, Alexandria, or
                       Rome? What can we learn from these
                       ancient cities to improve our own?

    Sept. 19/20   Review for exam. Bring your own questions.

    Sept. 21   Exam

III. CULTURE AND SOCIETY

    Sept. 24/25   LOVE AND SEX. Discussion of WW, chap. 5:
                       Where do our ideas of love and sex come from,
                          Greece or Rome?

    Sept. 26/27   WAR AND PEACE. Discussion of WW, chap. 6:
                       What can we learn from the Romans about the
                       causes of war and peace?

    Sept. 28   INDIVIDUALITY AND SOCIETY. Discussion of
                       chap. 7; What are the social "causes"
                       of individuality? Are we becoming more
                       or less individualistic?

IV. RELIGION: East and West

    Oct. 1/2   Discussion of Siddhartha, pp. 1-61. What
                     is "religious" here? How is this like
                     or different from what you know as
                     religion?

World Civilization I
Fall, 1984/Page 3

IV. RELIGION: East and West (continued)

Oct. 3/4 Discussion of Siddhartha, pp. 63-152 (conclusion). Who was Siddhartha? What was his message? How is it similar to, or different from, others you have heard.

Oct. 5 Video: The World: 6. The World Religions. Discussion: How are the religions of the world similar or different?

Oct. 9 HINDUISM AND BUDDHISM. Discussion of WW, pp. 153-163.

Oct. 10/11 ASIAN RELIGION. Discussion of WW, chap. 8, complete.

Oct. 12 Film: Asian Religion.

Oct. 15/16 The Bible: Genesis, chap. 1-5 and chap. 15; Exodus, chapters 19-21; Leviticus, chapter 1; Job, chapter 1; Psalm 23.

Oct. 17/18 The Bible: Isaiah, chapters 1, 5, 9. Daniel, chapters 1-4 and 11-12.

Oct. 19 The Bible: Mark, chapter 1. Matthew, chap. 1, 6, 23, 24. Acts, chapters 9 and 15. Romans, chapters 1 and 15.

Oct. 22/23 Exam

V. RELIGION AND SOCIETY: The Traditional World

Oct. 24/25 LOVE AND DEVOTION. Discussion of WW, pp. 183-192.

Oct. 26 Discussion of WW, pp. 192-204: Do we still practice "courtly love?" How is the tradition of love in the West different from that of Japan?

Oct. 29/30 Video: The World: The End of the Ancient World. Discussion of WW, pp. 205-212. Why did Rome and the ancient world decline?

Oct. 31/
Nov. 1 WAR AND VIOLENCE. Discussion of WW, pp. 212-230. Is Christianity a peaceful or violent religion? Video: The World: 9. Europe Recovers.

World Civilization I
Fall, 1984/Page 4

V. RELIGION AND SOCIETY: The Traditional World (continued)

Nov. 2	Introduction to Islam: Professor Osman Ahmed.
Nov. 5/6	ISLAM. Discussion of <u>The Sword and the Prophet</u>, pp. 16-49.
Nov. 7/8	Video: <u>The World</u>: 8. Islam. Discussion of <u>The Sword and the Prophet</u>, pp. 50-86.
Nov. 9	Discussion of <u>The Sword and the Prophet</u>, pp. 87-108. And WW, pp. 230-235. Are we less violent now?

VI. CITY AND COMMUNITY

Nov. 12/13	Video: <u>The World</u>: 13. China. Discussion of <u>WW</u>, pp. 239-249: The Chinese City.
Nov. 14/15	Video: The World: 10. The Mongol Onslaught. Discussion of <u>The Sword and the Prophet</u>, pp. 109-132.
Nov. 16	Video 11: The Expansion of Europe. THE EUROPEAN CITY. Discussion of WW, pp. 249-265.

VII. ECOLOGY AND EXPLORATION

Nov. 19/20	Discussion of WW, chapter 12.
Nov. 26/27	Video: <u>The World</u>: 14. China. Discussion of <u>The Book of Tea</u>, pp. 1-41.
Nov. 28/29	Discussion of <u>The Columbian Exchange</u>, chapters 1 & 2.
Nov. 30	Discussion of <u>The Columbian Exchange</u>, chap. 3 Video: <u>The World: 15. Americas</u>.
Dec. 3/4	Discussion of <u>The Columbian Exchange</u>, chap. 4
Dec. 5/6	Discussion of <u>The Columbian Exchange</u>, conclusion.
Dec. 7	Review. Bring your questions.

World Civilization II			Somerset County College
Kevin Reilly				Spring, 1985

READING:

Kevin Reilly, The West and the World, vol. II (or combined edition)

Chinua Achebe, Things Fall Apart

Daniel R. Headrick, The Tools of Empire: Technology and European Imperialism

Orville Schell and Joseph Esherick, Modern China

Louis Fischer, Gandhi

Erich Fromm, Escape From Freedom

This course is organized around seven important issues of modern society. Each issue is a shorthand for a number of questions that our society is currently asking. They might be briefly summarized in the following way:

1. POLITICS: Can politics be moral? Is the best government the least government? Can democracy work?

2. ECONOMICS: Is our economy fair? How can it become more productive? What are the causes of our economic difficulties?

3. ECOLOGY: How can we take better care of our environment? Can we become more independent of foreign energy? Will we survive?

4. RACISM: What breeds prejudice and discrimination? How can racism be curbed or eliminated? Can government end it?

5. COLONIALISM: What makes one country try to control another? Can we use the technological and political power of the U.S. for the good of other countries? Does power lead to involvement and war?

6. REVOLUTION: How should the U.S. respond to revolutions in the world? Can the U.S. accept communist revolutions? Can the U.S. accept independence movements?

7. INDIVIDUALITY: Are we losing our sense of individuality? Is modern culture too threatening? Are we giving up the search for hard solutions to social problems?

World Civ. II/Page 2
K. Reilly/Spring, 1985

The readings in the course are selected to provide a sense of the history of the problem, the past experience of others with similar problems, and an understanding of the directions of change. The more fully we can see each of these issues in a broader historical context, the better prepared we will be to act as intelligent citizens in a shrinking, fragile, and interdependent world.

CLASSES AND ASSIGNMENTS:

UNIT I: POLITICS

Jan. 16   Introduction to the course.

Jan. 18   Discussion of Achebe, part I, chapter 1. What is the political value in this society of the following: fame, personality, wealth, family, age, "titles"? How is this different from our own society?

Jan. 21   Discussion of Achebe, part I, chapter 2. How "democratic" is this society? How are public decisions made? What is the main unit of political authority?

Jan. 23   Discussion of Achebe, part I, chapters 3 and 4. How are economic decisions made here? What is the relationship between economic and political decisions? How is this different from our own society?

Jan. 25   Slide presentation on Cameroon, West Africa, and discussion of Achebe, part I, chapters 5 and 6.

Jan. 28   Discussion of Achebe, part I, chapters 7-10. What role does the family and clan play in politics? How important is the individual to the family, clan, or village?

Jan. 30   Discussion of Achebe, part I, chapters 11-13. What happens when an individual disobeys the clan? How would the events described in the novel occur differently if there had been a more centralized political authority like the state?

Feb. 1   Discussion of The West and the World, chapter 13 (pp. 297-308). How are the issues faced by Machiavelli similar to (and different from) those faced by Okonkwo?

World Civ. II/Page 3
K. Reilly/Spring, 1985

Feb. 4   Discussion of The West and the World, pp. 308-
            314. How has the modern state changed political
            behavior? How have different social classes
            changed traditional political behavior? What
            is meant by the "ethic of process?"

Feb. 6   Discussion of The West and the World, pp. 314-
            327. How is "market society" different from
            Umuofia? What did Hobbes see as the implications
            of market society for political behavior? Why
            did he think democracy was impossible? Why did
            Locke think it was possible?

UNIT II: ECONOMIES

Feb. 8   Discussion of The West and the World, chapter 14
            (pp. 329-339). What is capitalism? How did it
            develop? Was the economy of Umuofia capitalist?
            How did it work?

Feb. 11   Discussion of The West and the World, pp. 339-
            352. What have been the successes and failures
            of capitalism and capitalist industrialization?

Feb. 13   Film-strip on the Industrial Revolution.

Feb. 16   Discussion of The West and the World, chapter 17
            (pp. 411-418) and film-strip on The French
            Revolution.

Feb. 18   Discussion of The West and the World, pp. 418-428.
            How about Fourier? What's your passion? Should
            it have to pay? What is socialism?

Feb. 20   Discussion of The West and the World, pp. 428-445.
            Does Marx have anything to say to us today?

UNIT III: ECOLOGY

Feb. 23   Discussion of The West and the World, chapter 16
            (pp. 385-402). To what extent are our ecological
            problems economic?

Feb. 25   Discussion of The West and the World, chapter 20
            (pp. 507-522). What is the contemporary version
            of our ecological crisis? What are the causes?

Feb. 27   Discussion of article on Manville and asbestos,
            "Left in the Dust," in free copy of The Village
            Voice. What is the local version of the problem?
            What are the causes?

World Civ. II/Page 4
K. Reilly/Spring, 1985

    March 1   EXAM

UNIT IV: RACISM

    March 4   Introduction to problem of racism.
                      Selections from film: "Black History: Lost,
                      Stolen or Strayed."

    March 6   Discussion of The West and the World, chapter 15
                      (pp. 355-367). What were the cultural roots of
                      white racism? How significant do you think they
                      were in the development of prejudice?

    March 8   Discussion of The West and the World, pp. 367-
                      382. What was the burden of slavery? What has
                      been the relationship between racism and slavery?

    March 18   Discussion of The West and the World, chapter 18.
                      Has racism diminished since slavery, or merely
                      changed its form?

    March 20   Lecture: American Segregation and South African
                      Apartheid.

UNIT V: COLONIALISM

    March 23   Introduction and discussion of The Tools of Empire,
                      pp. 3-54.

    March 25   Discussion of The Tools of Empire, pp. 58-111.
                      Compare the role of quinine and arms in the
                      European conquest of Africa.

    March 27   Discussion of Achebe, Part II (pp. 119-156).
                      What did Christianity do for Africa?

    March 30   Discussion of Achebe, Part III (completion)
                      and The Tools of Empire, pp. 115-124.
                      Compare the role of religion and arms in the
                      conquest of Africa.

    April 1   Discussion of The Tools of Empire, pp. 129-164.
                      Did the European colonizers unify or divide the
                      world?

    April 3   Discussion of The Tools of Empire, pp. 165-210
                      (completion). What was the lasting legacy of
                      European imperialism?

World Civ. II/Page 5
K. Reilly/Spring, 1985

UNIT VI: REVOLUTION

April 8   Discussion of <u>Modern China</u>, chapters 1-3
           (pp. 1-59). What were the effects of Western
           involvement in China? What did the revolution
           of 1911 accomplish?

April 10   Discussion of <u>Modern China</u>, chapters 4-6
           (pp. 61-143). How did communism come to
           China? What did the communist revolution
           accomplish?

April 13   Slide lecture on contemporary China.

April 15   Discussion of <u>Gandhi</u>, part I (pp. 1-49). -
           The film "Ghandi" will be shown on video-cassette
           in the video lounge of the College Center at
           announced times. You will be expected to see
           the film at least once so that you are able to
           discuss the images and interpretation presented
           in class.

April 17   Discussion of <u>Gandhi</u>, part II, pp. 50-102.

April 20   Discussion of <u>Gandhi</u>, part II, pp. 102-153.

April 22   Discussion of <u>Gandhi</u>, part III (conclusion),
           and slide lecture on contemporary India.

UNIT VII: INDIVIDUALITY

April 24   Discussion of <u>The West and the World</u>, pp. 467-
           472, and <u>Escape From Freedom</u>, chapter III (pp. 56-
           122). Has modern culture increased our freedom
           and individuality, or not?

April 27   Discussion of <u>The West and the World</u>, pp. 472-486
           and <u>Escape From Freedom</u>, chapter IV (pp. 123-156).
           What have been the effects of capitalism, protestan-
           tism and industrialization on our feelings of
           individuality and freedom?

April 29   Discussion of <u>The West and the World</u>, pp. 286-493
           and <u>Escape From Freedom</u>, pp. 231-264. Excerpts
           from film: "The Twisted Cross". Did some Germans
           support Hitler? Why? Could that happen again?
           Could it happen here?

May 1   Discussion of <u>The West and the World</u>, pp. 493-502
           and <u>Escape From Freedom</u>, chapter VII (pp. 265-303).
           Are we free? Are we individuals?

World Civ. II/Page 6
K. Reilly/Spring, 1985

May 3   Discussion of The West and the World, chapter 21.
         How is our "modern culture" different from cultures
         of the past? What are the possible routes beyond
         "modernism," historicism, and uncertainty? Which
         are the better routes?

RECOMMENDED ADDITIONAL READINGS:

Students are encouraged to read more than the assigned readings
when time permits. Such additional readings can be the basis for
"extra credit" reports to the class, book reviews, or papers that
explain what you learned. There are innumerable possibilities for
such additional reading. Many suggested titles are listed in the
"For Further Reading" section at the end of each chapter of The
West and the World. The following is meant to be a short list of
suggestions.

UNIT I: POLITICS

    Francis Bebey,   King Albert (a novel set in Cameroon)
    N. Machiavelli,   The Prince
    Thomas Moore,   Utopia
    Carl Becker   The Declaration of Independence
    Alexis de Tocqueville,   Old Regime and the French Revolution

UNIT II: ECONOMICS

    Robert Heilbroner,   The Worldly Philosophers
    Karl Marx & Friedrich Engels,   The Communist Manifesto
    E.L. Jones,   The European Miracle

UNIT III: ECOLOGY

    William Cronon,   Changes in the Land: Indians,
                                    Colonists, and the Ecology
                                    of New England
    Morris Berman,   The Reenchantment of the World
    Carolyn Merchant,   The Death of Nature: Women, Ecology,
                                    and the Scientific Revolution

UNIT IV: RACISM

    Marvin Harris,   Patterns of Race in the Americas
    George M. Fredrickson,   White Supremacy: A Comparative
                                    Study in American and South
                                    African History

World Civ. II/Page 7
K. Reilly/Spring, 1985

UNIT V: COLONIALISM

   Eric R. Wolf,   Europe and the People Without History
   George Orwell,   Burmese Days (a novel)

UNIT IV: REVOLUTION

   Ida Pruitt,   A Daughter of Han: The Autobiography of a
                              Chinese Working Women
   Jean Chesneaux,   Peasant Revolts in China, 1840-1949
   Lucien Bianco,   Origins of the Chinese Revolution, 1915-1949
   Jonathan D. Spence,   The Gate of Heavenly Peace
   Gandhi,   An Autobiography

UNIT VII: INDIVIDUALITY

   Natalie Zemon Davis,   The Return of Martin Guerre (and the movie)
   Richard Sennett,   The Fall of Public Man
   Christopher Lasch,   The Minimal Self

Indiana University   B391 World History   Fall 1983
Mr. Brooks   TR 2:30-3:45

The books listed below serve as texts for the course. Additional readings
are assigned from books held on reserve at the Undergraduate Reserve Desk.
   World Map, National Geographic Magazine (December 1981)
   McNeill, W., A World History (C.U.P., 2nd ed. 1971 is preferable to
      3rd ed., 1979)
   Historical Atlas of the World (Barnes and Noble paperback)
   The Economist is required reading for the course. Current (via air mail)
      issues are available at the Periodical Room of the Library and the
      School of Business Library.

There will be a map quiz (T Sept. 22), a mini-exam (T Sept. 29), a mid-term
examination (T Oct. 20), a mini-exam (R Nov. 19), and a final examination
(R Dec. 17). Undergraduates are responsible for a short paper analyxing a
"less-developed" country. Graduate studengs have the option of a term paper
or preparing a lesson plan incorporating a World History topic. Papers are
due Thursday, Nov. 12. (See handouts concerning papers).

World outline maps (Denoyer--Geppert #24099 or #25099) are available at the
bookstore. Bring a map to class for the map quiz on September 22 and for each
examination. You will be tested from the following list. Not all the following
are on the map handout, which is intended only as a guide. Use other large
scale maps to ensure precise locations. You are also responsible for knowing
the world's principal ecological areas depicted n the Physical Environment Map
at the back of McNeill, A World History (1st and 2nd editions only)

OCEANS AND SEAS   ISLANDS

Black   Arabian   Ceylon (Sri Lanka)   Mozambique
Adriatic   Red   Crete   Arguim (Cape Blanco)
Baltic   Indian Ocean   Cyprus   Sao Tome
Persian Gulf   Caspian   Sicily   Singapore
South China Sea   Yellow   Philippines   Kilwa (Tanzania)
Agean Sea   Madagascar   Utica
                                     Sumatra   Canary
RIVERS   Socotra   Madeira
                                     Zanzibar   Hong Kong
Amazon   Ganges   Balearic
Nile   Indus   Cape Verde
Tigris   Hwang Ho   Macao
Euphrates   (Yellow)   Goa
Congo   Yangtze   Normuz
Zambezi   Rhine
Danube   Senegal
Jaxartes/Syr-Darya

CITIES

London   Benin   Goa   Florence   Nagasaki
Rome   Calcutta   Vienna   Nara   Genoa
Carthage   Peking/Beijing   Kano   Sarai   Hamburg
Alexandria   Tokyo   Elmina (Ghana)   Paris   Meroe (Sudan)

Athens	Singapore	Ceuta	Malindi	Old Delhi
Axum	Istanbul	Damascus	(Kenya)	Timbuctu
Jerusalem	Sofala	Kiev	Cadiz	
Mecca	Mexico City	Marseilles	Lixus	
Canton	Baghdad	Venice	(Larache)	
		Moscow	Lepcis/Leptis	

PLACE NAMES

Pyrennes Mountains	Macedonia	Mongolia
Balkans	Inca Empire	Fertile Crescent
Cape of Good Hope	Ethiopia	Caucasus
Cape Horn	Malacca	Sahara Desert
Aztec Empire	Hong Kong	Olduvai Gorge
Aragon	Phoenicia	Valley of Tehuacán (Mexico)
Castile	Peru	Gibraltar
Kush (Nile Valley)	Ghana, Mali & Songhai	Kongo Empire
Lake Turkana/Lake Rudolph	Empires (West Africa)	(West-Central Africa)
(NE Africa)	Monomotapa Empire	Bering Strait
Zimbabwe	(East-Central Africa)	
Akjoujt (Mauretania)	Benin Empire	
	(West Africa)	

Lectures and Assignments

It is _imperative_ that you read the assignments _before_ class to understand fully the lectures and participate intelligently in the discussion periods. If you are not prepared to comply with this prerequisite you should withdraw from the course.

The illustrations and maps in A World History are an integral part of the text and will amply repay you for frequent perusal and reflection. McNeill's Rise of the West (available in paperback) is an even richer historical master work and most rewarding readings. You are urged to obtain a copy and browse sections as they relate to your assignments.

A number of handsomely illustrated studies are included on the reading list. A few minutes perusal of the photographs and illustrations in these works will be of great help in remembering the names and places discussed in the assignments. Systematic reading and browsing will pay enormous dividends in mastering--and enjoying--the material assigned for the course. Note: some of the Reserve assignments are listed in my name under E431-E432 - African History. Journals are not placed on Reserve; use the call numbers.

Assignments

T Sept. 1   Introduction

R Sept. 3   The Contemporary--and Future--World
    Linton, R., "One Hundred Per Cent American," The American
         Mercury, AP2 A54 Vol. 40 (1937), 427-429
    Fuller, R. B., "Remapping our World," Today's Education
         L13 N165 U (Nov.-Dec. 1974), 40-44; 107-110.

Assignments   -3-

                Jastrow, R., "Post-Human Intelligence," Natural History
                  QH 1 N2 (U) (June-July 1977), 12-18
                Daly, M. & Wilson, M., "Sex and Strategy," New Scientist
                  Q1 N44 (4 January 1979), 15-17. On Reserve.
                Caiden, N. and Wildavsky, A., Planning and Budgeting in Poor
                  Countries, "Prologue" (i-iv) HC 59.7 C28
                The Economist, H1 E 22, May 13, 1978, 86-87, "Grabbing the
                Oceans," March 3, 1979, 56-57, "A Great Change has Started."
                Garreau, J., The Nine Nations of North America, 1-13, and maps
                  following p. 204, E38 C37

T. Sept. 8   Paleolithic to Neolithic "Evolution"
                McNeill, World History, 3-21
                Howell, F.C., Early Man (Time-Life), passim. QH 368 .H83
                Piggot, S. (ed.) Dawn of Civilization, 19-40 passim.
                  CB301 .P63
                Bacon, E. (ed.) Vanished Civilizations, "The Fertile
                  Sahara," passim. CB311 .B12
                Davidson, B., African Kingdoms (Time-Life), 33-57. 960 DAV
                The Epic of Man (Time-Life), 11-65. CB301 .L72 (shelv after Z)
                Went, F. W., The Plants (Life Nature Library) Ch. 8.
                  QK50 W43

R Sept. 10   The Secondary Neolithic: Tigris-Euphrates, Nile, and Indus
                  Valleys
                McNeill, chapter 2
                The Epic of Man (Time-Life), 66-95
                Piggott, Dawn of Civilization, 41-96 passim
                Casson, L., Ancient Egypt (Time-Life) DT60 .C34
                Shinnie, M., Ancient African Kingdoms, 23-42 passim
                  Dt25 .S551
                Watson, F., A concise History of India, 11-29 passim.
                  DS 436 W338

T Sept. 15   Eurasia to c. 500 B.C.; Indo-European Migrations
                McNeill, chapters 3, 4, 6, 7
                Epic of Man (Time-Life), 194-207 96-159 passim
                Bacon, E., Vanished Civilizations, 299-322 passim
                Piggott, Dawn of Civilization, 97-276 passim, 301-357 passim
                Bourliere, F., Eurasia (Time-Life) QH179 .B77
                Watson, India, 30-37 passim.

R Sept. 17   Mediterranean Civilizations: Phoenicians, Greeks, and Romans
                McNeill, chapter 5; 127-162/129-165
                Bovill, E.W., The Golden Trade of the Moors, Chapters 2, 3,
                passim
                Davidson, B., African Kingdoms, (Time-Life), 79-99
                Piggott, Dawn of Civilization, 329-357 passim
                Bowra, C.M., Classical Greece (Time-Life) DF78 .B78
                Hadas, M., Imperial Rome (Time-Life) DG272 .H12
                McEvedy, C., The Penguin Atlas of Ancient History is a
                useful study guide for those seeking a detailed knowledge
                of the area G1033 .M142

Assignments

T Sept. 22   Eurasian Social and Cultural Interchanges
McNeill, Rise of the West, 316-386 passim.
Bowra, C., M., Classical Greece, 69-78 157-171 passim.
Map Quiz
Watson, India, 39-70 passim.

R Sept. 24   The First Closing of the Ecumene; China and the Roman Empire
McNeill, chapter 10, 11
Wolpert, S., India, 35-46 passim DS436 .W86
Davidson, B., Lost Cities of Africa, chapter VI
Bacon, Vanished Civilizations, 251-278
Piggott, S., The Dawn of Civilization, 277-300
Critchfield, R., "Heirs of Confucious," Agenda (AID)
Sept. 1981, 15-20.

T Sept. 29   The First Closing of the Ecumene, II; Outrigger Adventurers
and Growth of the Indian Ocean Trading Complex to 1000 A.D.
Emory, C. and D. Lewis, National Geographic, G1 N2 (U) 146,
6 (December, 1974), 732-745, 747-778, passim.
MINI-EXAM

R Oct. 1   The Era of Muslim Ascendancy
McNeill, chapters 12, 13
Steward-Robinson, J. (ed.) The Traditional Near East, 6-35;
94-121 both passim
Bovill, E. W., The Golden Trade of the Moors, chapter 6 passim
Abdul-Rauf, M., "Pilgrimage to Mecca," National Geographic
G1 N2 (U) (Nov. 1978), 573-607 passim.
Simons, G., Barbarian Europe (Time-Life) D117 .S612 passim.
Sherrard, P., Byzantium (Time-Life) DF521 .S55 passim.
Esin, E., Mecca the Blessed: Madinah the Radiant passim.
BP 187.3 .E75
Stewart, D., Early Islam (Time-Life) D199.3 .S85

T Oct. 6   Eurasia, c. 600 A.D. to C. 1500 A.D.
McNeill, chapters 14, 15, 16; pp. 270-71/273-275
Riesman, D., et alii, The Lonely Crowd, 17-32

R Oct. 8   The Transmutation of Europe
McNeill, 239-327
Riesman, D., et alii, The Lonely Crowd, 17-32 BF755 .A5 R5
Pirenne, 17-74 153-167
Hale, John R., The Renaissance (Time-Life) DG533 .H16 passim.
Simon. E., The Reformation (Time-Life) BR305.2 .S58 passim.

T Oct. 13   East Africa and the Indian Ocean Trading Complex to c 1500
Bacon, Vanished Civilizations, "City of Black Gold"
Shinnie, M., Ancient African Kingdoms, 101-121 ("Lands of
the Zanj" and "Zimbabwe") DT 25 S551
Davidson, The African Past, 122-138. DT20 .D25

Assignments   -5-

R Oct. 15   West Africa and the Trans-Saharan Trade to c. 1500
                    Oliver, R.O., and C., Africa in the Days of Exploration
                        1-7; 8-26
                    Bovill, Golden Trade, Chapters 7-10; 16, passim DT356
                        B76 1968
                    Davidson, African Kingdoms, 79-99 ("Merchant Empires";)
                        100-119 ("Forest Kingdoms") 960 DAV (Shelved after Z)
                    Davidson, The African Past, 75-83 (Mali)
                    Shinnie, M., Ancient African Kingdoms, 43-88 passim (West
                        African States).
                    McIntosh, S. & R., "Finding Jenne-jeno," National Geographic
                        (Sept. 1982), 396-418

T Oct. 20   MID-TERM EXAMINATION

R Oct. 22   The Transformation of Western Civilization, "A Word in Your
                    Ear: A Study in Language." Tape Lab, BH 108, catalogue
                    number: Linguistics E09.01
                    Hall, E.T., The Silent Language, Introduction, Chapters 1
                        and 10. HM258 .H17
                    No Class meeting. Read ahead on next assignment.

T Oct. 27   The Americans to 1492 A.D.
                    McNeill, 274-78
                    Driver, Americas on the Eve of Discovery, 1-5; 19-23 passim.
                        69-79 passim 93-111; 134-155 E58 .D76
                    Miner, H., "Body Ritual among the Nacirema," American
                        Anthropologist, GNL A5 58 (1956), 503-507.
                    Bacon, Vanished Civilizations, 139-168 passim.
                    Piggott, Dawn of Civilization, 359-386 passim.
                    Leonard, J.N., Ancient America (Time-Life) passim.
                        E161 .L57

R Oct. 29   The Age of Reconnaissance, I
                    Review McNeill, 295-336
                    Crosby, A.W., The Columbian Exchange, Chapter 2: chapters 3
                        and 4 passim. E98 .D6 C94
                    Hale J.R., Age of Exploration (Time-Life) G80 .H18 passim.

T Nov. 3   The Age of Reconnaissance, II
                    McNeill, 329-352/333-358.
                    Wolpert, 64-100 passim
                    Driver, 156-164; 165-173 passim. 34-47 passim; 112-133 passim
                        (see page 19)

R Nov. 5   Inter-Locking World Economies: The Slave Trade
                    Davidson, B., Black Mother, Introduction Part I-III
                        DT352 .D25
                    Curtin, P.D., "The Atlantic Slave Trade, 1600-1800" in
                        J.F.A. Ajayi, and M. Crowder History of West Africa,
                        Vol. I, chapter 7 DT475 .A312
                    Haley, A., Roots, 1-131: 569-580. E185.97 .H24 A33

Assignments

T Nov. 10	The Transformation of Western Civilization, I McNeill, chapters 23, 24, 25 Wallerstein, I., "The Rise and Future Demise of the World Capitalistic System: Concepts for Comparative Analysis," Comparative Studies in Society and History H1 C68 XVI, 4 (Sept. 1974), 387-415 Gay, Peter, Age of Enlightenment (Time-Life) CB411 .G28 passim. Burchell, S.C., Age of Progress (Time-Life) CB417 .B94 passim.
R Nov. 12	The Transformation of Civilization, II McNeill, chapters 26, 27 Crosby, The Columbian Exchange, Chapters 5 & 6 passim. Read ahead on next assignment. GRADUATE AND UNDERGRADUATE PAPERS DUE.
T Nov. 17 and R Nov. 19	The Age of Imperialism I and II Brooks, G., "Africa and Europe to c 1870" and Gellar, S., "The Colonial Era," in Martin and O'Meara, Africa. Wallerstein, I., "The Three Stages of African involvement in the World--Economy," in P.C.W. Gutkind and I. Wallerstein, eds. The Political Economy of Contemporary Africa. Ellis, J., The Social History of the Machine Gun, 9, 79-90- passim. UF620 A2 E47 Brooks, G., "Tropical Africa: The Colonial Heritage," in Themes in African and World History DT20 B873 1982 Achebe, C., Things Fall Apart PR9387.9 .A2 T4 1969 Orvell, G., Burmese Days, chap. I-V MINI-EXAM ON NOV. 19
T Nov. 24	The Wofld since 1900 McNeill, chapter 29 Markandaya, K., Nectar in a Sieve (PR6063: A68N3 1971), Chapters 1-9. Arens, W., The Great American Football Ritual, Natural History, Oct. 1975, 72-80 QN1 N2 Read Ahead on next assignment.
T Dec. 1	The Nature of Underdevelopment, I McNeill, 416-437 Stryker, R., Development Strategies, in Martin and O'Meara, Africa. DT3 .A23 1977 Black, C.E., The Dynamics of Modernization, chapters 1 & 3 CB425 .B57 Deutsch, K.W. and W. Foltz, Nation-Building, Introduction chapter 8 JC131 .D40
R Dec. 3	The Nature of "underdevelopment," II Breese, G., Urbanization in Newly Developing Countries, 1-23 39-46 HT151 .B83 Howell, F.C., Early Man (Time-Life), 168-176 Jesus, C.M. de, Child of the Dark, passim HN290 S33 J52

Assignments

T Dec. 3

and

R Dec. 10

Contemporary World Political, Economic, and Social
    Interrerlationships, I-II
McNeill, 438-453 chapter 30
Hoffer, E., The True Believer, Part I NM231 .H6 1966
Riesman, The Lonely Crowd, 32-48
The Economist, H1 E22 Dec. 6, 1969 pp. 56-70, "The Cities
    that came too soon." May 7, 1977, Asia Survey: Two"
    November 2-8 1974 19-25 "The Fat Years and the Lean";
    May 22 1976; 41-42. The Cities of Men."
Desowitz, R.S., "How the Wise Men brought Malaria to Africa,"
    Natural History QH1 N2 (U) (October 1976). 26-44
Lappe, F.M. & J. Collins, "When More Food means more Hunger,"
    War on Hunger (Nov 1976), 1-15 (on Reserve)
Reread Caiden and Wildavsky assignment (Sept. 3) also Garreau.
Bukovsky, V., "The Soul of Man under Socialism," Commentary
67.1 (Jan. 1979), 34-42. BM1 C72
Galbraith, J.K., "The Second Imperial Requium," Harvard
    Magazine (Sept.-Oct. 1982), 29-33
"The Seething Caribbean," National Geographic (Feb. 1981),
    244-271, passim.

Indiana University   Mr. Brooks

B391/H425 World History

Undergraduate Papers

Undergraduates are responsible for a five page paper describing a "less-developed" country. Answer as many of the following features as you can; if information is not available explain why. Obtain the latest data possible.

- When did the country become independent?
- What form of government did it have at independence? Now?
- Who/what ethnic groups control the government, armed force, religious and educational institutions?
- What are the country's principal exports. Total amounts and %'s.
- Who owns the principal resources: mines, plantations, etc. ?
- The principal economic ties are with which countries?
- Does the country belong to a marketing arrangement for its primary product (s) ?
- What are the consequences of the "Green Revolution."
- What are the consequences of the OPEC price increases?
- Role in the North-South Dialogue?
- Role in the Laws of the Sea conferences?
- Foreign Aid: from which countries? How Much?
- Population and rate of population increase? % living in urban centers of over 100,000 population?

Selection of countries will be made following discussion of the project the second week of class.

Begin your research by reading encyclopedia articles on your country. Next consult the Topic Index files in the Graduate side of the Library. Look for recently published general studies; they or the volumes along side them on the shelf should provide all, or nearly all, the reference materials you need. Consult footnotes and bibliographies in the books you read to locate specialized books or articles. <u>Facts on File</u> and <u>World Almanac</u> are useful for statistics and specific facts. Be sure to check <u>The Economist</u> index for recent years; in many cases there will be a special report on the country you are studying, in addition to informative news reports. USFI Reports (Universities Field Staff International) are excellent sources for many countries.

Submit two copies of your paper. The first copy will be returned to you.

Indiana University   Mr. Brooks

                         B391/H425 World History

                          Graduate Student Papers

Graduate students have three options on papers, depending on their goals and interests.

(1) Graduate students intending to teach World History at the College or high school level are encouraged to prepare a lecture outline on a subject of special interest. The topic must incorporate a large geographical area and/or time period, such as the lectures for this course. Papers should be _five_ pages maximum and include the following: an outline of the main points of the lecture on the first page; discussion of the main points on the following three pages citing the sources for your statements; and page five should list your bibliography, no more than five sources--the most valuable sources you found. The objective of the paper is to identify the most important statements you can make about the topic you have chosen: statements that organize, describe, and highlight the significance of your topic. Include no more than five xerox pages of the maps, charts, graphs, etc., you would use in a lecture presentation either as slides or transparencies. Include the sources and page numbers for the xerox pages you submit.

(2) Graduate students may prepare ten page term papers on major groupings of "less-developed" countries in Africa, Asia, and Latin America, describing their inter-relationships, e.g., the ACP (African, Caribbean, and Pacific) countries associated with the European Economic Community or the Andean Pact countries in Latin America.

(3) Combine (1) and (2), following instructions for (1)

Consult with the instructor concerning your interests and preferences. Topics should be approved by the instructor by the eighth class meeting. Prepare a preliminary outline and 3 X 5 bibliography cards by the fourteenth class meeting. The paper is due at the twenty-second class meeting. Submit two copies; the original will be returned to you.

YOUNGSTOWN STATE UNIVERSITY

History 500
Introduction to World History
Summer, 1984
Lowell J. Satre

Office: ASOB 538
Hours: MTW 9:30-10:00
Th 12:10-12:30
And by appointmen

History 500 is designed for beginning college students who need an introduction to basic historical concepts. The course will focus on major themes and personalities in world history. <u>This course may not be applied to class requirements for a history major.</u>

Course Requirements:

1. Required reading:

    L. S. Stavrianos, <u>A Global History</u> (Prentice Hall, 3rd ed.)

    Additional reading material may be distributed to the students or placed on reserve in the university library. Students also will be required to consult newspapers, news weeklies, etc. to make reports on pertinent related events.

2. There will be three examinations during the quarter. The exams are a mixture of essay and objective, and are scheduled for July 31, August 14, and August 23. The first exam counts 15% of the final grade, the second 25%, and the last 30%.

3. Students will be regularly assigned short writing assignments and map quizzes. These will count for 20% of the final grade.

4. Class participation is worth 10% of the grade. Simple physical presence in the classroom does not constitute participation. Students must become involved in the class discussions.

5. Grading scale: 100-90 = A; 89-80 = B; 79-70 = C; 69-60 = D; 59 and below F.

6. Attendance will be taken regularly. Attendance is required. Anyone with more than four hours of unexcused absences will have the final grade dropped 1/3 of a letter grade (e.g., from B- to a C+) for each unexcused hour absent. The instructor will decide if the excuse for an absence is acceptable. Do not take this course if you believe you will have to miss many classes, even if the absences are work-related: <u>regular class attendance is mandatory.</u>

7. Students are encouraged to visit the instructor should any questions arise. Office hours are listed at the top of this syllabus.

TENTATIVE LECTURE TOPICS

(and reading assignments from Stavrianos)

1. Introduction to the Course.

2. What is History?

3. The Family in History (Stavrianos, pp. 3-22)
   a. The family today
   b. The family in other cultures (37-38, 44-45)

4. Religion--Explaining the supernatural. (56-58, 83-86, 94-96)
   a. Meaning of religion today
   b. The development of Christianity (54-56, 191-195)
   c. Native American
   d. Islam. (131-141)

5. Exploration--Explaining the natural (127-130)
   a. Discovery today
   b. The Spanish and the Aztecs (213-221, 263-275; and look over 276-287, 299-300)
   c. North America
   d. The search for the Nile (412-413)

6. The Impact of Disease
   a. Pandemic--the meeting of Europeans and native Americans (review pp. listed at 5b)
   b. Humans and Healing, Magic and Science: the Black Death (179-186)
   c. Medicine in the 19th and 20th centuries (315-320)

7. Nation--building and expansion
   a. The Roman Empire (42-43, 53-54, 59-81)
   b. Russia (288-297)
   c. India (384-394, 470-472, 537-538)

8. Slavery/Race Relations
   a. Afro-American slave trade (203-212, 298-304, 410-413)
   b. Hitler and the Final Solution (496-503)
   c. Apartheid in South Africa (413-415, 545-546)

9. Revolution and Social Change (421-429)
   a. French Revolution (335-353)
   b. Russian Revolution (353-356, 359-372, 449-454, 477-489, 492-496)
   c. Change in Latin America

10. Industrialization and Modernization
    a. England and the first Industrial Revolution (321-330)
    b. Japan, industry and cultural change (174-177, 396-408)
    c. European domination of the world (330-334, 413-420, 430-436)
    d. Industrialization in developing nations (413-416)

11. War and Peace
    a. Turco-Mongols (143-153)
    b. World War II (506-519, 520-534)
    c. War between developed and developing nations--Vietnam (536-541)
    d. Organizations for Peace (457-459, 554-556)

12. The Interdependent World (567-75)

DENISON UNIVERSITY

World History   Tim Bradstock
History 100   Michael Gordon
secs. 6,7,8,9   Fall, 1982

Books

Assignments will be made in the following books which are available in the Denison bookstore:

L.S. Stavrianos, Man's Past and Present: A Global History (Prentice-Hall)
Chinua Achebe, Things Fall Apart (Fawcett)
Ivo Andric, Bridge on the Drina (Chicago)
Yuan-Tsung Chen, Dragon's Village (Penguin)
Elizabeth Gaskell, Mary Barton (Penguin)
Carlo Cipolla, Clocks and Culture (Norton)
Selections from the Koran
Tales from the Thousand and One Nights (Penguin)
Giovanni Boccaccio, Decameron (Penguin)
Robert Van Gulik, The Chinese Gold Murders (Chicago)
Seneca, Letters from a Stoic (Penguin)
Arthur Waley, The Analects of Confucius (Vintage)
The Epic of Gilgamesh (Penguin)
V. Gordon Childe, The Urban Revolution
Robert Braidwood, The Agricultural Revolution (Scientific American reprint)

Also, assignments will be made from the Bible; any edition will do and the bookstore has copies of The Jerusalem Bible.

Requirements

Four take-home essays are required. Topics will be distributed well in advance of the due dates. Each paper must be typed, double-spaced, and may not exceed a maximum length. Extensions will not be granted and late papers will not be accepted. Following are the dates these papers will be due, their maximum length, and the percentage that each paper will count towards the final grade:

1. September 13, maximum length of five pages (20%)
2. October 6, maximum length of eight pages (25%)
3. November 15, maximum length of eight pages (25%)
4. Final exam period, maximum length of ten pages (30%)

In addition, students are expected to attend and participate in every class. Final grades will be adjusted to reflect attendance and participation.

THE RISE OF CIVILIZATION

9/1	The Urban Revolution	Stavrianos, chs. 1-3 Braidwood Childe
9/6	The First Civilization: Mesopotamia	Stavrianos, chs. 4-5 Epic of Gilgamesh

THE FORMATION OF THE CLASSICAL CIVILIZATION (1200 BC-500 AD)

9/13	Near Eastern Civilization	Stavrianos, ch. 6 Deuteronomy
9/20	Chinese Civilization	Stavrianos, ch. 10 Analects, bks. 1,2,7,10,12, 13,15,16,17,20 intro. pp. 14-20, 27-69
9/27	Greece-Roman Civilization	Stavrianos, ch. 8 Seneca, letters 2,5,7,8,15, 16,47,53,56,77,83,86,88,91, appendix
10/4	The End of the Ancient World	Stavrianos, ch. 11

CONTINUITY AND CHANGE IN THE MEDIEVAL CIVILIZATIONS (500-1800)

10/11	The Flowering of Chinese Civilization	Stavrianos, ch. 16 Van Gulik
10/18	The Growth of Islamic Civilization: Religion	Stavrianos, ch. 13 Koran
10/25	The Growth of Islamic Civilization: Society	Stavianos, ch. 14 1001 Nights, pp. 24-76, 113-162, 243-302, 372-407
11/1	The Elaboration of European Civilization	Stavrianos, ch. 17 Decameron, Days 1, 3
11/8	Technology and the Medieval Civilizations	Stavrianos, ch. 12 Cipolla

WORLD CIVILIZATIONS AND THE RISE OF INDUSTRIALISM (1800-PRESENT)

11/15	The Self-Transformation of European Civilization	Stavrianos, chs. 24-25 Gaskell
11/22	European Imperialism and its Consequences	Stavrianos, ch. 30 Achebe
11/29	Islam in the Modern World	Stavrianos, chs. 27, 33*, 34* Andric
12/6	The Transformation of Chinese Civilization	Stavrianos, chs. 29, 34*, 40* Chen
12/13	The Conclusion in which nothing is concluded	tba

DENISON UNIVERSITY

History 100   Amy G. Gordon, Fellows 426
World History   Donald G. Schilling, Fellows 405

SYLLABUS
Spring, 1982-83

The critical interdependence of the contemporary world effects the daily lives of average people everywhere. European civilization has related historically with the major civilizations in the rest of Eurasia, as well as in Africa and the Americas. This course will explore the development of and the relationships among the European, Chinese and African societies. We will examine the phenomenon of Europe's global dominance and its consequences, not only for the rest of the world but also for Europe itself. In this context we will seek to understand the roots of contemporary global issues.

Weekly Schedule. All our sections will meet together on Mondays in Fellows Auditorium for a lecture. During the remainder of the week we will meet in discussion sections. Dr. Gordon's sections will meet in Fellows 213 and Dr. Schilling's sections will meet in Fellows 321. The instructor in your particular section will evaluate your performance in the course, but you will be responsible for what transpires in lecture as well as in your individual section meetings.

Course Work. The weekly reading assignments are specified below. It will assist you to understand the lecture on Monday if you do the week's reading beforehand, but in any case this reading must be carefully done before your section meetings. Be sure to bring the readings assigned for the week to your section meeting, because frequent reference to texts is often necessary.

The course will have a take-home midterm (8 pp. maximum) due in class on March 18, and a take-home final (8 pp. maximum) due in your instructor's office by 11:00 A.M. on Thursday, May 19.

The course will also have two papers (3-5 pp.), due in class on February 21 and April 18, on topics which will be assigned by the instructors.

Finally, we will require a journal to be kept by each student. We are asking each of you to get a spiral notebook for exclusive use in this course, and we are giving this notebook the rather exalted title of "journal." You will use the journal for your lecture notes, notes and comments on the assigned readings, and for various short writing exercises that we will be requiring throughout the semester. We may, for example, have you take five minutes at the end of a lecture to summarize the major points of that lecture in your journal, or have you record the key questions which arise from the reading for that week. The basic purpose of this type of journal, then, is to use writing as a means to further your engagement in the course and, as a result, to enhance your learning. At the end of the semester, we will ask to see your journals, in order better to evaluate your performance and involvement in the course.

Grading. The two take-home examinations will each constitute 25% of your final grade. The first paper will make up 15% of your final grade, and the second paper will make up 20%. The combination of your journal and your work in class discussion will account for the remaining 15%. Regular attendance in both lecture and discussion sections is expected of all students. Any noticeable deviation from this standard will adversely effect your grade in the course. Instructors may weigh performance in somewhat different fashion, but in general these guidelines will prevail.

Reading.

L.S. Stavrianos, The World Since 1500: A Global History (Fourth Edition)
Robert Van Gulik, The Chinese Bell Murders
Karl Marx and Friedrich Engels, The Communist Manifesto
Chinua Achebe, Things Fall Apart
George Orwell, Coming Up For Air
Yuan-tsung Chen, The Dragon's Village
James Ngugi, Weep Not, Child

Weekly Schedule

Unit I: The World Pattern and the Emergence of Europe to 1700

Week of:	Topic:	Reading Assignments
Feb. 2	Introduction: States of Mind	Stavrianos, 1-7
Feb. 7	Classical China	Stavrianos, 21-29 Readings, The Hsiao Ching Start Chinese Bell Murders
Feb. 14	Imperial China	Finish Chinese Bell Murders
Feb. 21	The Commercial Revolution in Europe Paper: Due Feb. 21	Stavrianos, 49-79 Readings, The Commercial Revolution
Feb. 28	European Expansion	Stavrianos, 83-123, 138-160 Readings, China and Europe in the Age of Expansion
Mar. 7	State Formation in Early Modern Europe	Richelieu, 3-47, 71-79, 84-93, 103-128

Week of:	Topic:	Reading Assignments:
Mar. 14	Political Revolution and the Rise of Liberalism	Stavrianos, 191-218 Readings, Political Revolution in Europe and America

Take-Home Exam: Due March 18

Mar. 21 SPRING BREAK

Unit II: Patterns of Change, 1700-1900

Mar. 28	The Scientific and Industrial Revolutions	Stavianos, 163-189 Marx and Engels, Parts 1,2,4
Apr. 4	Transformation in 19th-Century China	Stavrianos, 285-296, 330-341 Readings, China and the World
Apr. 11	Change in Traditional Africa	Stavrianos, 302-317 Achebe - all

Unit III: Coping With Change, 1900-1982

Apr. 18	Global Conflict	Stavrianos, 345-369, 423-441, 461 Start Orwell

Paper: Due April 18

Apr. 25	Good-by to All That	Finish Orwell
May 2	China in Revolution	Stavrianos, 382-385, 498-502 Yuan-tsung Chen -- all
May 9	African Nationalism	Stavrianos, 463-66, 472-81 Ngugi - all
May 16	Conclusion	Stavrianos, 511-26

Take-home Exam: Due by 11:00 a.m. on Thurs. May 19.

DENISON UNIVERSITY

History 101   William Dennis
Fall, 1980   Amy Gordon
                                                                              Michael Gordon

WORLD HISTORY I: THE WORLD AND THE WEST

Assignments will be made in the following books which are available in the bookstore:

W.H. McNeill, <u>A World History</u> (3rd ed., Oxford)
Hung-hsiang Chou, <u>Chinese Oracle Bones</u> (Scientific American reprint)
W.H. McNeill, <u>The Ancient Near East</u> (Oxford)
W.H. McNeill, <u>The Classical Mediterranean World</u> (Oxford)
W.H. McNeill, <u>Classical China</u> (Oxford)
<u>The Bhagavad Gita</u> (Penguin)
<u>The Koran</u> (Penguin)
J. Strayer, <u>The Medieval Origins of the Modern State</u> (Princeton)
C. Cipolla, <u>Guns, Sails and Empires</u>
<u>Buddhist Scriptures</u> (Penguin)
<u>Tales from the Thousand and One Nights</u> (Penguin)
<u>Epic of Gilgamesh</u> (Penguin)
<u>Six Yuan Plays</u> (Penguin)

<u>Lecturers:</u>

William Dennis
Cornell Fleischer
Amy Gordon
Michael Gordon
Barry Keenan
Barry Strauss

Grades will be determined on the basis of the following components:

1. Each week we will distribute paper topics for the following week's work. In the course of the semester, you must hand in at least six papers. These must be handed in at the time of your discussion section and must be no longer than two pages. You are free to select which topics to write upon, but there is the following restriction: at least one paper must be submitted by week III, at least one additional one by week VII, and at least two more by week XI. These papers, along with participation in your discussion section, will comprise one-third of your final grade.

2. There will be in-class examinations on Friday, October 17 and Friday, November 14. These exams will comprise one-third of the final grade.

3. A final examination will be on Thursday, December 17. This will also be one-third of the final grade.

There will be no extensions or changes made in the dates of the examinations or the times that the papers are due.

Introduction

I.   9/3   The Neolithic Revolution

I: Early Civilization (to 1700 BC)

II. 9/8   Early Civilization: Mesopotamia   WH, ch. 1, Epic of Gilgamesh
III. 9/15 Early Civilization: China, Egypt, Indus WH, ch. 2, "Chinese Oracle Bones"

II: Eurasian Balance (1700-200 BC)

IV. 9/22 Middle Eastern Civilization   WH, ch. 3, Ancient Near East, secs. 2-3
V.   9/29 Indian Civilization   WH, ch. 4, Bhagavad Gita
VI. 10/6 Hellenic Civilization   WH, chs. 5,8, Classical Mediterranean World, pp. 3-44
VII. 10/13 Chinese Civilization   WH, chs. 6-7, Classical China, pp. 3-20, 32-91, 105-67

     10/17 EXAMINATION

III: Disturbance and Dynamism (200 BC-1000 AD)

VIII. 10/20 Hellenization: East and West   WH, ch. 9, Classical Mediterranean World, pp. 103-28, 241-81
IX.   10/27 Buddhism   WH, chs. 10-11, Buddhist Scriptures, tb
X.   11/3 Christianity   WH, ch. 12, Classical Mediterranean World, pp. 88-100, 128-75, 195-204, 281-300
XI.   11/10 Islam   WH, ch. 13, The Koran, tba
      11/14 EXAMINATION

IV: Eurasian Equilibrium (1000-1500 AD)

XII. 11/17 Medieval India and China   WH, ch. 14, Six Yuan Plays, tba
XIII. 11/24 Medieval Islam   WH, ch. 15, Arabian Nights, tba
XIV. 12/1 Medieval Europe   WH, chs. 16-17, Medieval Origins of the Modern State

Conclusion

XV.   12/8 A New Dynamic   Guns, Sails and Empires

DENISON UNIVERSITY

History 101　　　　　　　　　　Amy G. Gordon (Fellows 426)
Sections 2,4,6,8　　　　　　　　Kristen B. Neuschel (Fellows 408)
Fall 1981

THE WORLD AND THE WEST:
THE CIVILIZATION OF EURASIA TO 1500

This course is an introduction to the development and interaction of early civilizations, primarily those of China, the Middle East and Europe. Some of the goals of the course are

1. To help you understand why the study of the past is important and meaningful for your life.

2. To become acquainted with some of the many facets of human life which have varied over time and place, such as political and social organizations, religious beliefs, gender roles, and human sexuality.

3. To become more informed about other cultures and more willing to accept them on their own terms.

4. To have an understanding of the origins of civilization and how these origins influence the present.

Books
Assignments will be made in the following books which are available in the bookstore:

Kevin Reilly, The West and the World (Harper and Row)
Epic of Gilgamesh (Penguin)
Mary Renault, The Persian Boy
Letters of Abelard and Heloise (Penguin)
Tales from the Thousand and One Nights (Penguin)
Six Yuan Plays (Penguin)
Boccaccio, Decameron (Penguin)

Weekly Schedule

Our four sections will meet together on Mondays for a lecture. On Wednesday and Friday, section 2 will meet with Neuschel and section 4 with Gordon, for small group discussion. On Tuesday and Thursday, section 6 will meet with Neuschel and section 8 with Gordon for small group discussion. You are responsible for the material covered both in the Monday lecture and your discussion group.

Course Requirements

You are expected to complete all the assigned reading. Your understanding of the Monday lecture will be greatly enhanced if you do the reading beforehand, but in any case you must have the reading done, with care and thought, by the time your discussion group meets. Be sure to bring the assigned reading for the week to your section meeting.

Three essays, a take-home midterm exam and a take-home final exam are required. The first essay is due in class on Monday, September 14, the second on Monday, Oct. 5, and the third on Monday, Nov. 16. Each should be a maximum of 5 pages (typewritten and double-spaced). The midterm exam is due in class on Friday, Oct. 23 and the final is due at 9:00 A.M. on Thursday, Dec. 17. The exams should be a maximum of eight pages (typewritten and double-spaced). Final grades will be determined on the following basis: essays one and two will be 10% of the grade, essay three will be 20% of the grade, and the midterm and final will each be 30% of the grade.

Students are expected to attend and participate in every class. Final grades will be adjusted to reflect attendance and participation.

Rise of Civilization

9/2	Introduction	Reilly, ch. 1 & 2
9/7	Egypt and Sumer	Reilly, ch. 3, *Epic of Gilgamesh* (entire)

Classical Civilization

9/14	The Greek Cities (First essay due Mon., Sept. 14)	Reilly, ch. 4 *Thucydides*
9/21	The Attractions of Empire	Reilly, ch. 5 begin *Persian Boy* (to at least p. 190)
9/28	Male and Female in the Classical World	Finish *Persian Boy*
10/5	The Roman Empire: Classical and Christian (Second essay due Mon., Oct. 5)	Reilly, chs. 6 & 7 *St. Augustine*
10/12	China: Successful Empire	Reilly, ch. 8 *Three Ways of Thought in Ancient China*, pp. 3-79
10/19	China (cont'd.) (Take-home midterm due Friday, Oct. 23)	*Three Ways of Thought*, pp. 83-147

Medieval Civilization

10/26	Medieval Christian Society	Reilly, ch. 9 Abelard and Heloise, pp. 57-106, 127-156
11/2	Medieval Islam	Thousand and One Nights, 24-76, 243-302, 372-407
11/9	Christian against Muslim: The Crusades	Reilly, ch. 10, reading on the Crusades
11/16	Medieval China (Third essay due Mon., Nov. 16)	Reilly, ch. 11 Six Yuan Plays, plays 1,3 and 5
11/23	The City in Medieval Europe	Begin Decameron, 49-113 (Day I) and 231-323 (Day III)
11/30	Medieval Europe in Transition	Reilly, ch. 12 Finish Decameron (Days I and III)
12/7	The World in 1500	Cipolla, Guns, Sails and Empires
12/14	Conclusion and Evaluation (Take-home final due 9:00 A.M., Thurs., Dec. 17)	

UNIVERSITY OF WISCONSIN AT GREEN BAY

Syllabus: History 100
Professor Craig Lockard
MWF 10:10-11:05;
SE-222-24
Spring, 1984

HISTORY OF THE MODERN WORLD

Food for Thought:

"Awareness of the need for a universal view of history--for a history which transcends national and regional boundaries and comprehends the entire globe--is one of the marks of the present. Our civilization is the first to have for its past the past of the world, our history is first to be world history.,,As since 1945 the world has moved into a new phase of global integration, the demand for a history which reflects this new situation has become more insistent... The case for world history is undoubtedly very powerful."--Geoffrey Barraclough.

"I suppose that we are all aware of the fact that we live in the most catastrophically revolutionary age that men have ever faced...We are in fact living with ten or twenty such revolutions - all changing our ways of life, our ways of looking at things, changing everything out of recognition and changing it fast"--Barbara Ward.

"World history is no more difficult than national history. What one needs is a clear and distinct idea that will define what is relevent."--William H. McNeill

"Whether we consider the position of the rock layers that envelope the earth, the arrangement of the forms of life that inhabit it, the variety of civilizations to which it has given birth, or the structure of languages spoken upon it, we are forced to the same conclusion: that everything is the sum of the past, and that nothing is comprehensible except through its history."--Pierre Teilhard de Chardin.

Introduction

This course serves as an introduction to the history of the world during the past five centuries or so, and particularly since 1900. Roughly one-third of the course discusses the period since 1945. The global nature of modern historical change is emphasized, with special stress on the interaction of Europe and North America with the societies of Asia, Africa, and Latin America. The course must cover over 500 years of history of many peoples and countries in a

very brief time; because of this problem we cannot delve as deeply
into any one subject area as many of us would like. Indeed, it is
not possible to be comprehensive or complete. I have chosen instead
to concentrate on certain important themes so as to take maximum
advantage of history's power to illuminate and explain the present.
Specifically I asked myself: What does an educated American in the
last quarter of the twentieth century need to know about modern
global history in order to understand the interconnected and
interdependent , yet conflict prone and inequitable, world in which
he or she lives? This course also challenges much of traditional
historiography emphasizing narrative chronological change by
defining the subject in a more conceptual way, in this case by
deliberately restricting the foci and explicitly developing an
interpretation of how and why the modern world developed the way
that it did. To be sure, history happens as "one damn thing after
another" but the job of historical understanding is to make it, by
analysis, something more than that. The interpretation utilized in
this course relies partially on world-system theory (which
postulates the evolution of a world economy embracing and affecting
all societies) and on the notion that the interaction of
civilizations is a major force for historical change. My intention
is to create a meaningful, coherent, and hopefully pleasing tapestry
out of various diverse threads; such an approach requires sweeping
generalizations and a global overview, at the sacrifice of detailed
examination of events, trends and personalities, no matter how
fascinating. My hope is that you will emerge from this course with
as much understanding of the forest as of the individual trees.
Hence, in order for the whole to be greater than the sum of its
parts, we will be much less interested in names and dates than in
broad patterns of change.

The interpretative framework employed in this course allows us to
select the most revelant material from the bewildering data base of
modern world history; it defines to a considerable extent the content
of the lectures and selection of the texts from among many
available. Some of our material will come from the social sciences
so that the course takes a clearly interdisciplinary approach. Due
to time constraints we will also emphasize economic, social and
political history to the neglect of cultural, intellectual,
diplomatic, and military history. Among the major topics to be
considered are: the rise of capitalism, European expansion and
imperialism, the creation of new but differing societies in North and
South America, the evolution of colonial empires, the industrial and
scientific revolutions, the rise of socialism, the impact of
colonialism on Asia and Africa, nationalism and revolution in the
Third World, the role of the United States in the postwar world, the
evolution of communist societies, and contemporary Western-Third
World relationships.

Format:

The Format of the course is lecture and discussion. Because of the pressure of time and the need to cover much material it is important for you to keep up with the readings and lectures. Many phenomena in modern history are open to controversy in their interpretation; men and women of good will can and will disagree on their meaning and importance, a point exemplified by the different approaches to be found in the texts, films, and lectures. But debate and controversy should be encouraged, not ignored under the guise of "consensus" or "value-free objectivity" (which may or may not exist). This is not to deny the necessity for both students and instructor to maintain a "broad-minded" attitude open to many points of view. But one goal of the course is to demonstrate that the meaning of modern history can be perceived in different ways. I have opinions on many of the subjects under discussion and will try to make my biases clear. You need not accept my opinions or interpretations and are free to take issue them without penalty. This course has been designed with several purposes: to provide an introduction to modern social, political and economic change as well as historical processes; to provide necessary background for further coursework in history, social sciences, and international studies; and to encourage analytical thinking and intellectual growth. All that is required is an open mind and a willingness to learn about regions, countries and people outside the United States. On days with no films I will normally lecture for 40-45 minutes and will try to leave 10-15 minutes for questions and discussions. You are expected to obtain a preliminary background to the lecture topic by keeping up with the assigned readings. There are three paperback texts, all available at the campus bookstore and on reserve:

L.S. Stayrianos, The World Since 1500: A Global History, 4th ed., (Prentice-Hall)

Daniel Chirot, Social Change in the Twentieth Century (Harcourt Brace)

Richard Goff, et al, The Twentieth Century: A Brief Global History (Wiley)

The required texts are coded for reading as S, C and G. There is also a recommended paperback world atlas for this course, the Comparative World Atlas, New Revised Edition (Hammond). With or without the aid of this atlas, by the end of the second week you shouold have gained some sense of the regions and countries of the globe, including major cities, rivers, islands, mountain ranges, languages, religions, economic products, and distribution of resources and population. In my lectures I will assume that you have familiarized yourself with the various countries and regions. You will continually need this knowledge throughout the semester, indeed throughout life.
In addition to the lectures we will also tentatively have ten films

or slide presentations throughout the semester, normally scheduled for the Friday session. The films are listed in the tentative class schedule. One of these films, the three-part, Europe-produced "History Book," provides a radical intrepretation of modern history quite at variance with traditional American views; it differs as well from readings. Hopefully the film will spark controversy and discussion in the course. You are also strongly encouraged to take in as many as possible of the international films to be shown on campus this semester. I will also illustrate the lectures with overhead projections of maps, key terms, and other material.

Tentative Class Schedule:

The class schedule has been carefully planned so as to reasonably parallel the texts and erect a structure for interpretation and analysis. The first several weeks provide a background by resenting a framework for modern world history and briefly surveying the world before about 1450 A.D. The following five weeks concentrate on developments between 1450 and 1914, with an emphasis on the origins and emergence of the world-system. At this point we are ready for the mid term essay examination, scheduled for March 28.the second half of the semester covers the twentieth century world, with the final essay examination to be held on May 21. Barring unforeseen problems we will adhere closely to the class schedule listed below:

Session	Date	Topic (Reading Assignment)
1	Feb. 6	Introductory Remarks
	BACKGROUND TO MODERN WORLD HISTORY	
2	Feb. 8	World History: Why and What?
	Feb. 10	The Structure of Premodern World History (S:xvii-xx, 1-7, 257; G: 408-419)
4	Feb. 13	Contrasting Approaches to Modern World History: World-System and Modernization (C:2-15)
5	Feb. 15	Asia Before 1500 (S:8-33, 271-273, 258-260)

6	Feb. 17		Slides: "An Asian Mosaic"
7	Feb. 20		Africa and the Americas Before 1500 (S:35-48, 261-262)
8	Feb. 22		Europe Before 1450 (S:49-62, 263)

ORIGINS OF THE WORLD-SYSTEM, 1450-1770

9	Feb. 24		The Rise of Capitalism in Europe (C:18-23; S:64-81)
10	Feb. 27		Early Western Expansion in Americas (S:83-122)
11	Feb. 29		Early Western Expansion in Africa and Asia (S:124-159, 264-266)
12	Mar. 2		Film: "The History Book, Part I.

THE WORLD-SYSTEM EMERGES, 1770-1914

13	Mar. 5		Industrial Capitalism in Europe (S:161-185; G:6-11)
14	Mar. 7		Sociopolitical Transformation in Europe (S:191-218 G: 11-22)
15	Mar. 9		Film: "The History Book, Part 2"
16	Mar. 12		Imperialism and Colonialism in Southern Asia (S:185-189, 221-222: 302-317; G: 37-50
17	Mar. 14		Imperialism and Colonialism in Southern Asia (S:241-254, 273-284; G:68-76, 78-81)

18	Mar. 16	Film: "White Man's Africa"
19	Mar. 19	The Americas Take Different Paths (S:319-328; G:51-62)
20	Mar. 21	Imperialism and Development in East Asia (S:285-301): G: 63-67, 76-78, 83-90)
21	Mar. 23	Film: "The Japanese"
22	Mar. 26	The World-System in Early Twentieth Century (S:330-341; 266-268; C:23-93; 6:4-5, 22-25)
23	Mar. 28	Mid-term Examination (Sessions 2-22)

THE WORLD-SYSTEM IN TURMOIL, 1914-1945

| 24 | Mar. 30 | War and Russian Revolution in Europe (S:223-240, 343-369, 387-392; C:89-93; G:26-35, 92-110, 129-144) |

SPRING VACATION (Mar. 31-April 8)

25	Apr. 9	Fascism, Stalinism, and Depression (S:392-422; C:93-114; G:114-128, 144-149, 182-218)
26	Apr. 11	Colonialism and Nationalism in Third World (S:370-385; C:121-145; G:151-182)
27	Apr. 13	Film: "The Twisted Cross"
28	Apr. 16	Causes and Consequences of World War II (S:423-461); C:114-119; G:219-247, 273-277)

THE WORLD-SYSTEM IN TRANSFORMATION, 1945-PRESENT

29	Apr. 18		The Post-War World (S:463-466, 488-508; 511-522, 269; G:254-272, 277-313)
30	Apr. 20		**Film:** "The History Book, Part 3"
31	Apr. 23		The American World-System (C:147-202; G:328-331)
32	Apr. 25		Sub-Saharan African Struggle for Development (S:472-479; G:343-356)
33	Apr. 27		**Film:** "Last Grave at Dimbaza"
34	Apr. 30		The Communist World-System: Russia and Eastern Europe (C:227-242; G:372-381)
35	May 2		The Chinese Revolutionary Experience (S:506-509; C:242-245; G:314-324)
36	May 4		**Film:** "Shanghai: New China"
37	May 7		Latin American Struggle for Development (G:382-398)
38	May 9		South and Southeast Asian Struggle for Development (S:466-472; C:202-225; G:324-325, 331-341)
39	May 11		**Film:** "The Village of My Ann"
40	May 14		Middle Eastern Struggle for Development (S:479-486; G:358-367)

41	May 16	Capitalism, Cooperation, and the Welfare State in Western Europe and Japan (S:504-506; G:325-328, 369-372)
42	May 18	The World-System Today and Tomorrow (S:523-526; C:247-256; G:399-406)
	May 21	Final Examination (Sessions 24-42): 10:30-11:30 a.m.

Course Requirements:

Grading will be based on a flexible combination of factors; all students must complete certain common requirements, which include:

a) <u>Two essay examinations.</u> Tentatively the midterm exam is scheduled for March 28 and the final exam is scheduled for May 21 (10:30-11:30 a.m.). In each exam you will normally write on <u>two</u> questions out of <u>four</u> possible. Some of the questions will involve thought, interpretation, or comparison rather than just regurgitation of factual information. The final will only cover the material since the midterm. The exams will be graded on the assumption that you have read all the assigned readings and attended all the lectures and media presentations. Each exam will last <u>one</u> hour and be weighted equally. It is your responsibillity to keep abreast of any changes in exam dates or times.

b) <u>Class participation.</u> Satisfactory class participation as measured by reasonably regular attendance, completion of assigned readings, submission of the anonymous course evaluation and contributions to discussion can help your grade in cases where "benefit of doubt" comes into play. On the other hand, poor class participation can easily threaten otherwise satisfactory exam and project results. Students who are frequently absent without reasonable excuses can expect to be dropped several points, perhaps even a grade or more. While class participation does not merit a stated percentage of the grade, I reserve the right to add or subtract points from final grade based on class participation.

You can meet the written requirements of the course solely through the two exams; in this case the two exams each count for 50% of your final grade. Except in the most extraordinary circumstances no make-ups will be allowed.

In the interest of flexibility you can also satisfy the written course requirements by combining one of the following optional individualized projects with the two exams. The project grade will __only__ be counted toward your final grade if it helps your final grade (raises your exam average); in this case each of the two exams will count one quarter of your grade and the project will count one half. Thus, you have an incentive to complete the project since it may improve your grade; at the same time you lose time and energy but no points if your project falls short and also gain experience in preparing and writing academic projects. There is absolutely __no__ penalty for declining to undertake or complete a project. A wide choice of projects is open, depending on your talents and proclivities, such as:

1) __A research paper__ (8-15 pages, typed, double-spaced) on any topic of relevance to the course. Many topics are possible, as long as they discuss any broad historical theme or any global or semi-global pattern of any area of the world since about 1500 A.D. Comparative topics are welcome. The papers should be in a standard academic form, including the following: an introduction and conclusion; a conceptual framework or thesis (a research paper is not an encyclopedia article or mere compilation of information); footnoting and documentation of factual information, quotations, and paraphrasing (see below); complete footnotes, with author, title, publisher, and pages cited (footnotes may be grouped at end of paper); correct grammar, spelling and punctuation; numbered pages; bibliography (with complete bibliographic information); and use of sophisticated sources (academic books and periodicals rather than popular magazines or encyclopedias). You are advised to take these guidelines seriously. The Stavrianos text contains good bibliographical information.

2) __A Journal__ (20-50 pages) reflecting your impressions, criticisms, and evaluations of the assigned readings, relevant outside reading and experiences, relevant media presentations (TV documentaries and newscasts, radio programs, films, newspaper and magazine articles, etc.), class films, lectures and discussions. It should reflect the scope, direction, and depth of your involvement and growth with the subject matter during the semester; what have been the most interesting, challenging, upsetting, revealing, stimulating, relevant ideas and impressions that have emerged? A Journal should document what you have learned, how you react to what you are learning, what you would like to explore further, and how you feel you can apply the knowledge gained in this course. A journal is also a useful framework for mini-research papers and essays or for short reports on extra reading without the restrictions of more formal academic writing (as in options 1 and 3). An oustanding journal will normally include such material. A journal is not a one-shot affair but a growing record over the course of the term.

It may be typed or handwritten legibly. Illustrations, poems, and other creative materials may be included, as well as any quotations or sayings you find revealing and helpful. The first half of the journal should be submitted to me by the midterm exam; this will not be graded at that time but my feedback will give you an indication of how you are doing.

3) <u>A comparative and analytical review of books</u> (8-15 pages in length, typed, doublespaced), dealing critically with 2-4 books. Reviews could focus on a particular theme (such as Chinese communism, the depression of the 1930's, 19th century imperialism, the slave trade, or the Vietnam War), or on several themes. These books could include novels as well as scholarly studies and eyewitness accounts. I will be glad to suggest books for the review and to illustrate how an analytical book review differs from the traditional book report. Reviews should be in standard academic form, with quotations and paraphrasing footnoted. <u>Separate reviews</u> of 2 or 3 books (other than the texts) on different subjects will also be acceptable, providing that you get my prior permission for them.

4) <u>A work of imaginative/creative interpretation</u> dealing with some aspect of world history and civilization. You might submit a short story, or a play, or a group of poems, or several paintings, or a musical composition, or a photographic essay, or a series of political cartoons, or a collage or collage book--any creative product demonstrating conscious relationship with the subject matter of the course.

This is a suggestive, not an exclusive list of project options. In the interest of flexibility you can (through consultation with me) work out some combination of projects, do a more extensive project, or suggest alternative to the above list of options. The concept of the "project" is to link your aptitude and inclination to the subject. Advisement will be available to insure that conceptual rigor can be combined with personal virtuosity. The UWGB faculty has recommended strong penalties for plagiarism in papers; you must footnote or otherwise cite the sources from which you quote, paraphrase, or utilize factual or interpretative data. Submission of work prepared by others is a serious offense. I have prepared short hand-outs on how to prepare research papers, journals, and book reviews; these are available from me upon request. You <u>must</u> get my approval for your project and your topics, and should <u>have</u> selected your particular project by the end of the fourth week of class, earlier for those writing journals. A one-page (handwritten) outline of the project should be submitted by the end of the eighth week. Indeed, you are strongly encouraged to let me see some of your work at various stages during the semester (rough drafts, journals in progress, etc.). Projects must be handed in no later than the last class session, (earlier submissions are welcome). Except in the most exceptional circumstances later projects will not be accepted; on the other hand, failure to complete your project won't count against you either--your grade will be based on the two exams.

Grades

For those who choose not to do a project, each exam counts for 50% of your final grade. Only under extraordinary circumstances will a grade of incomplete be given; students should request incompletes in writing by the last class session.

Office Hours

My office is in the Community Sciences building (CS), room 350 (tel. 2714). My regular office hours are MWF 9:30-10:00, W 1:30-2:30; I am often there at other times as well, and am available by appointment. Please call me at home (468-0623) in a dire emergency; however, people who call me at home early in the morning, during the evening news or "Prairie Home Companion;" on weekends, or after 10 at night are subject to the "death by a thousand slices," an old Chinese favorite. Messages can be left for me with CCS secretaries (2355).

UNIVERSITY OF DENVER

16-104
Summer, 1983
Historical Introduction to the Modern World

General Information

Scope: The course will examine historical explanations of how, why, and in what varieties an epochal new form of human society has appeared during the past two centuries. In this study of "modernization," attention will be directed to the evolution of modernity in Western European states, and to its diffusion to, and sometimes strange careers in, Russia, China, Japan, India, and the Ottoman Empire.

Books: Each student should have a copy of:

    F. Roy Willis, World Civilizations Volume II (From the Sixteenth Century to the Contemporary Age)
    Michael Gasster, China's Struggle to Modernize
    Michael Howard, War in European History

Assignments are indicated on the attached Calendar.

Attendance: Because much of the information and analysis offered by the course will be presented only in the lectures, regular attendance will be more than usually necessary.

Examinations and Grades: There will be a Mid-Term and a Final Examination, both based entirely on the daily "Questions" indicated on the attached Calendar.

Procedures will be described orally during our first class meeting.

Grades will be determined:
    by the Mid-Term Essay - 20%
    by attendance and participation - 20%
    by the Final Examination - 60%

Instructor: Dr. Robert E. Roeder
    MRB 413   Tel: 753-2938, 753-2347
    Office Hours: Mon. - Thurs. immediately after class

16-104
Summer, 1983

CALENDAR
(The assigned reading should be completed by the day indicated)

Tues., June 14 1. Introduction: a. Concepts b. Overviews

Part One: The Old Regimes

Wed., June 15 2. East Asian Old Regimes
   a. China
      Reading: Willis, 731, 753-65; Gasster, Pref., Intro., 3-18
      Question: From what bases did the power of the 'gentry' elite of traditional China arise?

   b. Japan
      Reading: Willis, 765-777
      Question: Through what policies did Hideyoshi and his Tokugawa successors bring Japan's chronic civil wars to an end and convert it to a pacific 'centralized feudalism'?

Thurs., June 16 3. Islamic Old Regimes
   a. Mogul India
      Reading: Willis, 739-753
      Question: Why did the great Mogul Empire collapse in the early 18th century?

   b. the Ottoman Empire
      Reading: Willis, 732-739, 777-784
      Question: What were the defining characteristics and social roles of the ulema? of the Jannissaries?

Mon., June 20 4. European Old Regimes I
   a. Russia and Servile Europe
      Reading: Willis, 837-843
      Question: What were the defining characteristics of serfdom and why was it preserved (indeed strengthened) in 16th-18th century Russia?

   b. the Dutch Republic
      Reading: Willis, 785-821
      Question: Upon what was the 17th century economic ascendancy of Amsterdam and its mercantile oligarchy based?

16-104 - Summer, 1983

Tues., June 21 5. European Old Regimes II
   a. France
      Reading: Willis, 843-854, 823-837, 897-913
      Question: What were the principal elites of the Old Regime in France? What were their relations with one another and with the crown?

   b. England
      Reading: Willis, 854-867
      Question: Who were the oligarchs of oligarchic England and why may they be considered a single elite?

(NOTE: Mid-Term Essay Question will be designated)

Part Two: The Invention of Modernity

Wed., June 22 6. The Triple Revolution
   a. Overview

   b. Science and the Enlightenment
      Reading: Willis, 869-897
      Question: What was revolutionary in the political and social ideology of the Enlightenment? Why may it be considered an ambiguous ideology?

(NOTE: Mid-Term Essay due)

Thurs., June 23 7. The Emergence of the Egalitarian Nation State
   a. The American Case
      Reading: Willis, 915-927
      Question: What were the key problems of political order addressed by American constitution-makers? In what ways were their solutions novel?

   b. The French Case
      Reading: Willis, 927-947
      Question: Did Napoleon betray or fulfill the diverse aspirations which produced egalitarian revolution in France?

16-104 - Summer, 1983

Mon., June 27   8. The Industrial Revolution
- a. The Transformation of Production and Distribution
  Reading: Willis, 1013-1037
  Question: What essential features of the industrial system of production and distribution were manifest in the early 19th century history of Manchester?

- b. The Transformation of Urban Life
  Reading: Willis, 1037-1076
  Question: In what essential ways were the life patterns of the major urban classes changed by the coming into being of the industrial system?

Part Three: Modernity vs. The Old Orders, c1800-1918

Tues., June 28   9. The Contest in Europe
- a. Metternichean Containment
  Reading: Willis, 948-1011
  Question: To what extent and how did old elites of European areas east of France maintain their hold on social and political power during the first half of the 19th century?

- b. The Slow Transformation of War
  Reading: Howard, 1-93
  Question: Why did not the innovations in military organization, tactics and strategy produced by the French Revolution immediately destroy the capacity of the old regimes of the continent to survive?

Wed., June 29   10. 19th Century Imperialism
- a. The New Imperialism
  Reading: Willis, 1076-1131, 1149-1155
  Question: Why, after several centuries of contenting itself with establishing trading relationships, did Europe seek and acquire direct imperial control of so much of Asia and Africa during the last decades of the 19th century?

- b. The Survival of Independent Old Orders in the Ottoman Empire and China
  Reading: Willis, 1131-1145; Gasster, 19-31
  Question: How did the Chinese ruling elite react to the mid- and late 19th century threat of outside dominance?

16-104 - Summer, 1983

Thurs., June 30   11. Latecomers to Modernity
- a. Japanese and Russian Modernization Compared
  Reading: Willis, 1145-1149; 1265-1270
  Question: What were the principal similarities in the way Russia and Japan belatedly began to modernize in the half century from the 1860's to World War I? The principal dissimilarities?
- b. The Problem of Germany
  Reading: Willis, 1157-1179; 1205-1238
  Question: Did Germany's somewhat belated achievement of nation-statehood and industrialization leave it with a more volatile and fragile social and political order than those of France and England?

Tues., July 5   12. Europe's Catastrophe
- a. Military Evolution and the Coming of the Great War
  Reading: Willis, 1239-1250; Howard, 94-115
  Question: How did late-19th, early 20th century developments in military organization, equipment, and thinking complicate the tasks of diplomacy and contribute to the outbreak of World War I?
- b. The Political Effects of the Great War
  Reading: Willis, 1250-1257, 1270-1272; Gasster, 31-38
  Question: In which societies and to what extent did the Great War destroy the political power of previously-dominant and conservatively-inclined elites?

Part Four: Twentieth Century Turmoils

Wed., July 6   13. The Failed Restoration
- a. Overviews
- b. The 'Versaille' System and its Breakdown
  Reading: Willis, 1303-1347; Howard, 116-135
  Question: Why did 'liberal' statesmen's attempts to restore national and international order and progress fail in the 1920's and 1930's?

16-104 - Summer, 1983

Thurs., July 7   14. The End of Empire and the Beginning of Modernization in
                      Asia and Africa
                      a. Disintegration of European Empires
                         Reading: Willis, 1385-1386; 1409-1447
                         Question: What aspirations have driven the quest
                                   for independent nationhood in Asia,
                                   the Middle East, and Africa since World War I?

                      b. Strategies of Modernization
                         Reading: Same
                         Question: What alternative strategies of
                                   modernization have appeared desirable
                                   to the leading elites of the new nations?

Mon., July 11   15. Revolutions of the Left
                      a. Russia
                         Reading: Willis, 1261-1301
                         Question: What were the principal elements of
                                   Stalin's strategy of modernization?
                                   Could he rightfully claim to be Lenin's
                                   heir in pursuing this strategy?

                      b. China
                         Reading: Willis, 1386-1401; Gasster, 38-146
                         Question: How did Mao's modernization goals and
                                   strategy differ from those of his Russian
                                   Communist predecessors?

Tues., July 12   16. High Modernity
                      a. Variant Forms of Social and Economic Order in the
                         post-1945 Developed World
                         Reading: Willis, 1449-1485; 1401-1409
                         Question: Despite ideological and cultural
                                   differences, are there important common
                                   features in the economic and social policies
                                   of the developed nations of the post-1945
                                   era?

                      b. The Urban Order in the Developed World
                         Reading: Willis, 1349-1383
                         Question: Is it possible to create satisfactory
                                   communities in megalopolis?

                  (NOTE: Designation of questions eligible for the Final will
                  be made on this day)

16-104 - Summer, 1983

Wed., July 13   17. Dilemmas of Statecraft in the Nuclear Age
                    a. Origin and Conduct of the Cold War
                       Reading: None
                       Question: Was Franklin Roosevelt's grand design
                                 for peace doomed to failure?

                    b. Is Modernity Obsolete?
                       Reading: Howard, 136-143
                       Question: None

Thurs., July 14   FINAL EXAMINATION

Schematic Outline: Descriptions of Old Regimes

A. Preliminary Description.

   1. Territorial extent.
   2. Population trends.
   3. Economic geography of major regions.
   4. Basic framework of government.
   5. Chronological sketch of major developments.

B. Structure of Institutions.

   1. "Village" structure and functions.
   2. Other primary groups.
   3. Urban hierarchy.
   4. Elite networks.

      a. Aristocratic.
      b. Religious.
      c. Mercantile.
      d. Other, if any.
      e. Bureaucratic.

   5. "Camp": Military structure.

   6. "Court": Central government structure.

   7. Ideological structure: dominant legitimating and directing ideas, traditions, beliefs.

C. Dynamics.

   1. Examples of recurrent social problems and solutions.
   2. Special crises and responses to them.
   3. Important trends during the last generation of the old regime.

HAMPTON INSTITUTE

HISTORY 106 - WORLD CIVILIZATIONS II

Dr. Sarah S. Hughes
Office: MLK 212
Office Phone: 727-5750
Home Phone: 723-2394

Office hours:
MWF - 3:00-5:00

REQUIRED TEXTBOOKS:

L.S. Stavrianos, The World Since 1500, 4th edition (green cover)

Mary Berry and John Blassingame, Long Memory

Chinua Achebe, No Longer at Ease

During the semester you will be assigned chapters 11-28 pf Stavrianos and all of the other two books. Other brief readings on reserve in the Huntington Library may also be required.

Reading assignments should be completed prior to the class on which the topic is scheduled. That reading must be taken seriously, cannot be stressed too much. As you read, check maps in Stavrianos or an atlas at the library to be sure you know the region under discussion and its spatial relationships to other countries, continents and oceans.

COURSE OBJECTIVE AND CONTENT:

World Civilizations II focuses on the years from 1800 to the present, a period when many aspects of the contemporary world were shaped. The nineteenth century was a time when industrialized nations conquered and ruled much of the world. The rise of imperialism was accompanied by the abolition of slavery in the Americas. But racism became more virulent as it was used to justify white domination throughout the world. In the twentieth century conflicts between powerful nations led to World Wars I and II. European nations lost power as the United States and the Soviet Union became leaders of blocs engaged in perpetual cold war. Colonialism became obsolete as African and Asian nations gained political independence, but continued to struggle for economic parity. Particular attention will be paid to the historical development of the black community in the United States and the interaction of the West and Modern Africa.

PROCEDURES:

World Civilizations is primarily a lecture course. Attention, attendance, and careful note-taking are advised. If you are unfamiliar with methods of taking notes, see me in my office. There will be some class discussion, but it is not feasible to plan on daily student participation in large classes. Students should not hesitate to ask relevant questions after or during lectures, as well as in discussion sessions or privately in my office.

OFFICE VISITS:

Every student should see me in my office during the semester. If you have problems in the course, let me know immediately. Study groups and tutoring are more effective if begun early and pursued regularly.

ATTENDANCE AND ABSENCES:

Regular attendance at all classes es expected. Three tardies (coming after class has commenced) count as one absence. Eleven absences for any reason can cause you to fail the course.

STUDENT RESPONSIBILITY:

It is the responsibility of each student when absent to secure materials distributed in class, assignments, and other announcements from me in my office. The distribution or dissemination in class of any information or material indicates student responsibility for same for testing purposes. If you must miss a class, you should read the class notes of another student. Consult the bibliography, the reading lists at the end of each chapter in Stavrianos and in Berry-Blassingame, or ask me for additional sources that may clarify some topics or be of particular interest to you.

PAPER, EXAMS, AND GRADES:

A brief research paper of 5-6- typed pages is required. This assignment will be graded S/U. To receive a passing grade or better in the course, regardless of your test grades, you must receive a satisfactory grade on your paper. It is due on February 29, 1984. If it is unsatisfactory, the paper will be returned with suggestions for improvement. It can then be resubmitted any time before April 20 for re-evaluation without penalty. Further information on topics and sources for this paper will be demonstrated separately.

There will be three one-hour examinations, including the final. Each will incorporate materials from assigned readings, lectures and class discussions. Each of these three tests will count for one-third of your course grade.

All make-up exams will be given at a single announced time. Written excuses may be required for taking make-up exams. If a student misses a scheduled make-up exam, no further make-up will be allowed, and a grade of zero will be given for that test.

PLEASE READ THIS SHEET COMPLETELY AND CAREFULLY. RETAIN IT THROUGHOUT THE COURSE AND CONSULT IT FROM TIME TO TIME.

Sarah Hughes   Spring 1984

WORLD CIVILIZATIONS II - HISTORY 106

Course Outline

Industrialization
  Changes in Production Methods
  Impact on Society
    Labor, Migration, Families, Consumption, Environment
    Expansion of Markets and Erosion of Traditional Cultures
    The Rise and Collapse of Slave Economics

Ideas of the Industrial World
  Individualism, Liberalism, Romanticism
  Socialism and Anarchism
  Nationalism

Military, Economic and Political Power in the 19th Century
  Dominant Nations: England, France, Germany
  Emerging Powers
    Russian Expansion
    U.S. Expansion

Black Culture in the United States: Its Roots in Slavery and Freedom
  The African Contribution
  Free Blacks and Slaves
  Family and Church

Men, Women, and the Family in the Nineteenth Century

Colonialism and Imperialism
  India as a Colony of England
  Partition and Conquest of Africa
  U.S. Colonies and Protectorates
  The Black Struggle for Political Rights in the U.S.
  China and Japan

"Scientific Racism" and Social Darwinism

The Changing Industrial Economy of the West

Conflict Among Imperial Powers: World War I

The Aftermath of War
  Third World Nationalism
  Communist Revolutions

Segregation in the United States
  Jobs and Schools

World War II

Sarah S. Hughes					Spring 1984
			History 106 - World Civilizations II
ASSIGNMENTS - 1

Topic	Reading	Due for class of:
Industrialization	Stavrianos, 173-190 (review 163-173)	January 18
Ideas of the Industrial World	Special assignment in lieu of class	January 20
Liberalism, Individualism, and Romanticism	Stavrianos, 210-219	January 23
Socialism and Anarchism		January 25
Nationalism	Long Memory, 388-423	January 27

Military, Economic, and Political Power in the 19th Century

Dominant Nations: England, France and Germany		January 30
Emerging Powers: Russia	Stavrianos, 221-240	January 30
Emerging Powers: The United States		February 1

Black Culture in the U.S.
African Contribution	Long Memory, 3-32	February 3
Free Blacks & Slaves	Long Memory, 33-69	February 6
Family and Church	Long Memory, 70-113	February 8

Men, Women, and the Family in the 19th Century

		Barbara Welter, "The		February 10
		Cult of True Womanhood,
		1820-1860," copies
		on reserve at Huntington
		Library desk

FIRST EXAM						February 15

Sarah S. Hughes Spring 1984

History 106 - World Civilizations II

ASSIGNMENTS - 2

Topic	Reading	Due for class of:
Men, Women & the Family in the 19th Century	Barbara Welter, "The Cult of True Womanhood, 1820-1860," copies on reserve at Huntington Library desk	Feb. 17
Colonialism & Imperialism		
India as an English colony	Stavrianos, 271-284	Feb. 24
The Partition of Africa	Stavrianos, 302-318	Feb. 27
RESEARCH PAPERS DUE	- - - -	Feb. 29
U.S. Colonies & Protectorates	R. Hofstadter, W. Miller, & D. Aaron, The Structure of American History, 274-281. Copies on reserve at Huntington Library desk.	Mar. 2
The Black Struggle for Political Participation in the U.S.	Long Memory, 142-169	Mar. 12
China and Japan	Stavrianos, 285-301	Mar. 16
"Scientific Racism" & Social Darwinism	Stavrianos, 330-341	Mar. 19
Sex and Racism	Long Memory, 114-141	Mar. 21
The Changing Industrial Economy of the West	- - - -	Mar. 23 (end of drop period)
World War I	Stavrianos, 345-369	Mar. 26
Third World Nationalism	Stavrianos, 370-385	Mar. 28
SECOND EXAM	(covering all assignments on this sheet)	MARCH 30

Sarah S. Hughes   Spring 1984

                    History 106 - World Civilizations II

Assignments - 3

Topic	Reading	Due for class of:
World War I	Stavrianos, Chapter 20	April 2
Aftermath of War: Revolutions and Nationalism	Stavrianos, Chapter 21	April 4
Depression and the Beginning of Another World War	Stavrianos, Chapter 24	April 6
World War II	Stavrianos, Chapter 25	April 9
The Twilight of Colonialism: A Nigerian Case Study	Achebe, No Longer at Ease, pp. 1-65	April 11
	No Longer at Ease, pp. 66-159 Be prepared to write short essays in class to answer specific questions about this novel.	April 13
Segregation in the U.S: Jobs and Schools	Long Memory, pp. 195-226; 261-294	April 16
Demands for Equality: End of Empires in Asia and Africa	Stavrianos, Chapter 26	April 18
Demands for Equality: Black Protests and Black Power in the U.S.	Long Memory, pp. 169-194	April 20
	Long Memory, pp. 342-387	April 23
Cold War and Localized Wars in a Nuclear Age	Stavrianos, chapter 27	April 25

FINAL EXAM: Tuesday, May 1 at 10:10 a.m. Location to be announced.

Sarah Hughes

WORLD CIVILIZATIONS II - HISTORY 106

Bibliography

INDUSTRIALIZATION

    Phyllis Deane, The First Industrial Revolution
    W.W. Rostow, British Economy of the Nineteenth Century
    Thomas Cochran and William Miller, The Age of Enterprise
    James Gilbert, Designing the Industrial State
    Samuel P. Hays, The Response to Industrialism, 1885-1914
    Paul Barran and Paul Sweezy, Monopoly Capitalism

IDEAS OF THE WESTERN WORLD

    Douglas R. Hofstadter, Godel, Escher, Bach: An Eternal Golden Braid
    George Mosse, The Culture of Western Europe
    H. Stuart Hughes, Consciousness and Society: The Reorientation of European Social Thought
    Robert L. Heilbroner, The Worldly Philosophers
    P. Robertson, Revolutions of 1848: A Social History

MILITARY, ECONOMIC, AND POLITICAL POWER IN THE NINETEENTH CENTURY

    W.B. Wilcox, Star of Empire A Study of Britain as a World Power, 1485-1945
    A.J.P. Taylor, Bismarck: The Man and Statesman
    Eric J. Hobsbawn, The Age of Revolution, 1789-1848
    William A. Williams, The Tragedy of American Diplomacy
    Michael T. Florinsky, Russia, A History and Interpretation

BLACK CULTURE IN THE UNITED STATES

    Rayford W. Logan, The Betrayal of the Negro
    W.E.B. DuBois, Black Reconstruction in America, 1860-1880
    August Meier, Negro Thought in America, 1880-1915
    Okon Edet Uya, ed., Black Brotherhood: Afro-Americans and Africa
    Joyce Ladner, Tomorrow's Tomorrow: The Black Woman
    Robert Engs, Freedom's First Generation
    Lawrence Levine, Black Culture, Black Consciousness
    Filomena Steady, ed., The Black Woman Cross-Culturally
    (also refer to extensive bibliography in Long Memory)

MEN, WOMEN AND THE FAMILY

    Martha Vicinus, Suffer and Be Still
    Herbert Gutman, The Black Family in Slavery and Freedom
    Sheila Rowbotham, Hidden From History
    Sara Evans, Personal Politics
    Ester Boserup, Woman's Role in Economic Development
    Sharon Harley and Rosalyn Terborg-Penn, The Afro-American Woman

-2-

Michael Gordon, ed., The American Family in Social-Historical Perspective
Renate Birdenthal and Claudia Koonz, eds., Becoming Visible: Women in European History

COLONIALISM AND IMPERALISM

    Eric Williams, Capitalism and Slavery
    Percival Spear, India: A Modern History
    John K. Fairbank, ed., Chinese Thought and Institutions
    John Strachey, The End of Empire
    R.W. Van Alstyne, The Rising American Empire
    Thomas McCormick, China Market: America's Quest for Informal Empire, 1893-1901
    Hugh Borton, Japan's Modern Century
    Rosa Luxemburg, The Accumulation of Capital
    Walter Rodney, How Europe Underdeveloped Africa
    Eric R. Wolfe, Europe and the People Without History

RACISM AND SOCIAL DARWINISM

    Gxorge M. Fredrickson, White Supremacy: A Comparative Study of American and South African History
    John W. Cell, The Highest Stage of White Supremacy
    Richard Hofstadter, Social Darwinism in American Thought
    David M. Chalmers, Hooded Americanism, The History of the Ku Klux Klan
    John Higham, Strangers in the Land: Patterns of American Nativism, 1860-1925
    Thomas F. Gosset, Race: The History of an Idea in America

THE CHANGING INDUSTRIAL ECONOMY OF THE WEST

    Robert L. Heilbroner, The Future as History
    J.K. Galbraith, The New Industrial State
    Karl Polanyi, The Great Transformation
    James C. Abegglen, The Japanese Factory: Aspects of Its Social Organization

TWENTIETH-CENTURY WARS

    Raymond Aron, The Century of Total War
    Ernst Nolte, Three Faces of Fascism
    Gar Alperovitz, Atomic Diplomacy: Hiroshima and Potsdam
    C. Falls, The Second World War: A Short History
    Arthur Marwick, The Deluge

THIRD WORLD NATIONALISM AND REVOLUTIONS

    Edward H. Carr, The Bolshevik Revolution
    Edgar Snow, Red Star Over China
    Zeine N. Zeine, The Emergence of Arab Nationalism
    Frantz Fanon, The Wretched of the Earth

-3-

C.P. Fitzgerald, *The Birth of Communist China*
C.B. MacPherson, *The Real World of Democracy*
Immanuel Wallerstein, *Africa: The Politics of Unity*
Basil Davidson, *Which Way Africa?*
Margaret Randall, *Sandino's Daughters*
Jose Yglesias, *In the Fist of the Revolution: Life in a Cuban Town*
Robert A. Humphreys, *Tradition and Revolt in Latin America*
Walter LaFeber, *Inevitable Revolutions: The United States in Central America*

History 106

RESEARCH PAPER

Your paper is to be in the form of an essay discussing what you read. You need to describe enough of the book to assure me that you read it. If you read a historical work, for instance, explain what country, period of time, and problems were discussed. Try to explain the author's thesis, or main argument, either in your own words or in a brief quotation. After you do this, give some of the examples or facts you thought important to support the argument. If you read a novel, explain the plot in no more than one paragraph. If you read an autobiography, essay, or works of an influential person, give a brief biographical sketch of the person in one paragraph.

The focus of your essay, however, should be topics you found important in the context of world history. For instance, if you read the novel by Andre Malraux, Man's Fate, about communist revolutionaries in China in the 1920s, it would be important to indicate what you learned about Chinese society, the conflicts between nationalists and communists, the role of Europeans, and to perhaps speculate about the impact of the real events described in the novel on the government when the Chinese communists later assumed power. For this paper, in contrast to one in an English course, the author's style or manner of organizing the book are not so important as the setting and events. If you read a nonfiction historical work, either a monograph or the writings of an influential person, you need to discuss the events or ideas that seemed important to you in the context of world history. Thus, if you read The Souls of Black Folks by W.E.B. DuBois, your report should indicate what he thought of the situation of his people at the beginning of the twentieth century and what kind of reforms he proposed. You might then relate his ideas about the importance of education to those of other nationalist leaders in Africa or Asia. It is important to consider when the book was written (usually shown by the copyright date, unless it is a modern reprint), so that you can put it in historical perspective.

The purpose of this assignment is to enable you to explore some aspect of the human experience since 1800 in greater detail. The attached list of books includes a variety of topics, as well as styles of writing. Some are short, some long, some easy, some difficult. If you want to read a book that is not on this list, you must get my prior approval. The simplest way to do this is to check the book out of the library and bring it to my office.

Be sure that your paper is entirely in your own words. Do not copy or plagiarize what you read. When you cite brief excerpts from a book, enclose them in quotation marks and indicate the page number.

Example: "For the Puritans the extermination of the Pequots was proof of their political and military ascendancy." (85)

The most common reason for rejecting a paper as unsatisfactory is plagiarism. Few of you write as well as the authors you will read, so when you copy them if often "jumps out."

Neither footnotes nor bibliography are required. Begin your paper with the following information:

Author, title, publisher, copyright date (and date of original publication for a reprint edition).

Criteria for a satisfactory paper: five-six double-spaced, typed pages; content that indicates you did the reading, thought about it, and related it to world history; coherent organization, adequate grammar and spelling.

Novels

E. M. Forster, A Passage to India
Andre Malraux, Man's Fate
Alice Walker, The Color Purple
Zora Neale Hurston, Their Eyes Were Watching God
Francis Bebey, Ashanti Doll
Paule Marshall, Brown Girl, Brownstones
Dorothy West, The Living Is Easy
O.E. Rolvaag, Giants in the Earth
Hamlin Garland, Main Travelled Roads
Leo Tolstoy, War and Peace
Ignazio Silone, Bread and Wine
Ernest Hemingway, For Whom the Bell Tolls
Honore de Balzac, Eugenie Grandet
Maxine Hong Kingston, The Woman Warrior
Agnes Smedley, Daughter of Earth
Doris Lessing, Children of Violence (one part only)
Virginia Woolf, Orlando
Santha Rama Rau, Remember the House
Erich M. Remarque, All Quiet on the Western Front
Harvey Swados, On the Line
Jane Austen, Emma
Willa Cather, My Antonia
Karen Blixen (Isak Dinesen), Out of Africa
John Steinbeck, The Grapes of Wrath
R. Prawer Jhabvala, Amrita or A Stronger Climate
Nella Larson, Quicksand
Doris Lessing, The Grass Is Singing
Thomas Mann, Buddenbrooks
Alice Tisdale Hobart, Oil for the Lamps of China
V.S. Reid, The Leopard
Roger Mais, Brother Man
Chinua Achebe, Things Fall Apart
William Conton, The African
Cyprian Ekwensi, Survive the Peace
Ngugi Wa Thiong's Weep Not Child

Monographs, Historics, Travel

Margaret Mead, Coming of Age in Somoa
Ketih Schall, ed., Stony the Road
Carl Degler, Neither Black Nor White
Edgar Snow, Red China Today or The Long Revolution
Joshua S. Horn, Away With All Pests
Lawrence Levine, Black Culture, Black Consciousness
William Harris, The Harder We Run
Edmund Wilson, To the Finland Station
Melvin Kranzberg and Joseph Gies, By the Sweat of Thy Brow: Work in the Western World
R. W. Malcolmson, Popular Recreations in English Society, 1700-1850
Robert Heilbroner, Business Civilization in Decline
K. William Knapp, The Social Costs of Private Enterprise
Christine Obbo, African Women
Denise Paulme, ed., Women of Tropical Africa
Nawal el Saadawi, The Hidden Face of Eve
Nelson Reed, The Caste War of Yucatan
Leon Wolff, Flanders Fields
Norman E. Himes, Medical History of Contraception
Nell Painter, Exodusters
C. Vann Woodward, The Strange Career of Jim Crow
Ray Ginger, The Bending Cross, Eugene V. Debs: A Biography
David M. Chalmers, Hooded Americanism
Robert K. Murray, Red Scare
Gilbert Osofsky, Harlem: The Making of a Ghetto
Arthur F. Raper, Preface to Peasantry
Robert Jungk, Brighter Than a Thousand Stars: The Story of the Men Who Made the Bomb.
Dan T. Carter, Scottsboro
Monica Schuler, Alas, Alas, Kongo
Roger Bastide, The African Religions of Brazil
Samir Amin, Neo-Colonialism in West Africa
Harry Magdoff, Imperialism
Brian Weinstein, Eboue (a biography)
Ann and Neva Seidman, South Africa and U.S. Multinational Corporations
Roger Bastide, African Civilizations in the New World
Leo Spitzer, The Creoles of Sierra Leone, 1870-1945
Thomas Cripps, Slow Fade to Black: The Negro in American Film, 1900-1942
Edmund Wilson, Apologies to the Iroquois
Vine Deloria, Jr., Behind the Trail of Broken Treaties
George Woodcock, Mohandas Gandhi

Autobiographies, Essays, Writings of Influential People

Ray L. Billington, ed., The Journal of Charlotte Forten
John Reed, Ten Days That Shook the World
Rauli Murray, Proud Shoes
Ann Moody, Coming of Age in Mississippi
W. E. B. DuBois, The Souls of Black Folks
Alain Locke, The New Negro
Amy J. Garvey, ed., Philosophy and Opinions of Marcus Garvey
Sigmund Freud, Civilization and Its Discontents
Adolf Hitler, Mein Kampf
John Stuart Mill, On Liberty and Autobiography
Mahatma Gandhi, The Story of My Experiments With Truth
Charles Darwin, On the Origin of Species
William Graham Sumner, Social Darwinism
Thorsten Veblen, The Portable Veblen
Henry David Thoreau, Walden
V. I. Lenin, Imperialism
Marshall McLuhan, Understanding Media
Frantz Fanon, The Wretched of the Earth
Karl Marx and F. Engels, Collected Writings (many editions)
Eric Williams, Capitalism and Slavery
Kwame Nkrumah, Ghana: The Autobiography of Kwame Nkrumah
Elizabeth Gurley Flynn, The Rebel Girl
Naboth Mokgatle, The Autobiography of Chief Obafemi Awolowo (Nigeria)
Odinga Odinga, Not Yet Uhuru (autobiography, Kenya)
Paul Robeson, Here I Stand
Nelson Mandela, No Easy Walk to Freedom

BROOME COMMUNITY COLLEGE
Binghamton, New York

HIS100
The West and the World: Contemporary Problems
in Historical Perspective

Fall 1982
Mr. Higginbottom

REQUIRED READING: Readings should be completed by the dates indicated. There are two sources of course readings: the first is titled The West and the World by Kevin Reilly (R); the second is a series of short articles on aspects of social history by Peter Stearns (S).

SCHEDULE: Please follow this schedule of assigned readings, exams, and films closely.

Class/Date	Assignment (for next class)	Class Activity
1 T 8/31	Reilly - Preface (for 9/2 class) Stearns - Introduction (for 9/2 class)	Introduction Discussion
2 R 9/2	Reilly - Ch. 11 (for 9/7)	Discuss Stearns
3 T 9/7	R. - Ch. 11 (for 9/9) S. - Thomas, "Religion and the Decline of Magic" SEE FILM: "The Seventh Seal" -- 9/8	Discuss Ch. 11
4 R 9/9	SEE FILM: "The Good Earth" -- 9/9 R. - Ch. 12 (for 9/14)	Discuss "Seal" and Thomas. Write a short essay-review
5 T 9/14	R. - Ch. 12 (cont.) S. - Laslett, "The World We Have Lost," Hunt, "Pre-Modern Families," and Lasch, "The Family Besieged."	Discuss "Good Earth" and Reilly, Ch. 12
6 R 9/16	Write analysis of traditional and modern society, utilizing films and readings, theme to be assigned. (for 9/21)	Discuss readings and concepts of tradition and modernity
7 T 9/21	Read supplementary material on the Renaissance and Reformation to be assigned	Lecture on Renaissance Humanism
8 R 9/23	FILM: "The Majestic Clockwork" R. - Ch. 13 (for 9/28	Screen film in class
9 T 9/28	R. - Ch. 13 (cont.) SEE FILM: "Cromwell" -- 9/30	Discuss "Clockwork"
10 R 9/30	SuppTementary reading to be assigned R. - Ch. 14 (for 10/5) FILM: "Cromwell"	Lecture/discussion the Enlightenment
11 T 10/5	S. - Intro. to Part II on Early Industrialization R. - Ch. 14 (cont.)	Discuss "Cromwell" and reading
12 R 10/7	R. - Ch. 15 (for 10/12) S. - Langer, "The Population Revolution," and Tobias, "Crime and Industrialization in Britain."	Lecture on Industrial Revolution

HIS100   -2-

13 T 10/12 SEE FILM: "Max Haavelar"   Lecture on Colonialism
              R. - Ch. 15)cont.)   in non-western world

14 R 10/14 Write an essay on racism and colonialism; theme   Discuss Racism and
              to be assigned (for 10/19)   Colonialism
              *10/18 "The Atomic Cafe"
              *10/19 "Failsafe"
              *10/20 "Dr. Strangelove"
              *10/21 "The Missiles of October"

15 T 10/19 R. - Ch. 16 (for 10/21)   Lecture on Economics
                                                        and Ecology

16 R 10/21 R. - Ch. 16 (cont.)   Discuss and review,
                                                        Ch. 14 - 16

17 T 10/26 No Assignment   FIRST HOUR EXAMINATION:
                                                        Ch. 14 - 16

18 R 10/28 R. - Ch. 17 (for 11/2)   Screen film
              SEE FILM: "Drive for Power"

19 T 11/2   R. - Ch. 17 (cont.)   Lecture on early labor
              SEE FILM: "The Organizer"   organization

20 R 11/4   R. - Ch. 17 (cont.)   Discuss Ch. 17
              S. - Intro Part III.
              Stearns, "The Adaptation of Workers."
              Branca, "Middle-Class Women." (for 11/9)

21 T 11/9   R. - Ch. 18   Discuss "The Organizer"
              Write short essay on theme to be assigned
              relating to labor organization in the
              industrial revolution

22 R 11/11 R. - Ch. 18 (cont.)   Lecture on Caste, Class
              Prepare for second hour exam, 11/16   and Race

23 T 11/16 R. - Ch. 19 (for 11/18)   SECOND HOUR EXAMINATION:
              S. - Intro to Part IV   Chapters 17, 18, readings
                                                        and films

24 R 11/18 R. Ch. 19 (cont.)   Screen "Fallacies"
              SEE FILM: "Fallacies of Hope"
              S. - Schoenbaum, "Social Bases of Nazism"

25 T 11/23 R. - Ch. 19 (cont.)   Screen "Swastika"
              S. - Walvin, "Sports," and Inkeles, "Modern
              Man." Intro to Part V
              SEE FILM: "Swastika"

26 R 11/25 R. - Ch. 20 (for 11/30)   Discuss "Fallacies" and
                                                        "Swastika"

*During the week of October the college will sponsor a series of films, lectures,
and debates on strategic nuclear weapons and danger of nuclear war. Extra credit
can be earned for attendance at one or more of these events. See me for details.
The films particularly should be of great topical interest.

HIS100

27	T	11/30	R. - Ch. 20 (cont.) S. - Dubos, "Mirage of Health"	Lecture on the environment
28	R	12/2	R. - Ch. 21 (for 12/7) S. - Laing, "The Horror of Modernization," and Plumb, "The New World of Children."	Discuss environment, health, and environmental health
29	T	12/7	R. - Ch. 21 (cont.) S. _ Shorter, "Sexual Revolution" and Zehr, "Crime and the Development of Modern Society."	Review for final examination
30	R	12/9	FILM: "Knowledge or Uncertainty"	Screen film

EVALUATION AND GRADING: You will be evaluated by the quality of your thinking--expressed orally and in writing--on the various themes which we explore in the reading and in class. The final grade will be determined as follows:

```
Two hour examinations          50
Final examination              25
Quizzes, short essays, and
   class participation         25
```

ATTENDANCE: You are expected to attend all classes. You will not be downgraded for non-attendance, but it is certain to undermine your performance. Films which are full feature in format, and thus, longer than a single class session, will be screened several times during the day. You will be expected to attend one of the screenings.

OFFICE HOURS: I will be available in T121 to confer with you by appointment throughout the day. Mrs. Benko will be happy to schedule you.

THE JOHNS HOPKINS UNIVERSITY

The Department of History

THE WORLD AND THE WEST

80.329
Fall Semester, 1983
Mr. Curtin
Monday and Tuesday at 10 AM
Four Credits

This course departs somewhat from the usual pattern in either history, or anthropology, although, as a study of the ways peoples' cultures or ways of life change through time, it has elements of both. It also differs from both disciplines. The scope is too broad to leave room for an intimate picture of any culture or society, so that many anthropologists may feel unsatisfied. Nor will the course follow a sequence of events in any place through a substantial period of time, so that many historians may be equally unsatisfied. The course is episodic of necessity, being a series of case studies illustrating general patterns. This inplies a strong comparative element in approach and presentation.

The course also departs from the usual pattern in that most lectures are not delivered in the class room but are available on tape at the audio-visual desk, A level, Elsenhower Memorial Library. Audio-visual also lends casette recorders, if you do not have your own. Outlines and illustrative material for each lecture will be distributed early in the semester. The two class meetings each week will normally be used for discussion of the lectures and reading assignments for that week.

In preparation for these discussions, students are required to present each Monday Morning a brief (2 to 3 typed pages) and informal account of their reactions to the readings and lectures assigned for that week, or to the discussions of the preseeding week. For lack of a better name, these are called "intellectual journals." One purpose is to keep the instructor informed of class reactions. Another is to encourage students to express their own thoughts in writing. One way to think about this assignment is to consider it as an answer to this question--what did I learn this week that was significant, and why? If not, why not?

The intellectual journals are not returned until the end of the semester, but students are expected to meet with the instructor from time to time to discuss their work.

As compensation for the extra work of preparing these intellectual journals, any student who turns in his or her journal every Monday <u>without fail</u> for the entire semester is automatically excused from the final examination. The grade in that case will be based on the quality of the journals and of class discussion.

No term paper is required.

There is no formal text, but a considerable part of the following will be read in the course of the semester:
P.D. Curtin, Two Jamaicas, all assigned.
Percival Spear, A History of India, vol. 2 (Pelican A770), 88 of 288 pages assigned.

TOPIC I - THE WORLD AND THE WEST: A SURVEY OF PAST RELATIONS

First Week = Technology and Power in Europe

September 12 - Classroom lecture 1: Relations between Societies
September 13 - Classroom lecture 3: European Technology and European Power.

Assigned Reading and taped lectures for the second week should be read or heard this week in preparation for discussion on September 19. (Note that lectures are not necessarily assigned in order, and that lectures 6, 9, and 13 are not assigned at all this year.

Second Week = Technology and Power in World Perspective

September 19 - Discussion based on:
Lecture 2 - Societies beyond Europe: Agriculture and Population.
Lecture 4 - Technology and Power in Non-Western Societies.

September 18 - Discussion based on:
McNeill, William H., Plaques and Peoples, pp. 149-198.
McNeill, William H., The Pursuit of Power, pp. 24-62.
Wolf, Eric R. Europe and the People without History, pp. 24-72.

Recommended:

Elvin, Mark, The Pattern of the Chinese Past, esp. pp. 109-99.
Chaunu, Pierre, L'expansion europeene du XIIIe au XVe sieCle
Chaunu, Pierre, Conquete et exploitation des nouveaux mondes (XVIe sieÇle).
Braudel, Fernand, Civilization and Capitalism 15th-18th Century, 2 vols., (esp. vol. 1 on diffusion of technology and vol. 2, pp. 14 -37.
Cioppola, Carlo M., Guns and Sails in the Early Phase of European Expansion, 1400-1700.
Parry, J.H., The Age of Reconnaissance, pp., 19-127 for maritime technology.

Wallerstein, Immanuel, The Modern World System, volume 1.

TOPIC II _ ASIAN TRADE AND WESTERN SHIPPING

Third Week = The Fifteenth and Sixteenth Centuries in Asia
    September 26-27 - Discussions based on:
        Lecture 5 - Intellectual Consequence of Overseas Knowledge for Europe.
        Curtin, Cross-Cultural Trade (xerox mss., chapters 1, 6, and 7)

    Recommended:
    Meilink-Roelofsz, M.A.P., Asian Trade and European Influence
    Boxer, C.R., The Portuguese Seaborne Empire
    Steensgard, Niels, Carraoks, Caravans, and Companies
    Elliot, John., The Old World and the New

Fourth Week = Missionaries in Asia

    October 3-4 Discussions based on:
    Lecture 7 - Missionary Aims and Achievements
    Lecture 8 - Japan's Reception of Christian Missions
    Sansom, G. B., The Western World and Japan, pp. 54-86, 115-64.

    Recommended

        Boxer, C.R., The Christian Century in Japan
        Rowbotham, Missionary and Mandarin
        Elison, George, Deus Destroyed: The Image of Christianity in Early Modern Japan.

    Fifth Week = New Entrants and New Technology in Asian Trade

        October 10 - Slide lecture on Mughal India and Japan
        October 11 - Discussion based on:
            Lecture 10 - Technology and Trade in the seventeenth and eighteenth centuries.
            Curtin, Cross-Cultural Trade (mss. xeroxed chs., 8 and 9)
            Steinberg, D.J., and others, In Search of Southeast Asia, pp. 11-21, 48-58.
            Spear, Peroival, A History of India 2:40-80.

Recommended:

    Furber, Holden, Rival Empires of Trade in the Orient
    Chauduri, K.N., The Trading World of Asia and the English East India Company.

    Sixth Week = Adjustments in Agricultural and Political Structure

        October 17 - 18 - Discussion of:
        Lecture 11 - Asian Agricultural Adjustment

Lecture 12 - Transition to Territorial Empire: Java and Bengal.
Steinberg and others, Search of Southeast Asia, pp. 141-54
    Spear, History of India 2:81-128
    Curtin, Cross-Cultural Trade, xeroxed, ch. 11

Recommended

    Mauro, Frederick, L'expansion europeen, 1600-1870.
    McNeill, William H., The Rise of the West, chs. 11 and 12 (pp. 569-725) in original edition).
    Wallerstein, Immanuel, Modern World System, vol., 1, chs., 6-7 (pp. 199-239 in text edition)
    Sauer, Carl O., Agricultural Origins and Dispersals.
    Parry J.H., Trade and Dominion: The European Overseas Empires in the Eighteenth Century.

TOPIC III - THE RISE AND FALL OF THE SOUTH ATLANTIC SYSTEM.

Seventh Week - Medieval Origins

    October 24-25 - Discussion based on:
    Lecture 14 - Mediterranean Origins of Plantation Slavery.
    Lecture 15 - From Cyprus to the Atlantic Islands
    Knight, Franklin W., The Caribbean, pp. 3-49
    McNeill, W.H., Plaques and Peoples, pp. 199-234.
    Paul Bohannan and Philip Curtin, Africa and Africans, pp 223-76

Recommended

    Verlinden, Charles, The Origins of Modern Colonization

Eighth Week = Sixteenth-Century Transition

    October 31-November 1, Discussion based on:
    Lecture 16 - Africa and the Slave Trade
    Lecture 17 - Capitalism, Feudalism, and Brazilian Sugar Planting.
    Curtin, P.D., and others, African History, pp., 213-76
    Boxer, C.R., The Portuguese Seaborne Empire, pp. 84-127.
    Hoetink, H., "Colonial Psychology and Race, " Journal of Economic History, 21:629-44 (December 1961)

    Recommended

    Russell-Wood A.J.R., The Black Man in Slavery and Freedom in Colonial Brazil, pp. 267-103
    Furtado, Celso, The Economic Growth of Brazil pp 43-77

Ninth Week = The Spanish Empire on the American Mainland

    November 7-8 - Discussion based on:

Lecture 18 Bureaucrats and Free Lances
Lecture 19 - Imperial Theory and Demographic Fact
Gibson, Charles, Spain in America, pp. 24-159.

Tenth Week = The South Atlantic System Established

November 14-15 - Discussion based on:
Lecture 20 - The Sugar Revolution and Imperial Control
Lecture 21 - The Periphery of the South Atlantic System
Knight, F.W., The Caribbean, 50-120.
Russell-Wood, A.J.R., Slavery and Freedom, pp. 104-27.

Recommended:

Dunn, Richard S., Sugar and Slave, pp. 46-83, 188-262

Eleventh Week = Economic and Society in the Caribbean

November 21-22 - Discussion based on:
Lecture 22 - The Caribbean Economy in the Eighteenth Century
Lecture 23 - Coastal West Africa in the Eighteenth Century
Braithwaite, Edward, The Development of Creole Society in Jamaica 1770-1820, pp. 105-239.
Curtin, P.D., Two Jamaicas, pp. 3-80

Recommended:

Eltis, David, "Free and Coerced Transatlantic Migrations, "American Historical Review, 88:251-80 (1982)
Craton, Michael and James Walvin, A Jamaican Plantation
Paterson, Orlando, Sociology of Slavery
Debien, Gabriel, Les esclaves aux Antilles francaises
Morner, Magnus, Race Mixture in the History of Latin America
Craton, Michael, In Search of the Invisible Man

Twelfth Week = The Democratic Revolution

November 28-29 - Discussion based on:
Lecture 24 - Revolution in the Atlantic Basin
Lecture 25 - The French Revolution in the West Indies
Curtin, Two Jamaicas, pp. 81-121
Wolf, People without History, pp. 265-309

Recommended:

Geggus, David P., Slavery, War, And Revolution
McNeill, W.H., The Rise of the West, ch 12

Thirteenth Week = The End of the South Atlantic System

December 5-6 - Discussion based on

114

Lecture 26 - Readjustments of the Nineteenth Century
Lecture 27 - Liquidation of Slavery in the Americas
Wolf, People without History, 353-83
Curtin, Two Jamaicas, pp 121-209
Knight, F.W., The Caribbean, pp. 121-145

Recommended:

    Higman, Barry, Slave Population of Jamaica
    Conrad, Robert, The Destruction of Slavery in Brazil
    Knight, Franklin, Slave Society in Cuba during the Nineteenth Century.
    Moreno Fraginals, Manuel, The Sugarmill.

THE JOHNS HOPKINS UNIVERSITY
Department of History

Professor Curtin
History 80.330
The World and the West: The Revolution of Modernization
Fall, 1984
Four Credits

This course departs somewhat from the traditional pattern of historical study. Instead of relating the series of events that took place in a given period of time in some particular part of the world, it concentrates on a process. That process is the interaction of Western culture and the other major cultures of the world since about 1500. The first half was concerned principally with the period in which Europe gradually changed its position from that of being one among a number of equally technologically proficient societies to that of a world leadership. By 1800, Europe was not yet in a position to dominate on a world-wide scale, but it was clearly on the way to industrialization. The first industrial society in the world in turn set the standard of modernity which other societies had either to copy or to resist.

The second half will be concerned with the industrial age. The chronological break at 1800 is not sharp. Some forms of interaction, such as the South Atlantic System, were tracxd well beyond 1800 during the first semester. Others, arising out of the wholesale migration of Europeans overseas, are mainly a nineteenth-century phenomenon, though their origins must now be traced back to the period before 1800.

The world and the West interacted in many different ways during the past century-and-a-half. Needless to say, all of them cannot be traced in a one-semester course. The lectures and readings will therefore skip around among the multitude of possible examples, concentrating on culture change--on the manner in which people changed their ways of life in response to contact with culturally different environments. This subject not only takes in the non-Western people who respond to the impact of the west; it is also concerned with the changes in western culture among the settlers who went overseas.

This course is being taught with taped lectures, using the set of lectures originally taped for broadcast by the Wisconsin State Radio Service in 1970-71, now much revised. The reason for the tapes is to use mechanical means to convey information so as to make more time available for actual face-to-face interchange of ideas. The normal weekly pattern of the course will therefore consist of two lectures n tape and two hours of discussion, on Monday and Tuesday mornings--one hour mainly concerned with the two lectures assigned for that week, and one mainly concerned with the readings.

The tapes are available for loan at the audio-visual section of the Eisenhower Memorial Library. They can be played on a standard cassette tape recorder, which makes it possible to stop the lecture, make it repeat, and otherwise control the speed of information. Tape recorders may also be borrowed, for the use by those who otherwise have no access to one.

As a way of preparing for these discussions, students are required to present each Monday a brief (3-4 typed pages) very informal account of their reactions to the reading, lectures, and discussions of the week. For lack of a better name, these can be called "intellectual journals." They are not graded or returned until the end of the semester, though they are read each week as a way of keeping the instructor posted on what the class is thinking. Perhaps the best way to think of this assignment is to consider it an answer to an implicit question--what did I learn last week that is significant, and why? Or, why was the material less significant than it might have been?

Graduate students may not normally take the course for credit, but they are expected to read more than the assigned readings. The recommended readings are listed for some weeks which provide a point of departure. Any student should feel free to consult the instructor about further readings, subject matter that strikes his or her interest, and other extensions beyond the normal course. Office hours are Tuesday, 1:00 - 2:00.

There is no formal text, but the following paperbacks are assigned in part and may be useful purchases:

   Nelson, Reed, The Caste War in Yucatan (Stanford, 192), 182 pp., assigned;
   James R. Scobie, Argentina: A City and a Nation (Oxford paperback) 123 pp., assigned;
   E. Bacon, Central Asia Under Russian Rule, 124 pp., assigned (not in paperback);
   Michael Adas, Prophets of Rebellion (University of North Carolina Press, 1980), 94 pp., assigned

TOPIC I - SETTLEMENT

1st Week - Introductory

Sept. 10 Introductory Meeting

Sept. 11 Discussion based on assigned readings in:
          W.W. Rostow, "The Stages of Economic Growth: A Non-Communist Manifesto," The Economist, August 15 & 22, 1959
          C.E. Black, The Dynamics of Modernization, 1-34.
          Dean C. Tipps, "Modernization Theory and the Comparative Study of Societies," Comparative Societies, 15:199-206 (1973).

Recommended: C.E. Black, The Dynamics of Modernization, pp., 175-199 (Bibliographical essay on modernization theory)

2nd Week - Population and Settlement

Sept. 17 Discussion based on:
          Lecture 1 - Overseas Settlement before the Napoleonic Wars
          Lecture 2 - Growth and Movement of Populations

Sept. 18 Discussion based on assigned readings:
          McNeill, William H. "Human Migrations: An Historical Overview" in McNeill and Ruth S. Adams, Human Migration. Patterns and Policies, pp., 3-19.

Doveing, Folke, "The Opportunity to Multiply: Demographic Aspects of Modern Colonialism, Journal of Economic History, 21:559-612, (1961).
Thistlethwaite, Frank, "Migrations from Europe overseas in the Nineteenth and Twentieth Centuries," in Moller, Population Movements, pp., 73-92.
Akerman, Sune, From Stockhold to San Francisco, pp., 5-46
Moller, H., "Population and Society During the Old Regime," in Moller, Population Movements in Modern European History, pp., 19-42

Recommended: Uncut version of the Thistlethwaite article in XIe Congres International des Sciences Historiques, Stockhold 1960, Rapports V: Histoire Contemporaire, pp., 32-60

3rd Week - European Overseas

Sept. 24 Discussion based on:
Lecture 3 - Theories and Theorists of Colonization
Lxcture 5 - Emigration and Culture change

Sept. 25 Discussion: Trans-Frontier Cultures
D.R. Sarmiento, Life in the Argentine Republic, ch. 2.
Duncan Baretta, Silvio R. and John Markoff, "Civilization and Barbarism: Cattle Frontiers in Latin America," Comparative Studies, 20: 587-618 (Oct. 1978).
J.K. Howard, Strange Empire, pp., 23-45, 292-306.
Richard Elphick, The Shaping of South African Society,1652-1820, 41-71, 155-162.

4th Week - Frontier and Metropolis in Southern Africa

Oct. 1 Discussion: Trans-Frontier Cultures, plus slides of the environmental setting of South Africa

Oct. 2 Discussion based on:
Lecture 6 - Frontier Expansion in the Nineteenth Century
Lecture 7 - The Metropolises and New Frontiers
Marquart, A Short History of South Africa, pp., 56-156 (in 1968 edition)

5th Week - Frontier and Metropolis in Argentina

Oct. 8

Oct. 9 Discussion based on comparisons of South Africa and Argenhina and on:
Lecture 8 - The Port and the Pampa
Lecture 9 - The "Conquest and the Desert"
James R. Scobie, Argentina: A City and a Nation, pp., 36-159

-4-

TOPIC II - CONQUEST

6th Week

Oct. 15   Discussion based on:
           Lecture 10 - The Pattern of Territorial Empire
           Lecture 11 - Development, Technology, and Military Power

Oct. 16   P.D. Curtin (ed.), Imperialism, pp., ix-xxiii, 1-22
           (Cuvier and Knox), 132-65 (Carlyle), 177-191 (Macaulay).
           D.K. Fieldhouse, Economics and Empire 1830-1914, 63-87
           Ronald Robinson, "Non-European Foundation of European
             Imperialism Sketch for a Theory of Collaboration," in
             Roger Owen and Bob Sutclifte (eds.), Studies in Theory
             of Imperialism (London), pp., 117-142

Recommended: Further reading in Fieldhouse
              Michael Barratt Brown, Economics of Imperialism (esp. pp., 39-72)

7th Week

Oct. 22   Discussion based on:
           Lecture 12 - the Politics of Imperialism
           Lecture 13 - Conquest and Culture Change: Soviet Central Asia

Oct. 23   Discussion of Soviet Central Asia based on:
           Elizabeth Bacon, Central Asia Under Russian Rule, pp., 1-28, 92-188.

8th Week - Conquest and Culture Change

Oct. 29   Discussion based on:
           Lecture 14-The Hispanization of Mexico
           Lecture 15 - Administration and Social Change: Bengal and Java

Oct. 30   Discussion of Culture Change in Yucatan
           Nelson Reed, The Caste War in Yucatan, pp., 3-49, 159-296

Recommended: The remainder of Reed

TOPIC III - CONVERSION

9th Week - Missionary Movements

Nov. 5   Discussion based on:
           Lecture 16 - The Missionary Movement from Europe
           Lecture 17 - Missionaries Overseas: East Africa (1973)

Nov. 6   Discussion based on:
           Robin Horton, "The Rationality of Conversion," Africa, 45: 219-23
           Humphrey Fisher, "Conversion Reconsidered: Some Historical
             Aspects of Religious Conversion
             Reconsidered: Some Historical Aspects of Religious
             Conversion in Black Africa," Africa, 43: 27-40

-5- Peel, J.D.Y., "Conversion and Tradition in Two African Societies: Ijebu and Buganda," Past and Present, no. 7, pp., 108-417 (November, 1977).

Recommended: J.D.Y. Peel, Aladura: A Religious Movement among the Yoruba. C. Wrigley, "The Christian Revolution in Buganda," Comparative Studies in Society and History, 2; 33-48 (October, 199).

10th Week - Conversion from Within

Nov. 12 Discussion based on:
Lecture 18 - Varieties of Modernization
Lecture 19 - Meiji Japan: Selective Modernization

Nov. 13 Discussion based on readings:
Fairbank, Reischauer, and Craig, East Asia: The Modern Transformation, pp., 178-273

Recommended: G.B. Sansom, The Western World and Japan

11th Week - The Modernization of Turkey

Nov. 19 Discussion based on:
Lecture 20 - Ottoman Reforms
Lecture 21 - Radical Reforms

Nov. 20 Comparative Discussion of Japan and Turkey
Roderic Davison, Turkey, pp., 53-168

D.E. Ward and D. Rustow, Political Modernization in Japan and Turkey, pp., 434-468. (Catalogued under "Conference on Political Modernization.")

Recommended: Bernard Lewis, The Emergence of Modern Turkey (graduate students should substitute Lewis for Davison assignment).

TOPIC IV - THE REVOLUTION OF MODERNIZATION

12th Week - "Nationalism"

Nov. 26 Discussion based on:
Lecture 22 - Non-European Resistance and European Withdrawal
Lecture 23 - Economic and Social integration in the Post-Colonial World

Nov. 27 Discussion based on readings in:
R. Emerson, From Empire to Nation, pp., 89-104.
Karl Deutsch, "The Growth of Nations," World Politics, 5: 168-196
P.D. Curtin, Africa and the West, pp., 231-244
O. Pflanze and P.D. Curtin, "Varieties of Nationalism in Europe and Africa," Review of Politics, 28: 129-253, (April, 1960)

Recommended: J.A. Hobson in Curtin (ed.), Imperialism, pp. 319-337

-6-

13th Week - The Roots of Non-Western Revolt

Dec. 3   Discussion based on:
         Lecture 24 - Millennial Movements

Dec. 4   Discussion based on readings in Adas, Prophets of
         Rebellion, 3-91, 183-189

Recommended: Worsley, The Trumpet of Sound, pp., ix - lxix, 11 - 16,
              32 - 48, 75 - 92

Optional: The following two weeks of lectures and assignments are normal
           for the Spring version of this course but are not included in
           the Fall for lack of time.

14th Week - The Emergence of Indonesia

Dec. 10 Discussion based on:
         Lecture 25 - The Indonesian Revolution and its Setting
         Lecture 26 - Indonesia under the Early Republic

Dec. 11 Discussion based on the assigned reading:
         Bernard Dahm, The History of Indonesia in the Twentieth Century,
         pp., 20-109

15th Week - The Emergence of Ghana

Dec. 17 Discussion based on:
         Lecture 27 - The Creation of a Nation
         Lecture 28 - The Creation of Nationalism.

Dec. 18 Discussion based on assigned readings in:
         D. Austin, Politics in Ghana, pp. 1-48
         C.E. Black, The Dynamics f Modernization, pp. 1-128 (skim)
         Toynbee, A Study of History (abridgement of vols. vii-x by
              by D.C. Somervell), pp., 145-188, 219-240

Recommended: David Apter, Ghana in Transition.
              F.M. Bourret, Ghana: The Road to Independence,
              1919-1947, esp. pp., 53-202.
              Trevor Jones, Ghana's First Republic, 1960-1966

Ohio State University

C. Findley
Dulles 371
Extension: 2-7645
Office Hours: 2-3 Monday-Tuesday
　　　　　and by appointment

J. Rothney
Dulles 214
Extensions: 2-6594 or 2-2674
Office Hours: Wednesdays,
　　　　　2-4:30 and by appt.

HISTORY 209:   CRITICAL ISSUES OF THE 20th CENTURY WORLD

SPRING QUARTER 1983, 1 p.m.

This course will look from a global perspective at major issues which have made or are making the world we live in today. Each week will be devoted to one issue or set of issues. The three weekly lectures will explore major themes or examples illustrative of the weekly theme. The course will not attempt an exhaustive coverage of twentieth-century world history, nor will it cover every example of every issue. It will examine issues of particular importance, attempting in every case to draw out their global significance.

In addition to the lectures, the weekly two-hour lab will enable us to explore a variety of alternative approaches to understanding the world around us. We shall explore the evidence provided by films, works of literature, the pictorial record created by artists and photographers, and games simulating real life problems. A vital part of the course, the labs will help us to understand and identify with our subject by heightening our consciousness of the kinds of evidence and experience from which people form their worldviews, as each of us must do.

The ultimate goal of the course is not only to convey factual knowledge about the twentieth-century world, but to provide an interpretive framework in which this knowledge can be set, and to help us all to become well-informed and responsible citizens of a world which is now at a critical point in its history.

ASSIGNED READINGS

The following have been ordered through SBX:

　　Nigel Calder, Nuclear Nightmares
　　Richard Critchfield, Shahhat: An Egyptian
　　Richard Goff, Walter Moss, Janice Terry, and Jiu-Hwa Upshur, The Twentieth
　　　　Century: A Brief Global History
　　Arthur Koestler, Darkness at Noon
　　Naguib Mahfouz, Midaq Alley
　　Erich Maria Remarque, All Quiet on the Western Front

EXAMS AND GRADING

Exactly how the grades should be weighted in computation of the term averages is a matter that can be discussed and redefined, if there is general student interest in doing so. Barring such redefinition, expect the computation of grades to be as follows:

　　15% attendance and participation · labs
　　15% first mid-term
　　15% first paper
　　15% second mid-term
　　25% comprehensive final exam

Make-up examinations will br administered only in cases of compelling necessity and upon presentation of a valid written excuse. It is the responsibility of the student to take the make-up at the time determined by the instructors. Papers turned in late will be penalized one letter grade for each day late.

Exams may include both objective and essay-type elements. Exams will definitely cover material presented in labs. When we look at films or slides of play games, do not just be a spectator; actively participate in the process of drawing out what we can learn from these materials and experience. Make notes about things that you will not see again so that you can keep your impressions alive in your memory.

MEETING ROOMS

Lectures on Mondays, Tuesdays, and Wednesdays will be held in Page Hall 102, Labs from 1:00 to 3:00 on Thursdays will be held in Mendenhall Lab 200. On some Thursdays, the class will be broken up into two smaller groups, one of which will meet in Mendenhall 200 and the other in the room isted in the Course outline.

COURSE OUTLINE

I. THE EUROPEAN-DOMINATED WORLD SYSTEM AND THE CHALLENGE OF MODERNITY

READING: Goff et al., 4-91 begin Remarque, All Quiet on the Western Front

LECTURES:

28 Mar. M Introduction: Themes of the Course   Findley
29 Mar. T A Western Metropolis: Imperial Berlin, 1914   Rothney
30 Mar. W A Village in Egypt: Dinshawai, 1906   Findley

LAB:

31 Apr. R. Metropolis and Village in Film: "Berlin, Symphony of a Great City" (1927) and "Song of Ceylon" (1934)

II. CRISIS OF THE EUROPEAN WORLD SYSTEM: WAR AND REVOLUTION, 1914-1918

READING: Goff et al., 92-110: complete Remarque, All Quiet on the Western Front.

LECTURES:

4 Apr. M The European Civil War and its Global Impact   Rothney
5 Apr. T World War I and its Global Ramifications   Findley
6 Apr. W. The Collapse of Imperial Russia   Rothney

LAB:

7 Apr. R. Men of the Trenches: Discussion of All Quiet (Two groups, meeting in Mendenhall 200 and Derby 21A)

III. RESTRUCTURING THE SOCIAL AND POLITICAL ORDER: THE BOLSHEVIK CHALLENGE

    READING: Goff et al., 112-203; begin Koestler, Darkness at Noon

    LECTURES:

11 Apr. M. Lenin, Stalin, and the Attempt to Make the Future Work	Rothney
12 Apr. T Young Revolutionaries of the World	Findley
13 Apr. W The Great Depression: A Second Crisis of the European-Dominated World System	Findley

    LAB:

    14 Apr. R A Pictorial Study of Revolutionary Upheaval in Russia

IV. RESTRUCTURING THE SOCIAL AND POLITICAL ORDER: THE WELFARE STATE

    READING: Goff et al., 204-18; finish Koestler, Darkness at Noon

    LECTURES:

18 Apr. M. The Dilemma of Democratic Socialism	Rothney
19 Apr. T The New Deal in Global Perspective	Rothney
20 Apr. W FIRST MIDTERM	

    LAB:

    21 Apr. R Chaplin's "Modern Times"

V. FASCISM: RESTRUCTURING THE SOCIAL AND POLITICAL ORDER?

    READING: Goff et al., 219-30; begin Mahfouz, Midaq Alley

    LECTURES:

25 Apr. M Fascism in Europe	Rothney
26 Apr. T Nazi Society	Rothney
27 Apr. W Agression East and West	Rothney

    LAB:

    28 Apr. R. Mass Movement and Mass Murder; "Triumph of the Will" (1934-36) and "Night and Fog" (1955)

    FIRST PAPER DUE 1:00 PM, THURSDAY, 28 April

VI. TWILIGHT OF THE EUROPEAN WORLD SYSTEM

    READING: Goff et al., 231-313: complete Midaq Alley

    LECTURES:

2 May M The Reality of Global War	Rothney

3 May T The Drive for Indian Independence   Findley
4 May W The Middle East through 1948   Findley

LAB:

5 May R War Disturbs a Changing Society: Discussion of Midaq Alley
         (Two groups meeting in Mendenhall 200 and Derby 21A)

VII. INTERNATIONAL RELATIONS IN THE AGE OF THE NUCLEAR THREAT

READING: Goff et al., 314-57; begin Critchfield, Shahbat

LECTURES:

9 May M From European System to Balance of Terror   Findley
10 May T "Gulliver's Troubles" in an Era of Detente   Rothney
11 May W SECOND MIDTERM

LAB:

11 May R Brinksmanship: Holocaust or Compromise (simulation)
         (Two groups, meeting in Mendenhall 200 and Derby 21A)

VIII. ALTERNATIVE APPROACHES TO DEVELOPMENT

READING: Goff et al., 358-406; finish Critchfield, Shabhat

LXCTURES:

16 May M Mao's China and Nehru's India   Findley
17 May T Shaykhs and Ayatollahs   Findley
18 May W Subsaharan Africa: Closing the Gap, or
         Modernizing Poverty?   Findley

LAB:

19 May R "Full Moon Lunch" (1976, film)

SECOND PAPER DUE AT 1:00 PM, THURSDAY, 19 May

IX. INTERDEPENDENCE AMID SCARCITY: TOWARDS A REAL WORLD SYSTEM?

READING: Begin Nigel Calder, Nuclear Nightmares.

LECTURES:

23 May M Too Many People?   Rothney
24 May T Food and Energy   Findley

25 May W Vietnam viewed from the 1980's   Rothney

LAB:

28 May R Balanced Diet, or Starvation? "Baldicer" (simulation)
(Two groups, meeting in Mendenhall 200 and Derby 21A)

X. AFFLUENT NORTH AND HUNGRY SOUTH

READING: Complete Calder, <u>Nuclear Nightmares</u>

LECTURES:

31 May T The Freeway Megalopolis, 1983   Rothney
1 June W The Urbanization of Poverty, 1983   Findley

LAB:

2 June R Student Volunteers' Debate: For and Against Nuclear Weapons
7 June T FINAL EXAMINATION 8-9:45 A.M.

RUTGERS UNIVERSITY

510:111
The Twentieth Century
Spring 1984
Professor Adas

R =s on Reserve in
Douglass Library
pbk =s Available in
paperback the
Douglass Bookstore

I. The Age of High Imperialism and the Birth of the Twentieth Century

Jan. 23 - Introduction to a Century of Promise and Violence

Jan. 26 - The Core of the Global System: England, France, Germany
Required: L. Stavrianos, World Since 1500, chapters 11 (4-7), 12(6-8), 19 & pp. 339-41. (pbk)

Jan. 30 - Emerging Giants on the Periphery: The U.S. & Russia
Required: Stavrianos, chapters 13, 18.

Feb. 2 - The View from the Colonized World: Custer & Gordon, Little Big Horn and Khartoum
Required: Stavrianos, chapters 14, 15 (1-4), 17 (3-4).

Feb. 6 - Doubts of the Dominant: Discussion of Heart of Darkness
Required: Joseph Conrad, Heart of Darkness, entire (pbk).

Feb. 9 - Opening Rounds in the Global Revolt to Come
Required: Stavrianos, chapters 15 (5), 16.

II. The First World War and Its Impact

Feb. 13 - The March to War

Feb. 16 - Machines over Men: The Horror of Trench Warfare
M. Howard, War in European History, chapters 5 & 6
Stavrianos, Chapter 20 (1-3)

Feb. 20 - War Produces Revolution: Russia, 1917

Feb. 23 - Wilson's Dilemmas, American Intervention, Allied Victory
Required: Stavrianos, 20 (4-6), 22 (1-2).

III. Hollow Victory and Capitalist Collapse

Feb. 27 - The Victors Quarrel; The Lost Chance for Peace at Versailles
Required: Stavrianos, chapter 20 (7-8)

Mar. 1 - The Age of Illusion & Disillusionment: The Cultural Crisis of the West
Required: Selections from T.S. Elliot, G.B. Shaw and Others

Mar. 5 - War and the Crisis of the Colonial Empires

Mar. 8 - War and the Anti-Imperialist Revolt: Phase I
Required: George Orwell, "Shooting an Elephant" (R).
Stavrianos, chapter 21.

Mar. 12 - The Best of Times, The Worst of Times: The Roaring Twenties, Stalinist Winter in Russia

Mar. 15 - The New Empires: Japan & Italy
   Required: Stavrianos, chapter 22 (3-5), chapter 23 (1).
             F. Carsten, The Rise of Fascism, chapter 2 ((R).
             E. Reischauer, Japan, chapter 9 (R).

Spring Break

Mar. 26 - The Great Depression and the Crisis of the Capitalist Order
   Required: Stavrianos, chapter 23 (2).

IV. Desperate Solutions and a Second Global War

Mar. 29 - The Failure of Weimar and the Rise of Hitler and the Nazi State

Apr. 2 - Film "The Triumph of the Will" Discussion

Apr. 5 - A Second March to War, Munich and All That
   Required: Carsten, chapters 3 & 4 (R)
             S. Haeffner, The Meaning of Hitler (pbk)
             Stavrianos, chapter 24.

Apr. 9 - World War II in Europe

Apr. 12 - The War in the Pacific
   Required: Stavrianos, chapter 25.

Apr. 16 - Enter the Atomic Age: World War II and the Coming of the Cold War
   Required: Stavrianos, chapter 27.

Apr. 19 - Decolonization and Revolutions Betrayed

Apr. 23 - The Great Wave: Communist Victory in China
   Required: Stavrianos, chapter 26.

Apr. 26 - Whither the Third World?
   Discussion of V.S. Naipaul's Guerrillas.
   Required: V. Naipaul, Guerrillas (pbk).

Apr. 30 - Superpower Confrontation and the Fate of the Earth

May 3 - America Confronts a Revolutionary World: Cuba, Vietnam and the Next War
   Required: Stavrianos, chapter 28 & 523-6.

Much of the reading in the course will be taken from the following books which are available in paperback in the Douglass Coop.

L. Stavrianos, **The World since 1500**
V. Naipaul, **Guerrillas**
J. Conrad, **Heart of Darkness**
S. Haeffner, **The Meaning of Hitler**

All other readings will be on reserve in the Douglass Library.

Assignments: In addition to the assigned readings, there will be two **short** take-home essays and a final exam take-home essay.

RUTGERS UNIVERSITY

Global History   510-112   Bell, Stoianovich
Love in History   Roden
                                                             Fall 1983

Sept. 8   General Introduction
             The Invention of Europe: The Three Functions Examined

Sept. 12   Introduction to Japan

Sept. 15   Mythological Conceptions of Love
                Japan: The Kojiki
                Europe: Tacitus, Nibelungenlied, and Poetic Edda

Sept. 19   Buddhist Conceptions of Love

Sept. 22   Christian Conceptions of Love

Sept. 26   Saints and Lovers in the Christian World

Sept. 29   Song of Roland: Clans and Companions in early Feudal Europe

Oct. 3   The Letters of Abelard and Heloise: Europe's Earliest Story
                         of Passion and Love

Oct. 6   Tristan and Iseult, Courtly Love, and The Romance of the
                                 Rose (Lorris)

Oct. 11   The Tale of Genji: The Absence of Courtly Love in Japan?

Oct. 13   The Tale of Genji (II): Love without Heroism; Genji and
                            Tristan compared

Oct. 17   The Tale of Heike: Samurai Clans and Companions in Early
                            Feudal Japan

Oct. 20   The Tale of Heike (II): Heroism without a "Lady" Knighthood in
                            Japan and Europe compared: The reverse
                            Order of Courtly and Heroic Traditions

Oct. 24   Romance of the Rose (Meung)

Oct. 27   Dante and the Vita Nuova

Oct. 31   Dante and the Quattrocento

Nov. 3   Neoplatonic and Rabelaisian Love in the Sixteenth Century

Nov. 7   Patron and Client in Seventeenth Century France: The Three
                 Musketeers and the World of the Gentleman Swordsman

Nov. 10   Duty and Love in Seventeenth Century Japan: The Gentleman
                 Samurai and Dissolute Merchant

Nov.	14	Love in the Sixteenth and Seventeenth Centuries: The Gentlemanly Ideals of Japan and Europe Compared
Nov.	17	The Don Juan Hero in Mozart's Opera (<u>Don Giovanni</u>)
Nov.	21	The Romantic Vision in late Eighteenth and Early Nineteenth Century Europe
Nov.	28	The Impudence of Capitalism and the <u>Letters</u> <u>of</u> <u>Lady</u> <u>Montagu</u>
Dec.	1	From Romantic Sensibility to the Unconscious: Introduction to Sigmund Freud
Dec.	5	<u>Sons</u> <u>and</u> <u>Lovers</u>: D.H. Lawrence and the Freudian Vision
Dec.	8	"<u>Sons</u> <u>and</u> <u>Lovers</u>" (II)
Dec.	12	Tanizaki's "Bridge of Dreams": Genji in a Post-Freudian Age
Dec.	14	"Bridge of Dreams" (II) Tanizaki and Lawrence compared

* * * * * *

Welcome to Global History! This semester we will focus on love as a problem in the history of Europe and Japan from the early Middle Ages to the present. Through an examination of the modes and institution of love, we hope to illuminate the fundamental nature of European and Japanese culture: how men and women interacted with each other; how they expressed affection and hatred; how they confronted the universal challenges of life and death; how they distinguished the good from the bad, the beautiful from the grotesque. Our sources for this cross-cultural exploration are taken from some of the masterpieces of world literature. And while nearly all of these works are products of an aristocratic or upper-class culture, they also represent the aspirations and fears of a broad cross section of European and Japanese society.

We look forward to working with you this semester. Please feel free to raise questions at any time. The success of this course depends largely upon our collective efforts.

RUTGERS UNIVERSITY

510:111 Global History　　　　　　　　　Spring, 1984
Death in Japan and Europe　　　　　　　Bell, Roden, Stoianovich

Welcome to Global History! We shall focus during the Spring semester on death as a problem in the history of Europe and Japan from the moment of the constitution of these territories as autonomous civilizations (between the eighth and eleventh centuries) to the present.

Three practices have been common to all peoples living in partly permanent social groups: religion or ways of symbolizing community between a particular (or whole of) humanity and nature and the supernatural, and of linking past, present, and future; marriage and the constitution of a family as a means of assuring a group's ability to perpetuate itself ideologically and religiously and therefore socially; and socially and ceremoniously appropriate ways of mourning, disposing of, and honoring the dead. We shall deal during this semester with European and Japanese ways of death and mourning, consequently, with the symbols and codes of life and death by means of which European and Japanese civilizations achieved their respective identities.

Of all the Old World's civilizations or city cultures, the least direct contact until the nineteenth century was between the European and Japanese civilizations. That there should have been significant differences in the ways in which these two civilizations dealt with death needs less explanation, therefore, than the fact that there were amazing similarities, which can hardly be explained by the process of cultural diffusion. How then, do we explain the similarities? To what extent may an understanding of the European and Japanese civilizations enrich our understanding of other civilizations and of humanity in general?

Our sources for this cross-cultural exploration include some of the masterpieces of world literature. These works, true enough, are products of an aristocratic or elite culture. But aristocratic cultures are themselves in some ways products of popular culture even while acting in ways that lead to the transformation of popular culture. They thus provide clues to the past (popular culture) and to the future (again, popular culture). Whenever possible, we shall deal with the question of the ways of death and of civilization at the various levels of culture (warriors, priests, merchants, intellectuals, peasants, common people) and of the relationship between variations in the codes of death and variations in material culture.

We look forward to working with you this semester. Please feel free to raise questions at any time in class and do come and see us at the History Department (Van Dyck Hall) outside of class. The success of the course depends largely on our joint efforts.

DATE	TOPIC	READING ASSIGNMENT
Mon Jan 23	Introduction to the course	
Thu Jan 26	Early Japanese myth and religion	* "Myths and Legends," "Manyoshu"
Mon Jan 30	Death in Japan's courtly tradition	* "The Tosa Diary," * "The Rites" from Tale of Genji
Thu Feb 2	Popular Buddhism, Zen and early Samurai view of death	* "The Lotus Sutra," "Zen Stories," "Yoshitsune"
Mon Feb 6	Fate of the Gods and the human condition	* The Poetic Edda charts and maps
Thu Feb 9	Christianity and Resurrection	New Testament: Matthew 26-28; Mark 14-16; Luke 22-24; John 13-21
Mon Feb 13	Blest Martyrdom's Your Guerdon	Song of Roland, pp. 7-159 bring charts and maps
Thu Feb 16	Art of Dying and Funeral Rites	Song of Roland, 160-203; * Giambattista Vico, Tristan and Iseult; reviews of L'Homme devant la mort by Stoianovich and Bell
Mon Feb 20	Death as justice	Dante's Inferno
Thu Feb 23	Hell and lay culture	reread the Inferno
Mon Feb 27	Death denied	Boccaccio's Decameron, days 1 through 5
Thu Mar 1	Life defied	Decameron days 6-10
Mon Mar 5	Film: Passion of Joan of Arc	THE MIDTERM QUESTION WILL BE HANDED OUT
Thu Mar 8	Martyrdom of the Savior of France: The Maid of Orleans	* Joan of Arc ed. Wilfred T. Jewkes and Landfield, "The Trial"
Mon Mar 12	Between Heroism and Bureaucratism: Death and the Tokugawa Samurai	* Hagakure, Nitobe, Bushido YOUR MIDTERM ESSAY IS DUE

Thu Mar 15		From Tokugawa to Meiji	Natsume Soseki, Kokoro part I
Mon Mar 26		Egocentric versus Altruistic Suicide in Meiji Japan	Kokoro, parts II & III
Thu Mar 29		The Crisis of Western Christendom	* Erasmus' "The Funeral," selections from Jean Calvin
Mon Apr 2		Explaining the Inexplicable	Defoe, A Journal of the Plague Year
Thu Apr 5		A Young Woman's View of Death	Shelley, Frankenstein
Mon Apr 9		Death, Sociality, and the Expression of the Emotions	* Darwin's The Expression of the Emotions in Man and Animals; Spencer's The Principles of Psychology
Thu Apr 12		The Death of Death	Tolstoy, The Death of Ivan Ilych; bring charts, maps, and reviews by Bell and Stoianovich of Aries
Mon Apr 16		Oh, to Be a Child, a Woman, and Dead (That Is, Alive): Land of Lamentation and City of Pain	Rilke, Duino Elegies; * Erasmus, Preparation to Death and Calvin, selections
Thu Apr 19	Film:	Un chien andalous; Luis Bunuel, director, 1928; senario by Salvador Dali	
Mon Apr 23		The Samurai tradition in contemporary Japan	* selections from writings of Mishima Yukio
Thu Apr 26		The courtly tradition in contemporary Japan	Kawabata Yasunari, Sound of the Mountain
Mon Apr 30	Film:	Ikiru	FINAL EXAM HANDED OUT
Thu May 3		Film discussion and summary remarks	

* = on reserve in Alexander Library

Amherst College

Fall, 1980

History 11

SCARCITY AND PLENTY IN HISTORY

The books listed below are to be purchased at the College Bookstore located in Moore Dormitory.

All other readings in the course are contained in the volumes of multilithed materials for sale in the History Department office, Chapin 111, or are to be found on reserve.

Copying costs, copyright fees, and College rules make it necessary for us to charge each student for the set of readings. Please purchase the readings today in Room 111, Chapin Hall, between 2:00 p.m. and 5:00 p.m. (September 8).

1. Beals, Alan R., Village Life in South India, AHM Publishing Corp., $4.95.
2. Brown, Lester R., World Without Borders, Random, $2.95.
3. Cipolla, Carlo M., The Economic History of World Population, Penquin Books, $1.95.
4. Edgeworth, Maria, Castle Rackrent, Norton, $1.65.
5. Hobsbawm, Eric J., Industry and Empire, Penquin, $3.95.
6. Jennings, Francis, The Invasion of America, Norton, $4.95.
7. July, Robert, Precolonial Africa: An Economic and Social History, Scribner, $6.95.
8. McNeill, William H., Plagues and Peoples, Doubleday Anchor, $3.50.
9. Meek, Ronald L., ed., Marx and Engels on the Population Bomb, Ramparts, $3.50.
10. Morgan, Edmund S., American Slavery, American Freedom, Norton, $3.95.
11. O'Farrell, Patrick, Ireland's English Question, Schocken, $4.95.
12. Wallerstein, Immanuel, ed., The Modern World System, Academic Press, $6.50.
13. (Recommended) Handlin, Oscar, Boston's Immigrants, Atheneum, $3.25.

Copies of all books have been placed on reserve in Frost Library.

Fall, 1980

History 11

SCARCITY AND PLENTY IN HISTORY

I. The Malthusian Dilemma: Balancing Resources and Numbers in History

Sept. 8 Introduction: "What is Scarcity"--Prof. Gross

Sept. 10 Seminar

   Reading: Lester R. Brown, World Without Borders, pp. 3-57, 88-110 (buy)

   EVENING FILM SHOWING: Nanuck of the North and The Hunters

Sept. 12 Seminar

   Discussion of films
   Marshall Sahlins, "The Original Affluent Society," Stone Age Economics, pp. 1-39 (reserve)
   Begin: William McNeill, Plagues and Peoples, ch. 1, pp. 1-30 (buy)

Sept. 15 Seminar

   McNeill, Plagues and Peoples, chs. 2-3, pp. 31-131 (buy)

Sept. 17 Seminar

   McNeill, Plagues and Peoples, chs. 4-7, pp. 132-257 (buy)

   EVENING FILM SHOWING: The Seventh Seal

Sept. 19 Seminar

   Discussion of film
   Giovanni Boccaccio, The Decameron, pp. 4-11 (multilith)

   Daniel Defoe, A Journal of the Plague Year, pp. 46-59, 115-122, 141-145, 248-251 (multilith)

Sept. 22 Lecture: "World Population Growth"--

   Carlo M. Cipolla, The Economic History of World Population, pp. 82-133 (buy)

Sept. 24 Seminar

   S. Howard Patterson, ed., Readings in the History of Economic Thought, pp. 101-176 (Godwin and Malthus) (multilith)

136

History 11   - 3 -

    Sept. 26   Seminar

                    Ronald L. Meek, ed., <u>Marx and Engels on the Population
            Bomb</u>, pp. 53-124 (buy)

    Sept. 29   Seminar

                    Immanuel Wallerstein, <u>The Modern World System</u>, Introduction,
            chs. 4-5; pp. 3-11, 115-195 (buy)

    Oct. 1   FIRST PAPER DUE

II. Coping with Scarcity in Past Time: Case Studies

    A. England, America and Ireland

    Oct. 3   Lecture: "England and Its Colonies"--Prof. Gross

                    R. L. Schuyler, <u>The Fall of the Old Colonial System</u>,
            pp. 3-37 (reserve)

                    Thomas Mun, "England's Treasure by Foreign Trade," <u>Introduction
            to Contemporary Civilization in the West</u>, v. 1, pp. 828-841
            (reserve)

    Oct. 6   Seminar

                    Edmund S. Morgan, <u>American Slavery, American Freedom</u>, pp. 3-6,
            44-130 (buy)

    Oct. 8   Seminar

                    Edmund S. Morgan, <u>American Slavery, American Freedom</u>, pp. 133-179,
            295-337, 363-387 (buy)

    Oct. 10   Seminar

                    Francis Jennings, <u>The Invasion of America</u>, pp. 15-42, 58-84 (buy)

                    John Winthrop, "General Observations on the Plantation of
            New England," pp. 117-121 (multilith)

    Oct. 13   Seminar

                    Richard D. Brown, <u>Modernization</u>, pp. 23-48 (multilith)

                    Kenneth Lockridge, "Land, Population, and the Evolution of New
            England Society," <u>Past and Present</u>, vol. 39 (April 1968),
            pp. 62-80 (multilith)

                    James A. Henretta, "Families and Farms: Mentalité in Pre-
            Industrial America." pp. 3-32 (multilith)

History 11   - 4 -

Oct. 15   Seminar: England. The Industrial Revolution.

        Eric Hobsbawm, Industry and Empire, pp. 13-78 (buy)

Oct. 17   Lecture: "The Market and Laissez-faire Economics"--Prof. Halsted

        Eric Hobsbawm, Industry and Empire, pp. 79-108, 225-237 (buy)

        Karl Polanyi, "Our Obsolete Market Mentality," Man in Contemporary Society, v. 2, pp. 247-261 (reserve)

        "Corn Law Debate," ICC, v. 2, pp. 270-285 (reserve)

Oct. 20   Seminar: Ireland before 1800

        Patrick O'Farrell, Ireland's English Question, pp. 1-66 (buy)

        Jonathan Swift, "A Modest Proposal," The Works of Jonathan Swift, pp. 257-269 (multilith)

Oct. 22   Lecture: England and Ireland from the Union to the Famine--Prof. Hernon

        Patrick O'Farrell, Ireland's English Question, pp. 67-107 (buy)

        R. N. Salaman, The History and Social Influence of the Potato, pp. 273-288 (multilith)

Oct. 24   Seminar: Irish Society and Economic Policy

        Maria Edgeworth, Castle Rackrent (buy)

        R. D. Black, Economic Thought and the Irish Question, 1817-1870, pp. 3-11, 105-111, 134-144 (multilith)

        W. S. Trench, Realities of Irish Life, pp. 32-79 (multilith)

Oct. 27   Seminar: Contemporary Observations of Irish Society and the Famine

        Cecil Woodham-Smith, The Great Hunger, pp. 50-62, 75-77, 106-122, 171-205, 289-298 (reserve)

        R. N. Salaman, The History and Social Influence of the Potato, pp. 289-316 (multilith)

Oct. 29   Seminar: After the Famine--The Emigration

        Cecil Woodham-Smith, The Great Hunger, pp. 206-217, 241-252, 270-284, 406-413 (reserve)

        Patrick O'Farrell, Ireland's English Question, pp. 107-125 (buy)

        W. S. Trench, Realities of Irish Life, pp. 92-110 (multilith)

History 11   - 5 -

Oct. 31   Seminar

        Richard D. Brown, Modernization, pp. 122-158 (multilith)

        Edward Pessen, "The Egalitarian Myth and American Social
          Reality," American Historical Review, vol. 76, 4, Oct. 1971,
          pp. 989-1034 (multilith)

        Oscar Handlin, Boston's Immigrants, pp. 88-177, 207-237
          (buy or reserve)

Nov. 3   Seminar

    SECOND PAPER DUE

II. B. The Indian Experience

Nov. 5   Lecture: "Traditional India: Man, Land and Climate"--Prof. Lewandowski

        Bernard S. Cohn, India: The Social Anthropology of a
          Civilization, pp. 8-23 (reserve)

        Jawaharlal Nehru, The Discovery of India, pp. 33-78 (paperback)
          or pp. 58-113 (hardback edition) (reserve)

Nov. 7   Seminar: Village Life

        Premchand, Gift of a Cow (a novel), pp. v-xiv, 15-70 (multilith)

Nov. 10 Seminar: The Village Community: Ecology, Economic Relations and
         Society

        Alan R. Beals, Village Life in South India, pp. 9-26, 45-91 (buy)

Nov. 12 Seminar: Colonialism and Its Impact on India

        Jawaharlal Nehru, The Discovery of India, pp. 136-141, 181-250
          (paperback) or pp. 233-237, 274-336 (hardback) (reserve)

        Prakash Tandon, Punjabi Century: 1857-1974, pp. 7-38 (multilith)

    EVENING FILM SHOWING: Distant Thunder

Nov. 14 Seminar: Economic Transformations

        Discussion of film

        B. M. Bhatia, Famines in India, pp. 1-57 (multilith)

        Beals, Village Life in South India, pp. 134-147, 160-174 (buy)

History 11   - 6 -

II. C. Africa

Nov. 17   Lecture: "The African Context"--

         Robert W. July, <u>Pre-Colonial Africa. An Economic and Social History</u>, pp. 3-68 (buy)

Nov. 19   Seminar

         July, <u>Pre-Colonial Africa. An Economic and Social History</u>, pp. 69-119 (buy)

         EVENING FILM SHOWING: Films on Africa

Nov. 21   Seminar

         July, <u>Pre-Colonial Africa. An Economic and Social History</u>, pp. 123-143, 255-272 (buy)

THANKSGIVING RECESS

Dec. 1   "The Colonial Context" (Discussion)

         Gerald W. Hartwig & K. David Patterson, eds., <u>Disease in African History. An Introductory Survey and Case Studies</u>, pp. 3-24, 118-152 (multilith)

Dec. 3   Seminar

         Ralph H. Faulkingham, "Where the Lifeboat Ethic Breaks Down," <u>Human Nature</u> (Oct. 1978), pp. 32-39 (multilith)

         Robin Palmer, "The Agricultural History of Rhodesia," Palmer and Parsons, <u>The Roots of Rural Poverty in Central and Southern Africa</u>, pp. 221-254 (multilith)

Dec. 5   Seminar

         Gordon Harrison, <u>Mosquitoes, Malaria and Man: A History of the Hostilities since 1880</u>, chs. 26, 27, pp. 239-260 (multilith)

         LeRoy Vail, "Railway Development and Colonial Underdevelopment: The Nyasaland Case," in Palmer & Parsons, <u>Roots of Rural Poverty</u>, pp. 365-395 (multilith)

III. The Modern World Order and the Future

Dec. 8   Lecture: "Post Colonialism and Its Impact"--Prof. Mugomba

         Lester R. Brown, <u>World Without Borders</u>, pp. 132-154, 183-208, 321-364 (buy)

Dec. 10   Seminar

Dec. 12   FINAL PAPERS DUE AND COURSE ASSESSMENT

HISTORY 201

Graduate Seminar on

COMPARATIVE MILITARY SYSTEMS

Professor Peter Karsten
University of Pittsburgh

This is a reading seminar, designed to stimulate a research project of one's choice, on the nature of military systems throughout the world. Needless to say, while it should appeal to the sociologist and political scientist, it has a strong historical dimension. The literature we will be considering concerns: the social origins of military personnel; their recruitment, their training; the process of value inculcation; inter- and intra-service rivalries; mutinies; coups d'etat, civil-military relations; and the role of the military in "nation-building." We will also spend a week on a related topic, the laws of warfare and war-crimes. You will be asked to read a common reading and one other work each week.

The sorts of questions we will be asking in the next two months may be of interest to you now as you begin the readings. These questions include (but are by no means limited to) the following:

Stanislav Andreski (in *Military Organization and Society*) argues that the type of military organization or innovation a society adopts may cause sweeping changes in that society's political and social organizations. To what extent is this valid?

The readings reveal relationships between recruitment practices and the roles military systems play in society? What are they?

What consistent evidence exists of a "militarist" who tends to offer his services or to emerge from training?

Why do military coups occur? Of the several different causes which are associated with particular societies or conditions?

How does one evaluate the claim that "the military is a natural nation-builder"?

What values appear malleable in training? Does military training differ from culture to culture? If so, give examples and explain the differences.

What accounts for the emergence of any particular "law" or "rule" of warfare? What accounts for the fact that any particular "law" is not observed as scrupulously by some military personnel as its drafters had hoped?

You will each be asked to select a particular topic, formulate a question or hypothesis (not necessarily any one of those I've just jotted down, of course), and answer it either with an extensive analysis of the existing literature, or with original research.

141

WEEKLY TOPICS

Week	Subject	Common Reading (in addition to each individual's)
1.	Introduction: the Military & Society	S. Andreski, *Military Organization & Society* (skim read)
2.	Civil-Military Relations (in general)	S. Huntington, *The Soldier & the State*, pp. 1-97
3.	Recruitment & Social Background	P. Karsten, *Soldiers & Society*, pp. 1-20, 51-125
4.	Training & Value Inculcation	P. Karsten, *Soldiers & Society*, pp. 21-22, 126-144
5.	The "Military Mind" & Inter-Service Rivalries	A. Vagts, *A History of Militarism*, pp. 1-74
6.	The World of Combat	P. Karsten, *Soldiers & Society*, pp. 22-31, 145-231
7.	The Laws of Warfare & War Crimes	P. Karsten, *Law, Soldiers & Combat*, chpts. 1 & 2
8.	Mutinies	C. J. Lammers, "Strikes & Mutinies," *Admin. Science Q* (Dec. 1969)
9.	Coups d'Etat	Wm. Thompson, *The Grievances of Military Coup-Makers*
10.	"Nation-Building"	Lucien Pye, "Armies in the Process of Political Modernization," in John Johnson, ed., *The Role of the Military in Underdeveloped Countries*
11.	Veterans	P. Karsten, *Soldiers & Society*, pp. 32ff, 232ff.
12.	Office Hours	
13.	Presentation of Papers	

Basic Comparative Military Systems Literature, Organized Topically

1. The Military and Society: General Intro. Readings

Stanislav Andreski, *Military Organization and Society*
F. Voget, "Warfare & the Integration of Crow Indian Culture," in W.H. Goodenough, eds., *Explorations in Cultural Anthropology*, pp. 483-509

Peter G. Foote & David M. Wilson, The Viking Achievement
Victor Alba, "Stages of Militarism in Latin Amer.," in John Johnson, ed., The Role of the Military in Underdeveloped Countries
Thomas Barker, The Seige of Vienna
Ben Halpern, "Role of the Military in Israel," in Johnson, ed., Role of Military
Philip Kuhn, Rebellion & its Enemies in Late Imperial China: Militarization and Social Structure, 1796-1864.
Stanley Spector, Li Hung-Chang and the Huai Army: 19th Century Chinese Regionalism
P. J. Vatikiotis, Politics and the Military in Jordan
Ramsay MacMullen, Soldier and Civilian in the Late Roman Empire
M.D. Feld, "Middle-Class Society and the Rise of Military Professionalism: The Dutch Army, 1589-1609," Armed Forces & Society, I (1975), 419ff.
Bopegamage chapters in Jacques van Doorn, ed., Military Professions & Military Regimes and in Van Gils, ed., The Perceived Role of Military
Scott and Graczck chapters in On Military Ideology, eds. Morris Janowitz & J. van Doorn
Ayad Al-Qazzas, "Army & Society in Israel," Pacific Sociological Review, XVI (Apr. 1973), 143ff
S. Encel, "The Study of Militarism in Australia," in Jacques van Doorn, ed., Armed Forces & Society, 126-147.
Leonard Humphreys, "The Japanese Military Tradition," in James Buck, ed., The Modern Japanese Military System, 21-39.
J. Bayo Adekson, "Army in a Multi-Ethnic Society: Ghana," Armed Forces & Society, II (1976), 251ff. Chapter on Mamelukes in Ira Lapidus, Muslim Cities in the Late Middle Ages
Nikolai Galay, "The Relationship between the Structure of Society & the Armed Forces in the U.S.S.R.," Bulletin of the Institute for the Study of the U.S.S.R. (Nov. 1966).
Jeffrey Fadiman, Mountain Warriors: The Pre-Colonial Meru of Mt. Kenya
Andrew Vayda, "Maoris and Muskets in New Zealand," Political Science Quarterly, LXXXV (1970), 550-584
Thomas Forster, The East German Army
L.J.D. Collins, "The Military Organization & Tactics of the Crimean Tartars during the 16th and 17th centuries," in War, Technology & Society, ed. Vernon Parry & M.E. Yapp, 257-276
John Shy, "A New Look at Colonial Militia," William & Mary Quarterly (1963), 175-183
Marcus Cunliffe, Soldiers & Civilians
Dennis Skiotis, "Mountain Warriors & the Greek Revolution," in War, Technology & Society in the Middle East, ed. Vernon Parry & M.E. Yapp, 308-329
M.E. Yapp, "Middle Eastern Armies & Modernization," in Parry & Yapp, War, Technology & Society..., 343-366.
Joseph Smaldone, Warfare in the Sokolo Caliphate
Gwyn Harries-Jenkins, The Army in Victorian Society, chs. 1 & 2.
Jonathan Adelman, The Revolutionary Armies
Richard Divale, Warfare in Primitive Societies (introduction only)
Allan Millett, Guardians of the Dynasty
Halil Inalcik, :The socio-political effects of the diffusion of fire-arms in the Middle East," in War, Technology & Society, ed., Vernon Parry & M.E. Yapp, 195-217
Janes Guyot, "Ethnic Segmentation & the Function of the Military in Burma & Malaysia" I U.S. paper 1474.
Richard Hellie, Enserfment and Military Change in Muscovy
Tim Colton, "Impact of the Military on Soviet Society," in S. Bialer, ed., Domestic Context of Soviet Foreign Policy. 119-38

2. Civil-Military Relations

I. Deak, "An Army Divided: Loyalty Crisis in Haps. Off. Corps, 1848," Jahrbuch des I. fur Deut. G. VIII ('79)

Claude Welch and Arthur Smith, Military Role and Rule
E. Joffe, Party and Army: Professionalism and Political Control in the Chinese Officer Corps
Louis Perez, Army Politics in Cuba, 1898-1958
A. Mazrui chapter in Jacques van Doorn, ed., Military Professions and Military Regimes
Nelson Kasfir, "Civilian Participation under Military Rule in Uganda and Sudan," Armed Forces and Society, I (1975), 344ff.
C. Moskos chapter [on U.N.] in Van Gils, ed., The Perceived Role of the Military
Charles Moskos, Peace Soldiers and Moskos essay in J.van Doorn and Morris Janowitz, eds., On Military Ideology
Gabriel Ben-Dor, "The Politics of Threat: Military Intervention...," Journal of Political and Military Sociology, I (1973), 57ff
Gabriel Ben-Dor, "Civilianization of Military Regimes in the Arab World," Armed Forces and Society, I (1975), 317ff.
Edwin Lieuwen, Mexican Militarism
Anton Bebler, The Military in African Politics
D. Herspring and I. Volgyes, "Political Reliability in Eastern Europe Warsaw Pack Armies," Armed Forces and Society, VI (1980), 270-296
Jorge Dominques, "The Civic Soldier: The Military as a Governing Institution in Cuba,," 1973 IUS paper
Roman Kolkowicz, "Interest Groups in Soviet Politics: The Case of the Military," Comparative Politics (April 1970), 445-472.
Cynthia Enloe, Ethnic Soldiers

3. Recruitment

Richard Smethurst, A Social Basis for Prewar Japanese Militarism
Ithiel de Sola Pool, Satellite Generals
Summer Shapiro, "The Blue-Water Soviet Naval Officer" U.S. Naval Institute Proceedings (February 1971), 19-26
Christopher Duffy, The Army of Fredrick the Great 24-68
Shelby D vis, Reservoirs of Men: Black Troops of French West Africa
John Erickson, "Soviet Military Manpower Policies," Armed Forces and Society, I (Fall, 1974), 29ff.
H. Moyse-Bartlett, The King's African Rifles
Edward Lowell, The Hessians
Chapters by Dudley, Wiatr,Graczyk, and Cvrcek in Military Professions and Military Regimes, ed. Jacques van Doorn
D. Ayalon and S. Vryoni on recruitment, in War, Technology and Society in the Middle East, ed. Vernon Parry and M. E. Yapp, 44-68, 125-152
Coulombe chapter in On Military Ideology, eds., Morris Janowitz and J. van Doorn
Thomas Brendle, "Recruitment and Training in the SDF:," in James Buck ed., The Modern Japanese Military System
G. T. Griffith, The Mercenaries of the Hellenistic World
H. W. Parke, Greek Mercenary Soldiers
Peter Karsten, The Naval Aristocracy, chapter 1 and religion chapter 3
Peter Karsten, Soldiers and Society, (section on "The Recruitment Process")
Moskos, Davis-Dolbeare, and Wamsley essays in Roger Little, ed., Selective Service and American Society
Sylvia Frey, "Common British soldier in late 18th century," Societas (1975 (or '76)
Holger Herwig, "Feudalization of the Bourgeoisie: Role of Nobility in German Naval Officer Corps, 1890-1918," The Historian ('75-'76), 268ff.

Michel Martin, "Changing Social Morphology of French Mil. Est., 1945-75" (Mimeo)
Alan R. Skelley, The Victorian Army at Home
George Chessman, Auxilia of the Roman Imperial Army
Douglas Wheeler, "African Elements in Portugals' Armies in Africa," Armed Forces and Society, II (1976), 233ff.
John Schlight, Monarchs and Mercenaries
Michael Powicke, Military Obligation in Medieval England
Gianfranco Pasquino, "The Italian Army," Armed Forces and Society, II (1976), 205ff
JJ Sanders, Feudal Military Service in England
Fritz Redlich, The German Military Enterpriser and his work force (2 volumes)
F. Kazemnadeh, "The Origin and Early Development of the Persian Cossack Brigade," American Slavic and East European Review, XV, 351-63
D. Mantell, "Doves v. Hawks," Psychology Today, September 1974
G. Kourvetaris, "Greek Service Academies: Patterns of Recruitment and Organization Change," in G. Harries-Jenkins, ed., The Military and the Problems of Legitimacy, 113ff
E. H. Norman, Soldier and Peasant in Japan
E. Waldman, The Goose Step est Verboden
H. Desmond Martin, The Rise of Chingis Khan, 11-47
John Bassett, The Purchase System in the British Army, 1660-1871
Michael Lewis, A Social History of the Royal Navy, 1793-1815
F. Harrod, Manning The New Navy
Richard Gabriel, The New Red Legions, Volumes I and II
G. R. Andrews, "The Afro-Argentine Officers of B. A. Prov., 1800-1860," Journal of Negro History, 64 (1979), 85-100
Steven Cohen, "The Untouchable Soldier: Caste, Politics and the Indian Army," Journal of Asian Studies, XXVIII (May 1969)
Roger N. Buckley, Slaves in Red Coats: The Br. N.I. Regiments, 1795-1815
John Keegan, "Regimental Ideology," in War, Economy and the Military Mind, ed. G. Best, 3-18
Michael Lewis, The Navy in Trasition, 1814-1864
Michael Lewis, England's Sea-Officers
H. Hanham, "Religion and Nationality in Mid-Victorian Army," in Foot, ed., War and Society, 159ff
Norbert Elias, "Studies in the Genesis of the Naval Profession," British Journal of Sociology, I (1950), 291-309
C. B. Otley essay in Armed Forces and Society, ed., Jacques Van Doorn
P. Razzell, "Social Origins of Officers in the Indian and British Home Army," British Journal of Sociology, XIV (1963), 248ff.
Peter Karsten, et al., "ROTC, Mylai and the Volunteer Army," Foreign Policy, 1 (1971), 135-60

4. Training and Value Inculation

Roghmann and Sodeur, "Impact of Military Service on Auth. Attitudes in W. G." American Journal of Soc. (September 72)
John Farris, "Recruits and Boot Camp," Armed Forces and Society, (Fall, 1975)
James Kelley, "The Education and Training of Porfirian Officers," Military Affairs (October 1975), 124-28
Peter Karsten, The Naval Aristocracy, chapters 2 and 5
W. Cockerham: "Selective Socialization: Airborne Trainees," Journal of Political and Military Sociology, 1 (1973), 215-29
Correlli Barnett, "The Education of Military Elites," in Rupert Wilkinson, ed., Governing Elites, 193-214
Charles Firth, Cromwell's Army
Peter Karsten, "Ritual and Rank: Religious Affiliation, Father's "Calling" and Successful Advancement in the U.S. Officers Corps of the 20th Century", Armed Forces and Society (Fall, 1981)

Law, Radine, The Taming of the Troops, Social Control in U.S. Army
Morris Janowitz, "Changing Patterns of Org. Auth." Admin. Science Quarterly
   (1957)
William D. Henderson, Why The Vietcong Fought: Motivation and Control
Hassanein Rabie, "The Training of the Mamluk Faris," in War, Technology,
   and Society in the Middle East, ed. Vernon Parry and M. E. Yapp, 153-163
Harold Wool, "The Armed Services as a Training Institution," in
   Eli Ginsberg, The Nations Children, II, 158-185
Herbert Goldhammer, The Soviet Soldier
C. Lammers, "Midshipmen...," Sociologica Neerlandia, II (1965), 98-122
G. Wamsley, "Contrasting Institutions of AF Socialization," Amer. Journal of Soc.
   (Sept.72)

   5. "Militarism" and Military Ideologies

Hans Herzfeld, "Militarism in Modern History," in Germany History, ed.
   Hans Kohn, 108-121
Alfred Vagts, A History of Militarism, 1-74
Peter Karsten, The Naval Aristocracy, chapters 3, 5 and 6
Hansen and Abrahamsson chapters in On Military Ideology, eds. Morris
   Janowitz and J. van Doorn
Martin Kitchen, The German Officer Corps, 1890-1914
Francis Carsten, "From Scharnhorst to Schleicher: The Prussian Officer
   corps in Politics, 1806-1933, in Michael Howard, ed., Soldiers and
   Governments, 73-98
Stanley Payne, Politics and the Military in Modern Spain
Bengt Abrahamson, "The Ideology of an Elite...the Swedish Military," in
   Armed Forces and Society, ed. Jacques van Doorn, 71-83
Morris Janowitz, The Professional Soldier
Roman Kolkowicz, "Modern Technology and the Soviet Officer Corps," in
   Jacques van Doorn, ed., Armed Forces and Society, 148-168
Richard Smethurst, A Social Basis for Prewar Japanese Militarism
chapter on Italy in Stephen ward, ed., The War Generation
Maurice Keen, "Brotherhood in Arms," History, XLVII (1962)
Marcus Cunliffe, Soldiers and Civilians (chapters on volunteers and on North-
   South comparison)
Wallace Davies, Patriotism on Parade

   6. Inter - and Intra - Service Rivalries

Louis Morton, "Army and Marines on the China Station," Pacific Historical
   Review, X (1960), 51ff
Peter Karsten, The Naval Aristocracy, chapter 5, part 2
Fred Greene, "The Military View of American National Policy," in
   American Historical Review (1961), 354ff
Perry Smith, The Air Force Plans for Peace
Vincent Davis, Postwar Defense Policy and the U.S. Navy, 1943-1946
Robert Gallucci, Neither Peace nor Honor
Lewis Dexter, "Congressmen and the Making of Military Policy," in
   Nelson Polsby, ed., New Perspectives on the House of Representatives
Paul Hammond, Supercarriers and B-36s

   7. The World of Combat

Peter Karsten, Soldiers and Society, pp. 22-31, 145-231
John Baynes, Morale
John Keegan, The Face of Battle
S. L. A. Marshall, Men Against Fire
Peter Bourne, Men, Stress, and Vietnam
Art Bareau, The Unknown Soldiers

J. E. Morris, The Welsh Wars of Edward I
M. Barton, Goodmen: Civil War Soldiers
R. Grinker and J. Spiegel, Men Under Stress
"Cincinatus," Self-Destruction
Pete Maslowski, "A Study of Morale in Civil War Soldiers," Military
  Affairs, (1970), 122-125
Cecil Woodham-Smith, The Charge of the Light Brigade
Albert Biderman, March to Calumny
Eugene Kinkead, In Every War But One
Ron Glasser, 365 Days
John Beeler, Warfare in Feudal Europe, 730-1200
J. Glenn Gray, The Warriors
John Mahon, The Second Seminole War
Peter Paret, The Vendée, 1789-1796
Eric Leed, No Man's Land: Combat and Identity in World War I
Dennis Winter, Death's Men
Shils and Janowitz, "Cohesion and Disintegration in Wehrmacht," in
  W. Schramm, ed., Process and Effects of Mass. Comm

8. The Laws of War and War Crimes

Peter Karsten, Law, Soldiers and Combat
Maurice Keen, The Laws of War in the Late Middle Ages
Raymond Schmandt, "The Fourth Crusade and the Just War Theory,"
  Catholic Historical Review (1975), 191-221
Stan Hig, The Sand Creek Massacre
Seymour Hersh, Mylai 4
The Sand Creek Massacre, ed., John Carroll
Leon Friedman, ed., The Laws of War, Volumes I and II
John R. Lemis, comp., Uncertain Judgement: A Bibliography of War Crimes Trials
The Mylai Massacre and Its Coverup, ed., Burke Marshall, et al
W. H. Parks, "Crimes in Hostilities," Marine Corps Gazette (August 1976)

9. Mutinies

C. Lammers, "Strikes and Mutinies: A Comparative Study," Admin. Science
  Quarterly (December 1969)
J. A. B. Palmer, Mutiny Outbreak at Meerut (1857)
Christ. Hibbert, The Great Mutiny, India, 1857
Daniel Horn, The German Naval Mutiny of WWI
John Williams, Mutiny, 1917
50 Mutinies
Carl Van Doren, Mutiny in January
A. P. Ryan, Mutiny at the Curragh
Hayford, The Somers Mutiny Affair
Richard Watt, Dare Call It Treason
Ronald Spector, "The Royal Indian Navy Strike of 1946," Armed Forces and
  Society," VII (1981), 271-284
Peter Karsten, "Suborned or Subordinate? Irish Soldiers in the British
  Army, 1792-1922," AHA paper, 1981
Allan Wildman, The End of the Russian Imperial Army....Soldier's Revolt
John Prebble, Mutiny: Highland Regiments in Revolt

10. Military Corps d'Etat

William Thompson, The Grievances of Military Coup-Makers
Richard Kohn, "The Inside History of the Newburgh Conspiracy," William and Mary Quarterly (April, 1970), 1987-220
Harold Hyman, "Johnson, Stanton and Grant," American Historical Review, (October 1960), 85ff
Alfred Stepan, The Military in Politics...Brazil
John Ambler, Soldiers Against the State
Ph. Schmitter, "Liberation by Golpe...Portugal," Armed Forces and Society (Fall 1975), 5-33
Luigi Einandi, "U.S. Relations with the Peruvian Military," in Daniel Sharp, ed., U.S. Foreign Policy and Peru, 15-56
J. Rothschild, "The Military Background of Pilsudski's Coup d 'Etat," Slavic Review, XXI (1962), 241-260
Egil Fossum, "Factors influencing....military Coups d 'etat in Latin America," Journal of Peace Res. (oslo), III (1967), 228-251
Douglas Porch, "Making an Army Revolutionary: France, 1815-1848," in Geof. Best, ed., War, Economy and the Military Mind
Morris Janowitz, Military Institutions and Coercion in Developing Nations, ch. 3
Fuad Khuri and G. Obermeyer, "The Social Bases for Military Intervention in the Middle East," in Catherine Kelleher, ed., Political-Military Systems, pp. 55ff

11. Nation - building

Donald Jackson, Custer's Gold
D. Lerner and R. D. Robinson, "Swords and Ploughshares: Turkish Army as Modernizing Force," World Politics, XIII (October 1960)
Henry Bienen, ed., The Military and Modernization [on L.A., Asia, Turkey, Soviet Union, Africa, and Huntington's caveat]
Willard Barber and C. N. Ronning, Internal Security and Military Power: Counterinsurgency and Civic Action in L.A.
Ellen K. Trimberger, Revolution from Above: Military Bureaucrats and Development in Japan, Turkey, Egypt and Peru
Theophilus O. Odetola, Military Politics in Nigeria: Economic Development and Political Stability
Stephen Cohen, The Indian Army: Its Contribution to the Development of a Nation
Charles Corbett, The L. A. Military Force as a Socio-Political Force: Bolivia and Argentina
R. L. Clinton, "The Modernizing Military: Peru," Inter-American Economic Affairs, 24:4 (1971) 43-66
Francis Prucha, Broadax and Bayonet
William Goetzmann, Army Exploration in the American West
Lucien Pye, "Armies in the Process of Political Modernization," in John Johnson, ed., The Role of the Military in Underdeveloped Countries
Jae Souk Sohn, "Political Dominance and Political Failure: The Role of the Military in the Republic of Korea," in Henry Bienen, ed., The Military Intervenes 103-121
S. E. Finer, "The Man on Horseback-1974," Armed Forces and Society, I (Fall, 1974), 5ff
Hugh Hanning, The Peaceful Uses of Military Forces
Moshe Lissak, Military Roles in Modernization: Thailand and Burma
Robert Athearn, W. T. Sherman and the Settlement of the West

12. Veterans

H. Browning, et al., "Income and Veteran Status," American Sociological Review (1973), 74
Rodney Minott, Peerless Patriots
Steven Ross, "The Free Corps Movement in Post World War I Europe," Rocky Mountain Social Science Journal (1968), 81-92
Forrest McDonald, "French Veterans..." Agricultural History (1951)
G. Wooton, The Politics of Influence: British Ex-Servicemen, Cabinet Decisions and Cultural Change, 1917-1957
Mary Dearing, Veterans in Politics: The Story of the G.A.R.
William Benton, "Pa. Reve. Officers and the Federal Constitution," Pa. History (1964), 419-35
Peter Karsten, Soldiers and Society (section on veterans)
Al. Biderman and L. Sharp, "Convergence of Military and Civilian Careers," American Journal of Sociology (1968).
N. Phillips, "Militarism and Grass-Roots...," Journal of Conflict Resolution (December 1973), 625-655
Stephen Ward, ed., The War Generation
Isser Woloch, The French Veteran From the Revolution to the Restoration

THE JOHNS HOPKINS UNIVERSITY
GOLD AND SOCIETY IN COLONIAL BRAZIL
A COMPARATIVE APPROACH

A.J.R. Russell-Wood
History 10.397
Spring semester

This course will examine in detail socio-economic aspects of the discovery and exploitation of mineral resources in colonial Brazil. This development will be placed within the general Brazilian context. Students will be encouraged, and expected, to engage in independent reading about the gold mining industry in Canada, South Africa, Austrailia, Siberia and the United States of America.

The course will comprise formal lectures, group discussions and written assignments. A thematic approach to different aspects of gold mining will be adopted in the lectures, whereas the discussions and written assignments will be characterized by the establishment of comparisons between the technique, development and repercussions of gold mining in the various regions. Grades will be given on the basis of the student's contribution to the general discussions and the satisfactory completion of two written assignments.

Students should make full use of the bibliography, which is intended to serve as an indication of source materials for independent study, and not confine themselves to the weekly reading assignments. Students are requested to consult references in periodicals within the library or on overnight loan in order not to inconvenience their colleagues. They are reminded that the holdings of the Enoch Pratt Library, the Library of Congress and of other libraries (through Inter-Library loan) may be consulted.

The course will meet on Mondays 2-4 in Gilman 40. My office is at Gilman 302; office hours 11:30-12:00 daily, or by appointment with the secretary at Gilman 312.

January 31   Lecture: 'The Eldorado myth and Brazil, 1500-1825'

February 7   Lecture: 'The Brazilian gold rushes'
Reading assignments: Francois Balsan, 'Ancient gold routes of the Monomotapa Kingdom', Geographical Journal, vol. 136 (1970) pp. 240-246
George D. Hubbard, 'The influence of the presence, discovery and distribution of the precious metals in America on the migration of people', Bulletin of the American Geographical Society, vol. 44 (1912) pp. 97-111
George D. Hubbard, 'The influence of the precious metals on American exploitation, discovery, conquest and possession', ibid, vol. 42 (1910) pp. 594-602
Francile B. Oakley, 'Arkansas-golden army of '49', The Arkansas Historical Quarterly, vol. 6 (1947) pp. 1-85
Alan Cooke, 'Canada's first gold rush', The Beaver. Magazine of the North, outfit 295 (Summer, 1964) pp. 24-27
R.P. Bieber, 'The Southwestern trails to California', The Mississippi Valley Historical Review, vol. 12, no. 3, pp. 342-75
M.E. Martin, 'California emigrant roads through Texas', Southwest Historical Quarterly, vol. 28, pp. 287-301
R.M. Morse, The Bandeirantes (New York, Knopf, 1965)
E. Bradford Burns (ed.) A documentary history of Brazil (New York, 1966) pp. 89-92 and 155-163

February 14 Lecture: 'Mining camps in Brazil: man and nature'
Reading assignments: Robert S. Platt, 'Mining patterns of occupance in five South American districts', Economic geography, vol. 12 (1936) pp. 340-350

February 14
(continued)
G.D. Hubbard, 'The precious metals as a geographic factor in the settlement and development of towns in the United States', The Scottish Geographical Magazine, vol. 26 (1910) pp. 449-466
Isaiah Bowman, 'Planning in pioneer settlement', Annals of the Association of American Geographers, vol. 22 (1932) pp. 93-107
Richard Finnie, Canada moves North (New York, 1942) pp. 113-15 and 132-145
M. Cardoso, 'The Guerra dos Emboabas, civil war in Minas Gerais', 1708-1709, Hispanic American Historical Review, vol. 22, no. 3 (1942) pp. 470-192
M. Clark (ed) Sources of Australian history (London, O.U.P., 1957) pp. 278-313
Yuri Semyonov, The Conquest of Siberia (London, 1944) pp. 274-6
M.G. Bryan, 'The gold rush in Georgia', Georgia Review, vol. 9 (Winter 1955) pp. 398-405
W.A. Chaney, 'A Louisiana planter in the gold rush', Louisiana History, vol. 3 (1962) pp. 133-144
Carl L. Lokke, 'A Madison man at Nome', Wisconsin Magazine of History, vol. 33 (1949) pp. 164-183
J. McKevitt, 'Gold rush myth brought civilization to Plumas County', Journal of the West, vol. 3, no. 4 (1964) pp. 489-500
W.R. Kenny, 'Mexican-American conflict on the mining frontier', 1848-52', Journal of the West, vol. 6, no. 4 (1967) pp. 593-603
P.F. Sharp, 'Three frontiers: some comparative studies of Canadian-American, and Australian settlement', American Historical Review, vol. 24 (1955) pp. 369-77

February 28
Lecture: 'Mining towns'
Reading assignments: John C. Weaver, 'Silver peak and Blair: desert mining communities', Economic geography, vol. 15 (1939) pp. 80-84
Donald R. Patterson, 'The Witwatersrand. A unique gold-mining community', Economic Geography, vol. 27 (1951) pp. 209-221
L. Hanke, The Imperial City of Potosi. Boom Town Supreme.
D. Wharton, 'Stampede towns of the Upper Yukon', The American West, vol. 4, no. 4, pp. 45-52 and 73-75
R. Olmsted and others, 'In San Francisco and the mines; 1851-56', The American West, vol. 4, no. 3 (1967) pp. 40-49
E.M. Eriksson, 'Sioux city and the Black Hills gold rush: 1874-77, Iowa Journal of History and Politics, vol. 22 (1922) pp. 319-47
J.D. Hill, 'The Early mining camp in American life', Pacific Historical Review, vol. 1 (1932) pp. 295-311
B. Kent, 'Agitations on the Victorian gold fields, 1851-54', Historical studies of Australia and New Zealand, vol. 6 (1953-55), pp. 261-281

February 28   L.H. Carlson, 'Nome: from mining camp to civilized
(continued)   community', Pacific Northwest Quarterly, vol. 38,
               pp. 233-242
               H.A. Innes, 'Settlement and the mining frontier',
               in W.A. Mackintosh and W.L.G. Joerg (eds.)
               Canadian frontiers of settlement, vol. 9
               (Toronto, 1936)

March 6   Lecture: 'Local government in mining communities'
               H.A. Hoffmeister, 'Central City mining area',
                 Economic Geography, vol. 16 (1940) pp. 96-104
               G.S. Dumke, 'Mission station to mining town. Early
                 Las Vegas', Pacific Historical Review, vol. 22
                 (1953) pp. 257-70
               C.R. Boxer, Portuguese Society in the tropics
                 (Madison and Milwaukee (1965), chapter on Bahia
                 municipal council

March 13   Lecture: 'Royal government in mining communities'
               Reading assignments: 'The gold colony of British
                 Columbia', The Canadian Historical Review,
                 vol. 2 (1921) pp. 340-59
               D.R. Morrison, 'The politics of the Yukon Territory,
                 1898-99 (Toronto, 1968)
               J.L. Mecham, 'The Real de Minas as a political
                 institution', Hispanic American Historical
                 Review, vol. 7 (1927) pp. 45-83
               J. Ellison, 'California and the nation, 1846-69;
                 a study of the federal relations of a frontier
                 community', Southwestern Historical Quarterly,
                 vol. 30 (1926) pp. 83-113
               E. Pomeroy, 'California, 1846-1860, Politics of a
                 representative frontier state', California
                 Historical Society Quarterly, vol. 32 (1953)
                 pp. 291-302
               G. Blainey, 'The gold rushes: the year of decision',
                 Historical Studies of Australia and New Zealand,
                 vol. 10 (1961-63) pp. 129-140
               G. Blainey, 'Gold and governors', ibid, vol. 9
                 (1959-61) pp. 337-50

March 20   Lecture: 'Gold: types, technique and processing'
               H.A. Hoffmeister, 'Central city mining area',
                 Economic Geography, vol. 16 (1940) pp. 96-104
               R.C. West, 'Folk mining in Columbia', Economic
                 Geography, vol. 28 (1952) pp. 323-330
               'Gold in the Yukon district', The Scottish Geographical
                 Magazine, vol. 13 (1897) pp. 421-426
               G.D. Hubbard, 'Gold and silver mining and reduction
                 processes as responses to geographic conditions',
                 The Scottish Geographical Magazine, vol. 27,
                 pp. 417-26 and 470-74
               H.R. Wagner, 'Early silver mining in New Spain',
                 Revista de História de América, vol. 14 (1942)
                 pp. 49-71

March 20 (continued)	M.F. Lang, New Spain's mining depression and the supply of quicksilver from Peru, 1600-1700, Hispanic American Historical Review, vol. 48 (1968) pp. 632-641 C.E.W. Bromehead, 'The evidence for ancient mining', The Geographical Journal, vol. 96 (1940) pp. 101-120 D.A. Brading, 'Mexican silver-mining in the eighteenth century', The revival of Zacatecas', Hispanic American Historical Review, vol. 50, no. 4 (1970) pp. 665-681 William Ogilvie, 'The geography and resources of the Yukon basin', The Geographical Journal, vol. 12 (1898) pp. 21-41 C.M.H. Clark, Select documents in Australian history, 1851-1900 (Sydney, London, etc., 1955) pp. 26-30
April 3	Lecture: 'Gold and administration' Reading assignments: E. Bradford Burns (ed.) A documentary history of Brazil (New York, 1966) pp. 155-163 A.S. Aiton, 'The first American mining code', Michigan Law Review, vol. 23 (1924) pp. 105-113 A.S. Aiton, 'Ordenancas hechas por el Sr. Visorrey Don Antonio de Mendoca sobre las minas de la Nueva España. Ano de MDL', Revista de História de América, vol. 14 (1942) pp. 73-95 A.S. Aiton, 'The first American mint', Hispanic American Historical Review, vol. 11 (1931) pp. 198-215 M.S. Cardozo, 'The fifths in Brazil, 1695-1709', Hispanic American Historical Review, vol. 20 (1940) pp. 359-379 Joseph Ellison, 'The mineral land question in California, 1848-66', The Southwestern Historical Quarterly, vol. 30 (1926) pp. 34-55 H.E.S. Fisher, 'Anglo-Portuguese trade, 1700-1770', Economic Historical Review, 2nd series, vol. 16 (1963) pp. 219-233 C.R. Boxer, 'Brazilian gold and British traders in the first half of the eighteenth century', Hispanic American Historical Review, vol. 49 (no. 3) pp. 454-472 C.M.H. Clark, Select documents in Australian history, 1851-1900, pp. 8-21 Earl J. Hamilton, 'American treasure and the rise of capitalism, 1500-1700', Economica, no. 27, pp. 338-57 C.A. Fracchia, 'The founding of the San Francisco mining exchange, California Historical Society Quarterly, vol. 48 (1969) pp. 3-16 T.H. Marshall, 'The miners laws of Colorado', American Historical Review, vol. 25 (1919) pp. 426-39

April 10   Lecture: 'Society in mining communities and
              living conditions'
              Reading assignments: C.M.H. Clark, Select documents
              in Australian History, pp. 21-23, 30-46, 52-75
              Charles Camsell, 'The Yellowknife mining district',
              Canadian Geographical Journal, vol. 18, no. 6
              (June, 1939) pp. 311-19
              J.M.L. Bescoby, 'Society in Cariboo during the gold
              rush', Washington Historical Quarterly, vol. 24,
              no. 3 (1933) pp. 195-207
              R.M. Crawford and G.F. James, 'The gold rushes and
              the aftermath, 1851-1900' in C. Hartley Grattan
              (ed.) Australia (Berkeley and Los Angeles, 1947)
              pp. 47-64
              J.W. Covington (ed.) 'Letters from the Georgia gold
              regions', Georgia Historical Quarterly, vol. 39
              (1955) pp. 401-409
              H.O. Brayer, 'Insurance against the hazards of
              Western life', The Mississippi Valley Historical
              Review, vol. 34, pp. 221-236

April 17   Lecture: 'Racial prejudice, nationalist discrimination
              and slave labour in the gold mines'.
              Reading assignments: T.A. Rickard, 'Indian participa-
              tion in the gold discoveries', British Columbia
              Historical Quarterly, vol. 2 (1938) pp. 3-18
              E.D. and A. Potts, 'The negro and the Australian gold
              rushes, 1852-57, Pacific Historical Review, vol.
              37 (1968) pp. 381-400
              R.M. Lapp, 'The negro in gold rush California',
              Journal of Negro History, vol. 49 (1964)
              R.M. Lapp, 'Negro rights activists in gold rush
              California', California Historical Society
              Quarterly, vol. 45 (1966) pp. 3-20
              L.G. Churchward, 'Australian-American relations
              during the gold rush', Historical Studies of
              Australia and New Zealand, vol. 2 (1940) pp. 11-24
              L.G. Churchward, 'The American contribution to the
              Victorian gold rush', Victorian Historical Magazine,
              vol. 19 (1942) pp. 85-95
              R.H. Morefield, 'Mexicans in the California gold mines,
              1848-53', California Historical Society Quarterly,
              vol. 35 (1956) pp. 37-46
              Neil Coughlan, 'The coming of the Irish to Victoria',
              Historical Studies of Australia and New Zealand,
              vol. 12 (1965-7) pp. 68-86

April 24   Lecture: 'Soldiers, missionaries and the arts.'
              Reading assignments: A.P. Whitaker, 'The Elhuygar
              mining missions and the enlightenment', Hispanic
              American Historical Review, vol. 32, no. 4,
              pp. 557-85
              M.R. Booth, 'Gold rush theaters of the Klondike',
              The Beaver, Magazine of the North (Spring, 1962)
              pp. 32-37

April 24 (continued)	Lynn I. Perrigo, 'Law and order in early Colorado mining camps', The Mississippi Valley Historical Review, vol. 28, no. 1 (1941) pp. 41-62 M.R. Booth, 'Gold rush theater: The Theater Royal, Bakerville, British Columbia', Pacific Northwest Quarterly, vol. 51, pp. 97-102 H.S.C. Baker, 'The book trade in California, 1849-59', California Historical Society Quarterly, vol. 30, pp. 97-115, 249-67 and 353-67 W. Hanchett, 'The question of religion and the taming of California 1849-54', ibid, vol. 32 (1953) pp. 49-56, 119-44 R.D. Hunt, 'Pioneer Protestant preachers of early California', Pacific Historical Review, vol. 18 (1949) pp. 84-96 W. Hanchett, 'The Blue Law gospel in gold rush California', ibid, vol. 24 (1955) pp. 361-68 H. Kirker, 'Eldorado Gothic. Gold rush architects and architecture', ibid, vol. 38 (1959) pp. 31-46 J.B. McGloin, 'A California gold rush padre. New light on the "Padre of Paradise flat"', ibid, vol. 40 (1961) pp. 49-67 C.V. Hume, 'First of the gold rush theaters', ibid, vol. 46 (1967) pp. 337-44
May 1	Lecture: 'Supply trade and commerce' Reading assignments: 'G.B. Cobb, 'Supply and transportation for the Potosí mines: 1545-1640', Hispanic American Historical Review, vol. 29 (1949) pp. 25-45 J.H. Atkinson, 'Cattle drives from Arkansas to California prior to the Civil War', Arkansas Historical Quarterly, vol. 28 (1969) pp. 275-81 C.M. Love, 'History of the cattle industry in the Southwest', Southwestern Historical Quarterly, vol. 19 (1916) no. 4, pp. 370-99 W.S. Somderlin (ed.) 'A cattle drive from Texas to California: the diary of M.H. Erskine 1854', ibid, vol. 67 (1963-4) pp. 397-412 J.G. Bell, 'A log of the Texas-California cattle trail, 1854', ibid, vol. 35, pp. 208-37, 290-316 and vol. 36, pp. 47-66 W.D. Wyman, 'The outfitting posts', Pacific Historical Review, vol. 18 (1949) pp. 14-23
May 8	Lecture: 'The repercussions of gold on national and international trade and politics'. Reading assignments: Earl J. Haring, 'Imports of American gold and silver into Spain, 1503-60', Quarterly Journal of Economics, vol. 43, pp. 436-72 C.H. Haring, 'American gold and silver production in in the first half of the sixteenth century,' ibid, vol. 29, pp. 433-74 K.R. Maxwell, 'Pombal and the nationalization of the Luso-Brazilian economy', Hispanic American Historical Review, vol. 48, no. 4, pp. 608-31 A. Christelow, 'Great Britain and the trades from Cadiz and Lisbon to Spanish America and Portugal, 1759-83', ibid, vol. 27 (1947) pp. 2-29

Ancient History Expanded, 1200 B.C.E.-600 C.E.,
A Macro-Historical Survey

Lee Daniel Snyder
Fall Semester, 1982-83
New College of USF

Course Outline:
A. Theoretical Approach to Ancient History

1) Aug. 30 - Introduction: various approaches to Ancient History
2) Sept. 2 - Macro-History theory
3) Sept. 6 - An overview of the Second Era

B. Formative Cycles:

4) Sept. 9 - The Mesopotamian Heritage: Divine Kingship and Law
5) Sept. 13- Age of Hittites and Patriarchs
6) Sept. 16- India, A Slow Beginning: Tribe and Ritual
7) Sept. 20- The Greek Heroic Age
8) Sept. 23- A Wandering King: Man against Nature, Disc. of Oddyssey

C. Classical Cycles:
9) Sept. 27-Rise of Classical Greece: Age of the Polis
10) Sept. 30- Athenian Empire, Democracy and Rationalism
11) Oct. 4 - Assyria and Isreal, An Age of Small States
12) Oct. 7 - A Religious King: The Epic of David, Disc of I and II Samuel
13) Oct. 11- India Reorganized in States and Empire: The Age of Buddha and the Maurays
14) Oct. 14- A Questing King: The Epic of Rama, Disc. of Ramayana

D. Renewal Cycles:
15) Oct. 25 - Reshaping of India: Foreign Invasions and the Resurgence of Religion
16) Oct. 28 - Turning Inward, Disc. of Bhagava Gita
17) Nov. 1 - Assyrian Imperialism and the Prophetic Protest against Injustice
18) Nov. 4 - Turning Upward. Disc. Amos
19) Nov. 8 - Crisis and Reorganization in the Greek World
20) Nov. 11 - Turning Rational, Disc. of Plato's Symposium
21) Nov. 15 - Rise of Rome and Hellenistic Monarchies

E. Secularization Cycles:
22) Nov. 18 - Roman Civil War, Struggle for a New Constitution
23) Nov. 22 - Roman Empire: Climax and Exhaustion:
24) Nov. 24 - The Persian Empire, Unification of the Near East.
25) Nov. 29 - Age of the Guptas in India

F. Post Secularization Developments:
26) Dec. 2 - India and the Mediterranean Contrasted
27) Dec. 6 - Persia, The Parthian Frontier Empire and the Sassanian Renewal.
28) Dec. 8 - Conclusions: The Broad Comparison of Cultural Traditions

San Diego State University

Syllabus

Society and Culture in the Fourteenth Century: A
Global Approach to a Medieval Age

Fall 1981

R. Dunn

This course is an experiment in world history. Its aim is to take the continent of Eurasia as well as part of Africa as a single field of historical investigation and to study an "age," what we may call the Mongol Age, as it embraces this world region. The history of mankind is more than the sum of the histories of its nations or empires. In the Old World (Eastern Hemisphere) the most important events and developments in history have not taken place within the limits of particular countries or cultural areas. Their geographical and social range has almost always been greater than that, drawing peoples of different languages and cultures into a common historical experience. Moreover, the peoples of the Old World have been interacting with one another for some thousands of years on a larger scale and over greater distances than we commonly recognize.

This semester we will study a number of themes in the history of Afro-Eurasia during the period from about 1250 to 1350, an age characterized most conspicuously by the rise and decline of the Mongol world empire and its successor states. The focus of our study will be the Islamic dominated areas but will embrace the region of cities and relatively high population extending form Europe and Northern Africa on the west to China on the east. We will stress themes in social, cultural, and economic history--trade, commications, urban life, education, religion, art, and architecture--rather than political or military history. We will be especially concerned about one aspect of fourteenth century society: the life and values of an international cosmopolitan class. To what degree did a cosmopolitan social order exist in that century transcending the frontiers of particular countries or ethnic regions? How were cosmopolitan values and relationships given expression? How does fourteenth century cosmopolitanism compare with the world-mindedness of today?

Examinations: We will have one midterm examination (30%), a final exam (30%), and a map quiz (which you must pass with a score of 72 out of 100 or repeat). Exams will be essay-type. Plus and minus grades will be awarded.

Paper: Everyone will write a research paper or bibliographical essay of nine to twelve pages. I will provide a list of topics from which you may choose. You may also propose a topic not on the list. Please work closely with me in developing your paper. Papers will be due Novenber 25. They must be typed and squeaky clean.

Classes: I will lecture on most Mondays and Wednesdays, but interruptions for questions are welcome. On most Fridays we will discuss the readings assigned for that week. Assignments should be completed before the discussion hour each week.

Office: AH 3152, tel. 265-5187
       Hours: MW 3:00-4:30, F 3:00- 4:00

Readings: The following books should be available in the bookstore:

    Farmer, et al, Comparative History of Civilizations in Asia, vol. 1
    Hamdun and King, Ibn Battuta in Black Africa
    Latham, Marco Polo
    McNeill, Plagues and People
    Tuchman, A Distant Mirror

Society and Culture in the Fourteenth Century

Some reading assignments will be placed on Limited Loan in the library. You must be prepared to go to the library to read these assignments, as they will in most cases be placed on two-hour loan.

Week 1

Aug.	31	A World-Historical approach to the past
Sept.	2	Defining the world region and the age
	4	Discussion

        Marshall G. S. Hodgson, "The Interrelations of Societies in History," from *Comparative Studies in Society and History*, 1962

Week 2

Sept.	7	Holiday
	9	Islam as a Social Order
	10	Discussion

        Farmer, Introduction (xvii-xxix) and 221-241

Week 3

Sept.	14	Dawn of the Mongol Age
	16	The Mongol world empire and its successor states
	18	Discussion

        Farmer, 283-307, 358-382

Week 4

Sept.	21	The political shape of the Ecumene in the early fourteenth century
	23	Political fragmentation of mid century and the end of the age.
	25	Discussion

        Farmer, 382-398

Week 5

Sept.	28	Society and Culture in the Islamic Heartland
	30	Institutions of Islamic Cosmopolitanism
Oct.	2	Discussion of paper topics

        Work on Papers

Week 6

Oct.	5	The Islamic Pilgrimage
	7	The Life and Times of Ibn Battuta
	9	Discussion

        "Hadjdj," in *Encyclopedia of Islam* (reference room)
        H.A.R. Gibb, *The Travels of Ibn Battuta*, vol. 1 (limited loan)

Week 7

Oct.	12	Patterns of World Trade and Communication
	14	Discussion
	16	Examination

        Review for Examination

Society and Culture in the Fourteenth Century   Page 3

Week 8

Oct. 19   European Responses to the Mongol Age
     21   Marco Polo assessed
     23   Discussion

           Latham, Marco Polo, 7-73
           William McNeill, A World History, 256-269 (limited loan)

Week 9

Oct. 26   Cosmopolitan patterns in the Mediterranean world
     28   Mediterranean world (continued)
     30   Discussion

           J.H. Parry, The Discovery of the Sea, pp. ??? (limited loan)

Week 10

Nov. 2   The Indian Ocean world
     4   Indian Ocean (continued)
     6   Discussion

           Hamdun and King, Ibn Battuta in Black Africa, 12-21
           Dunn, "The World of the Western Sea," ms. in progress (limited loan)

Week 11

Nov. 9   The Saharan World
     11   Saharan world (continued)
     13   Discussion

           Hamdun and King, Ibn Battuta in Black Africa, 22-62
           P.D. Curtin and P. Bahannan, Africa and Africans, 223-248 (L.L. or handout)
           Bovill, The Golden Trade of the Moors, pp. ??? (limited loan)

Week 12

Nov. 16   Europe in the Fourteenth Century: Origins of World Domination
     18   China's Role in the Ecumene
     20   Discussion

           Barbara Tuchman, A Distant Mirror, 3-69
           Farmer, 328-344, 382-389
           Latham, Marco Polo, 113-162

Week 13

Nov. 23   Portraits of Cosmopolitan Cities: Cairo
     25   Portraits: Delhi
     27   Holiday

           Farmer, 307-320

Week 14

Nov. 30   Discussion: Portrait of Fez
Dec. 2   Review of Papers
Dec. 4   Review of Papers

Society and Culture in the Fourteenth Century   Page 4

Week 14 (continued)

        Farmer, 307-320

Week 15

Dec. 7   Social Effects of the Plague
      9   The Meaning of Cosmopolitanism
    11   Discussion

        Tuchman, <u>A Distant Mirror</u>, 70-125
        McNeill, <u>Plagues and People</u>, pp.???

COLUMBIA UNIVERSITY

HISTORY W4801y (Spring 1979) William R. Roff
MW 2:40-3:55   1129 I.A. Bldg. x4725

                           Richard W. Bulliet
                           1115 I.A. Bldg. x3581

THE INDIAN OCEAN

The course, to consist of twice-weekly lectures given by faculty drawn from several disciplines, will survey human contact and interaction in the Indian Ocean region, seen in ecological, cultural, social, economic and political perspective from earliest times to the present.

Students taking the course for 'E' credit will be asked to write two expository or analytical papers, one around the middle of the term and the other at the end.

The course outline that follows lists, in general terms, the topics that will be covered. The reading list includes required readings (all of which are on reserve in the College Library, and some of which are recommended for purchase), and a selection of additional material of relevance or interest.

Outline

A. The Indian Ocean as a physical unit

1. Mon. 22 Jan. Introduction to the course

2. Wed. 24 Jan. The ocean and its shores (geomorphology of the seabed; relation to continental land masses; isles and inlets; oceanography; fisheries and other oceanic natural resources)

3. Mon. 29 Jan. The ecologies (ecosystems) of the littoral (types of coastal terrain; coast-hinterland relations; basic settlement patterns; climatology)

4. Wed. 31 Jan. Seafaring and its constraints (navigation and knowledge (itineraries, cartography); coasts as river banks; sails and hulls; currents and winds; dimensions and distances)

B. Contact and interaction

5. Mon. 5 Feb. Anthropology and the pre-history of the Indian Ocean littoral

6. Wed. 7 Feb. Movement of plants, animals and technologies

7. Mon. 12 Feb. Movement of peoples: pre-history to 1800 (special topic: migrations of Indonesians to Madagascar)

8. Wed. 14 Feb. Movement of peoples: 1800 to the present (special topic: labor migration, Indians to East Africa)

9. Mon. 19 Feb. The spread of Indian religions in the eastern Indian Ocean

10. Wed. 21 Feb. The spread of Islam - the Indian Ocean as an Arabic-speaking Mediterranean

11. Mon. 26 Feb. Language: the development of the Arabicized trade languages - Swahili in the West and Malay in the East

12. Wed. 28 Feb. Music: Africa and Indonesia - the evidence of the xylophone

13. Mon. 5 Mar. DISCUSSION PERIOD

C. Systematic relationships

14. Wed. 7 Mar. Littoral state patterns to 1500

15. Mon. 19 Mar. The trans-Indian Ocean economy: the spice trade to 1500

16. Wed. 21 Mar. The trans-Indian Ocean economy: trade patterns from 1500 to 1800

17. Mon. 26 Mar. Alliance, warfare and empire, 1500-1800

18. Wed. 28 Mar. The trans-Indian Ocean economy: trade patterns 1850-1950

19. Mon. 2 Apr. DISCUSSION PERIOD

20. Wed. 4 Apr. High imperialism in the Indian Ocean region, 19th to early 20th centuries

21. Mon. 9 Apr. Nationalism as an unshared problem

D. Political and economic systems in the modern world

22. Wed. 11 Apr. The island states - population, tourism, strategic pawns

23. Mon. 16 Apr. The littoral states: economic networks (sea-bed exploitation, fishing (states as isolates); trade relations - interlocking or competing (bilateralism, regional groupings); the Indian Ocean as an economic order (rank and dependency))

24. Wed. 18 Apr.   The littoral states: networks of people (the minorities - 'Indians' in Africa, Southeast Asia - Arabs - Chinese; laborers and the Mid-East oil boom; post-colonial new metropoles - Indian doctors, Pakistani pilots, Singapore bankers)

25. Mon. 23 Apr.   The littoral states: political networks (bilateral/subregional, ties/conflicts; the political region - Indian Ocean, Indonesian Ocean, or Malagasy Sea

E. The Indian Ocean in global politics

26. Wed. 25 Apr.   Oil, energy and the Indian Ocean

27. Mon. 30 Apr.   The Indian Ocean as a nuclear free zone or zone of peace

28. Wed. 2 May.   FINAL DISCUSSION

Reading List

Required readings (those recommended for purchase marked*)

*Auguste Toussaint. History of the Indian Ocean. Chicago: University of Chicago Press, 1966. (There is no 'text' for the course, but this is the nearest available thing)

*Indian Ocean Atlas. Washington: Central Intelligence Agency, 1976. (Indispensable - and cheap)

Alan Villiers. Monsoon seas: the story of the Indian Ocean. New York: McGraw-Hill, 1952. (a good read)

James Hornell. Water transport: origins and early evolution. Cambridge: University Press, 1946. (Classic, standard work on early seafaring)

*George Hourani. Arab seafaring in the Indian Ocean in ancient and early medieval times. Princeton: University Press, 1951; repr. Beirut: Khayats, 1963; repr. New York, Octagon, 196 . (Short and useful, if not the last word)

Alan Villiers. The sons of Sinbad. London & New York: 1940. (On dhows)

*Sauer, Carl. Seeds, spades, hearths and herbs. Cambridge, Mass.: M.I.T. Press, 1965. (Agricultural technology, plant diffusion etc.) p/b

Chittick, H.N. & R.I. Rotberg. East Africa and the Orient: cultural synthesis in pre-colonial times. London: 1975

Ibn Battuta. Travels in Asia and Africa (transl. by H.A.R. Gibb). Routledge & Kegan Paul: London, 1929 (The inimitable - and the best edition for this course)

Joseph DeSomogyi. A short history of oriental trade. Hildesheim: Olms, 1968. (Excellent survey history in short compass)

J. Innes Miller. Spice trade of the Roman Empire. London: Oxford University Press, 1968. (Well-organized treatment of commodities, routes, and carriers)

*Niels Steensgard. The Asian trade revolution of the seventeenth century: the East India companies and the decline of the caravan trade. Chicago: University of Chicago Press, 1974. (Self-explanatory title - important book) p/b

J.C. van Leur. Indonesian trade and society: essays on Asian social and economic history. The Hague: Van Hoeve, 1955. (Influential book on the seaborne commerce of further Asia)

F.B. & C.P. Martin. Cargoes of the East. London: Elm Tree Books, 1978 (A recent general treatment, with the emphasis on the African-Arabian side of the Indian Ocean)

G.A. Ballard. Rulers of the Indian Ocean. London: Duckworth, 1927. (An old-fashioned but standard work on the politics of empire).

*Ferenc Vali. Politics of the Indian Ocean region: the balances of power. New York: Free Press, 1976. (A good, and up-to-date work on the contemporary scene)

THE INDIAN OCEAN   W4801y

SUPPLEMENTARY READING LIST

Required readings

(As with the first list, all materials are on Reserve in the College Library)

Edward A. Alpers. The East African slave trade. Nairobi: Historical Association of Tanzania, 1967. (A brief, 27 pp, introduction)

H.N. Chittick & R.I. Rotberg (eds.) East Africa and the Orient. London 1975 (A collection of research papers on a variety of topics).

Frederick-Cooper Plantation slavery on the East African coast. New Haven 1977

Richard Critchfield The golden bowl be broken. Bloomington, Ind. Indiana University Press, 1973

Holden Furber. Rival empires of trade in the Orient. Minnesota; University of Minnesota Press, 1976 (Covers the period 1600-1800, and is regarded by the revelant lecturers as the best general work.)

Chandra Jayawardena. "Migration and change: a survey of Indian communities overseas". Geographical Review, 58 (1968), 426-449

Michael Pearson. Merchants and Rulers in Gujerat. Berkley, Cal.: University of California Press, 1976

J.E.G. Sutton. Early trade in eastern Africa. Nairobi: East African Publishing House, 1973. (Useful, short survey, 42 pp.)

D.W. Phillipson. The later prehistory of eastern and southern Africa. New York: Africana Press, 1977

Hugh Tinker. Under the banyan tree: overseas emigrants from India, Pakistan and Bangladesh. New York Oxford University Press, 1977 (now the big standard work).

Please note that for those students taking the course for "E" credit, the first of the two expository or analytical papers, on a topic of the student's choice but drawn from roughly the first half of the course will be due directly after the mid-term break that is to say, on Monday, 19 March.

Bryn Mawr College
Spring 1984

Arthur P. Dudden
Patrick Manning

History 113
History of Three Worlds--- Africa, America, Europe

This course seeks to correct existing Euro-centered biases for understanding Western Civilization's interconnections with Africa and America by demonstrating the influences of Africa and America in Europe and upon each other. There is no textbook for this course. Required weekly reading assignments range from about 100 to about 200 pages, but you may find it desirable to read beyond the assigned pages. The lectures will develop the continuity and interrelated structures of the course, while illuminating each particular topic in turn. The map assignment is designed to provide an essential geographic familiarity early in the course. The statistical exercise emphasizes that many of the most significant historical sources, for our purposes, are quantitative rather than qualitative. The essay on interactions is assigned to encourage your analysis and interpretation of interrelations among Africa, America and Europe in the modern period. The midterm and final exams require you to review and synthesize the materials presented in the course.

You are expected to complete all of each topic's reading before the Monday and Wednesday discussion class meetings. Each Friday meeting will be devoted to a lecture on the topic for the week. The following books are required and recommended for purchase:

Required:
   Alfred Crosby, Jr., The Columbian Exchange
   Eric R. Wolf, Europe and the Peoples without History
   Daniel Headrick, The Tools of Empire
   Chinua Achebe, Things Fall Apart
   and any one of the following five:
      Chinua Achebe, A Man of the People
      Richard Critchfield, Shahhat, an Egyptian
      Carolina Maria de Jesus, Child of the Dark
      Graham Greene, Our Man in Havana
      V. S. Naipaul, A Bend in the River

Recommended:
   Eugene D. Genovese, From Rebellion to Revolution
   Edmund Morgan, American Slavery, American Freedom
   J. M. Roberts, History of the World Since 1500
   Dankwart A. Rustow, Oil and Turmoil

Topic 1. The Three Worlds.

   A cross-sectional survey of the cultures and civilizations of Africa, America and Europe in the 15th century.

   Readings:
      Fernand Braudel, The Structures of Everyday Life, 172-78, 227-65.
      Eric Wolf, Europe and the Peoples without History, 1-125 (recommended).

Topic 2. Establishing Contacts.

The voyages of discovery as an extension of Christian-Muslim confrontation in Europe and the Mediterranean. The voyages of discovery are chronicled, along with their initial impact in Europe. The Columbian exchange of food crops and disease across the Atlantic. The initial impact of Christian missionary work in Kongo, Benin, Mexico and Peru.

Readings:
    Georges Balandier, Daily Life in the Kingdom of Kongo, 19-24, 42-63.
    George Sanderlin, Bartolomé de Las Casas, 3-24, 86-102.
    Alfred Crosby, Jr., The Columbian Exchange, 3-121.
    Eric Wolf, Europe and the Peoples without History, 129-57 (recommended).

Topic 3. Mercantile Policy, Commercial Reality, and Slavery.

Sixteenth-century Spanish mercantile policy as an aspect of Charles V's bid for world empire. European rivalries at home and overseas, 16th and 17th centuries. Colonial conquest and mercantile policy for Holland, France and England. The rise of sugar and slavery in the 17th century.

Readings:
    Eric Wolf, Europe and the Peoples without History, 158-94.
    J. H. Parry, The Age of Reconnaissance, 243-56, 274-89.
    Edmund Morgan, American Slavery, American Freedom, 1-24, 133-57, 196-211.
    J. M. Roberts, History of the World Since 1500, 499-554 (recommended).

MAP ASSIGNMENT:
    For Africa, America and Europe, at approximately 1700 A.D., use a blank outline map or maps to display 1) climatic zones, 2) altitudes of terrain, 3) population densities and characteristics, 4) major crops, and 5) trade routes.

Topic 4. The Demography of World Interaction.

The decline and partial recovery of New World populations. The drain of the slave trade on Africa's population. Migration from Spain, Portugal and England to the colonies. American families in the 17th century. Urbanization in the three worlds.

Readings:
    Alfred Crosby, Jr., The Columbian Exchange, 122-221.
    Franklin Mendels, "Proto-Industrialization" Journal of Economic History, vol. 32 (March 1972), 241-61.
    Eric Wolf, Europe and the Peoples without History, 195-263.

Topic 5. Eighteenth-Century Society, Family, and Work.

A comparison of family structures and labor systems in Africa, the Americas and Europe, emphasizing ties among the systems: peasant producers in Africa and mainland Latin America, slave plantation society in the Caribbean, yeoman farmers in North America, hunters in North America, peasants and townspeople in Europe.

Readings:
  James Axtell, The Indian Peoples of Eastern America, 3-31.
  Georges Balandier, Daily Life in the Kingdom of Kongo, 153-79.
  Michael Craton, Searching for the Invisible Man, 197-208, 223-43.
  Andre Gunder Frank, Latin America: Underdevelopment or Revolution, 3-17.
  Howard Lamar and Leonard Thompson, The Frontier in History, 237-69.

Topic 6. The Democratic Revolutions.

The rise of Enlightenment thinking and the challenge to feudal and monarchical institutions as a world movement. Interrelations among the American Revolution, the French Revolution, the Haitian Revolution, the movements for independence in Latin America, the spread of Enlightenment thinking to the African coast, and the formulation of the anti-slavery movement.

Readings:
  Eric Hobsbawm, The Age of Revolution, 74-100, 163-79.
  J. M. Roberts, History of the World Since 1500, 636-660.
  Edmund Morgan, American Slavery, American Freedom, 250-70, 363-87.
  Eugene Genovese, From Rebellion to Revolution, 82-125.
  Simón Bolívar, Selected Writings, vol. 2, 596-606.
  Elie Kedourie, Nationalism in Asia and Africa, 153-89.

Topic 7. Industrialization.

Comparisons of technological change, changes in European social structure, and influences of the world economy as causes for the rise of industrial production: the lecture will give emphasis to the latter in addition to the usual interpretation of industrialization. It will also complete the narrative of the abolition of slavery.

Readings:
  Eric Hobsbawm, The Age of Revolution, 44-73, 202-17.
  Eric Wolf, Europe and the Peoples without History, 265-95.
  Eric Williams, Capitalism and Slavery, 154-77.
  Rolando Mellafe, Negro Slavery in Latin America, 124-45.
  Forbes Munro, Africa and the International Economy, 40-63.
  J. M. Roberts, History of the World Since 1500, 615-35. (recommended).

MID-SEMESTER EXAM -- on topics to date.

Topic 8. Changing Popular Culture.

The formation and mutual influences of popular culture in the Atlantic basin, including the growth of Afro-American culture, the impact of Afro-American culture on Europe, cultural exchanges between Native Americans and whites in the U.S.A., and the impact of Victorian culture in Africa.

Readings:
  Eugene Genovese, Roll Jordan, Roll, 309-24; 566-84.
  James S. Roberts, "Drink & Industrial Work Discipline in 19th Century Germany", Journal of Social History (Fall 1981), 25-38.
  Philip D. Curtin, Africa and the West, 99-138.
  Horatio Alger, Ragged Dick. (recommended).

Topic 9. Frontiers.

The expansion of frontiers in North America, South America, and Africa, with the dynamic nature of frontier societies.

Readings:
Roger Owen and Bob Sutcliffe, Studies in the Theory of Imperialism, 295-311.
Howard Lamar and Leonard Thompson, The Frontier in History, 14-40.
Michael Crowder, West African Resistance, 111-43.
Frederick Jackson Turner, "The Significance of the Frontier in American History," A.H.A. Annual Report (1893), 199-227.
J. M. Roberts, History of the World Since 1500, 661-702 (recommended).

Topic 10. Industrialization and Imperialism.

Economic and political motives for additional expansion in the age of the new imperialism. Responses and resistance by those peoples invaded.

Readings:
Eric Wolf, Europe and the Peoples without History, 296-353.
Daniel Headrick, The Tools of Empire, 129-64, 192-203.
Roger Owen and Bob Sutcliffe, Studies in the Theory of Imperialism, 35-70, 93-116.
J. M. Roberts, History of the World Since 1500, 703-39. (recommended).

STATISTICAL EXERCISE I
You will analyze the family and occupational structures of black and white Philadelphians in 1880 using data stored in the HP3000 computer and analyzing it with the Statistical Package for the Social Sciences (SPSS). You will perform a FREQUENCIES analysis.

Topic 11. Families under Pressure.

Comparisons of the impacts of industrialization and imperialism on family life in Europe, America, and Africa. The great migrations of the nineteenth century will be incorporated within this theme.

Readings:
Eric Wolf, Europe and the Peoples without History, 359-89.
Franklin Knight, Slavery in Cuba during the Nineteenth Century, 85-120.
Tamara Hareven, Family Time and Industrial Time, 38-68.
Chinua Achebe, Things Fall Apart (entire).

STATISTICAL EXERCISE II
A continuation of the previous exercise on Philadelphians. You will perform a CROSSTABS analysis.

Topic 12. Democracy, Nationalism, and Socialism.

The rise of each of these strands of thought in Europe, and the contentions among them in the twentieth century. The spreading impacts of the Russian Revolution, fascism, zionism, and nationalist movements in Latin America and Africa.

Readings:
> Eric Wolf, Europe and the Peoples without History, 385-91.
> Elie Kedourie, Nationalism in Asia and Africa, 372-87, 488-539, 552-61.
> Colin Legun, Pan-Africanism, A Short Political Guide, 228-36.
> J. M. Roberts, History of the World Since 1500, 771-815; 841-63.
> (recommended)

Topic 13. Oil and Turmoil.
> The formation of the United Nations Organization, the emergence of two great power blocs in the Cold War, and the subsequent formation of the Third World bloc.

Readings:
> Dankwart Rustow, Oil and Turmoil, 91-179.
> J. M. Roberts, History of the World Since 1500, 902-52. (recommended).
>
> Read one of the following books:
> > Chinua Achebe, A Man of the People
> > Richard Critchfield, Shahhat, an Egyptian
> > Carolina Maria de Jesus, Child of the Dark
> > Graham Greene, Our Man in Havana
> > V. S. Naipaul, A Bend in the River

ESSAY ON INTERACTIONS: 1850 to date.
> An analysis of interactions between regions, populations, nations, empires, and/or cultures. Due at end of semester.

FINAL EXAMINATION:

Bryn Mawr College   Mr. Johnson
Spring Semester   Mr. Dudden
1983-1984   History 113
         History of Three Worlds-Africa, America, Europe
                     LECTURES AND DISCUSSIONS

Topic 1 The Three Worlds (Jan. 23)
     Lec.   Mediterranean Europe in the 15th century   (Johnson)
     Disc. Africa   (Johnson)
     Disc. America's Indians   (Dudden)

Topic 2 Establishing Contacts (Jan. 30)
     Lec.   Gold from the Indies   (Dudden)
     Disc. Portugese Missionaries in Central Africa   (Johnson)
     Disc. Spanish Mission and Land Policy   (Dudden)

Topic 3 Mercantile Policy, Commercial Reality, and Slavery(Feb. 6)
     Lec.   Sugar and Slaves   (Johnson)
     Disc. France in the Age of Louis XIV   (Johnson)
     Disc. Elizabethan England   (Dudden)

Topic 4 The Demography of World Interaction(Feb. 13)
     Lec.   Colonizing the New World   (Dudden)
     Disc. Impacts of the Slave Trade on Africa   (Johnson)
     Disc. Seaport Cities   (Dudden)

Topic 5 Eighteenth Century Society, Family and Work(Feb. 20)
     Lec.   Enlightened Science and Reason   (Johnson
     Disc. Slavery in the New World   (Johnson)
     Disc. Indians in a Changing World   (Dudden)

Topic 6 The Democratic Revolutions (Feb. 27)
     Lec.   Man in Various States of Nature   (Dudden)
     Disc. Jefferson to Bolivar   (Dudden)
     Disc. Robespierre to Toussaint L'Ouverture   (Johnson)

Topic 7 Industrialization:I (Mar. 5)
     Lec.   The First Industrial Revolution   (Johnson)
     Disc. The Abolition of Salvery   (Johnson)
     Disc. The Continuing Industrial Revolution   (Dudden)

Topic 8 Changing Popular Culture (Mar. 19)
     Lec.   Technological, Artistic, Religious &
            Educational Interchanges   (Dudden
     Disc. The Arts of Painting, Sculpture and Music   (Johnson)
     Disc. Schools and Churches   (Dudden)

Topic 9 Frontiers (Mar. 26)
     Lec.   Southern Africa   (Johnson)
     Disc. Europe's Outposts in Africa and America   (Johnson)
     Disc. America in Frontier Theory   (Dudden)

History 113
Page -2-

Topic 10 Industrialization: II (April 2)
    Lec. Globalizing the Industrial Revolution   (Dudden)
    Disc. The Theory and Practice of Imperialism   (Johnson)
    Disc. Industry's Colonies   (Dudden)

Topic 11 Families under Pressure (April 9)
    Lec. The Demography of Industrialization   (Manning)
    Disc. Slavery in Cuba   (Johnson)
    Disc. The Industrial Family   (Dudden)

Topic 12 Democracy, Nationalism, and Socialism (April 16)
    Lec. Nationalism in the Colonial World   (Johnson)
    Disc. The American and French Revolutionary Models   (Johnson)
    Disc. Nkrumrah and Castro   (Dudden)

Topic 13 Oil and Turmoil (April 23)
    Lec. OPEC   (Dudden)
    Disc. The Middle East and the Three Worlds   (Johnson)
    Disc. Cold War in the Three Worlds   (Dudden)

510:114, GLOBAL HISTORY: THE MAKING OF THE MODERN WORLD, 1000-1984

Fall 1984
Lectures Monday, Thursday 2;

Professors John Gillis & Allen Howard
Rutgers University
Discussions to be arranged for Level III students

Office: Tillett Hall room 241
Office Hours: Prof. Gillis - Thursday, 3rd period
Prof. Howard - Monday, 3rd period

Description and Goals of the Course:

Through lectures, readings, and discussions this course will explore the origins of the relationships between three of the world's great regions: West Africa, Western Europe, and the Americas. It will begin with the regions before significant contact occurred, exploring their characteristics and defining their differences and similarities. Attention will then shift to the post-1500 period of exploration, colonization, and slave trade, focusing on how these created a new Atlantic economic system and at the same time altered each of the regions involved. The final weeks of the course will be concerned with the origins of the modern economic and political revolutions which created the patterns of development and underdevelopment which are the background to the present world crisis. The course is historical but the questions it deals with are starkly contemporary. It is through the past that we understand the world as it is and how it must be changed if we are all to survive.

To be an educated person, one must not only master a certain body of material and become an expert in a specialized field. One must also learn to think about the world at large and be able to express oneself effectively on critical issues. Therefore this course stresses oral and written expression as well as historical knowledge. We do not equate history with mere memory. Historical perspective is the ability to deal with the past analytically, not simply narrating what happened but understanding why things have turned out as they have. The successful student will complete this course with a deep and enduring understanding of the following:

The nature of world development in its many aspects: economic, political, social, and cultural.
Key differences, similarities, and interrelationships between the civilizations of West Africa, the Americas, and Western Europe, including religion, family life, and urban culture.
World-wide historical forces, including trade, slavery, feudalism, imperialism, colonialism, industrialization, revolution, the nation-state, and modern capitalism.
Reactions of ordinary people to these forces ranging from accommodation to resistance and revolution.
How the history of the Atlantic world has created the present condition of development and underdevelopment.
Some ways in which the current crisis of world inequalities and tensions might be overcome using historical understanding.

Requirements:
The course fulfills Livingston College's Level Three standards, but may also be taken as an ordinary course. It counts both toward a history major and as a fulfillment of distribution requirements. It is open to students of any college or level.

The following books are to be purchased at the Livingston Bookstore:
D.T. Niane, Sundiata: An Epic of Old Mali
Franklin Knight, The Caribbean
Hans Koning, Columbus: His Enterprise
Rowland Parker, The Common Stream
Tarikh, "The African Diaspora"
Eric Wolf, Europe and the People Without History

Other readings will be handed out in class or placed on reserve at the Livingston Library. These are to be read in the week assigned, as they are absolutely essential to understanding the lectures and participating in discussion as well as writing the papers.

The three required papers are listed on the syllabus and must be handed in on the day indicated. In addition, those doing the course for Level III credit will write a research paper (explained in detail on another handout), and those not doing Level III will write a final examination. Instructions will be available as the course goes along. The papers are carefully designed so as to develop your analytical and narrative skills. The first are essentially descriptive; the later papers are more comparative and analytic. We will be assisting you in developing both your thinking and writing abilities, and will ask you to re-write those papers which do not meet the required standard. You should not hesitate to consult with us on a regular basis about your work, for this is a normal part of the learning process.

Discussion in the lecture period is an integral part of that same process. You are expected to be prepared to contribute your ideas, to raise questions, and to inform the discussion. Students taking the course for Level III credit will participate in an extra meeting during certain weeks. These sessions will deal with methods of researching and writing longer papers.

Each student should make a point to consult with his or her instructor at mid-term and just before writing the final paper. This provides an opportunity to discuss progress in the course and deal with any problems that may have arisen. Take advantage of this opportunity. We are ready to help in any way we can to see to it that you successfully fulfill the goals of the course.

Grading:
Each paper will receive extensive comments and the final grade will be based on the progress a student has made in mastering the material and the concepts essential to the course. Learning is an active process and thus participation in discussion is also an indication of just how well you are learning not only to understand but express what you have understood. Remember that an educated person is also an articulate individual who contributes to the common good by sharing his or her thought with the larger community. If education is to have any real value it must be both a private and public enterprise.

510:114 -- page 3

The Syllabus:

PART I: THE WORLD OF 2000

Week I   Introduction to the Course

  Sept. 6   Organization of the course, including the adding of an
             additional hour of conveniently scheduled class time for those
             who are taking the course for Level III credit. They will
             sign up for additional course credit under 090:299, handing in
             add slips to Dean Christine Abdella of Livingston College.

Week II   The World We Have Inherited

  Sept. 10   North, South, and other Inequalities

  Sept. 13   Concepts and Perspectives

             The world as we know it is the product of complex changes
             taking place over hundreds of years. There is nothing
             inevitable about the present imbalance in world resources,
             capabilities, and power. Indeed, if we take the year 1000 as
             our starting point, those parts of the world which now enjoy a
             privileged position were by no means predominant then. If so,
             how did the present North/South imbalance come about? How did
             present class and gender inequalities develop? We will also
             be suggesting the terms of analysis most appropriate to
             answering these questions.

             Read selections from the Brandt Report, **North-South: A
             Program for Survival**

PART II: THE WORLD, 1000-1500

Week III West Africa, 1000-1500

  Sept. 17   The Rise of West African Empires

  Sept. 20   Population, Social Structure, and Economy of Mali

      Readings: Niane, **Sundiata**, 1-38
                Curtin, "Trade and Politics South of the Sahara,"

                Cohen, "The Kanuri of Bornu,"
                Wolf, **Europe and the People Without History**, 24-32

      For discussion think about the following questions:
      What social obligations did family members and others have in
      Mali and Bornu? How does the African definition of family
      differ from our own? How were production and distribution
      organized in Mali? The first **paper** will be **due Monday, Oct. 1**.
      Instructions will be available this week.

Week IV   West Africa, 1000-1500

Sept. 24   Religion and Politics in Mali

Sept. 27   West African Towns, Trade, and Empires

Readings: Complete Niane, <u>Sundiata</u>
            Davidson, "A Science of Social Control," 109-130
            147-156

For discussion think about the West African views of reality and the supernatural. What are the social and scientific methods used by their healers, and how are these similar to and different from our own? How were elders and kings responsible for the health and welfare of their people? What legitimated rulers, in other words, what gave them the right to rule? (Be sure you understand the notion of "ancestral charter.") How were great empires held together? What role did trade play in the growth of the empires? How were cities important? Were ordinary cultivators exploited in Mali and other kingdoms (was much of their product taken from them)?

Week V   Western Europe, 1000-1500

Oct. 1   From Roman Imperium to European Feudalism
          FIRST PAPER DUE TODAY

Oct. 4   Lords, Manors, and Peasants

Readings: Parker, <u>The Common Stream</u>, pp. 21-39, 54-88
            Einhard, <u>Life of Charlemagne</u>, selections

The discussion will focus on the nature of feudalism and how it differed from the Roman imperial system. How did Charlemagne exercise authority without a bureaucracy, a professional army or a body of written law? Compare him to Sundiata. Rowland Parker's marvelous research on the English settlement of Foxton will allow you to trace the change from Roman villa to feudal manor. What were the distinctive features of the medieval village and its inhabitants?

Week VI   Western Europe, 1000-1500

Oct. 8   Rise of Towns and Economic Growth to the Fourteenth
          Century

Oct. 11   Crisis of the Fourteenth Century

Readings: Parker, <u>The Common Stream</u>, 89-106
            Hilton, <u>Bond Men Made Free</u>, selections

            Documents relating to the Peasant Revolt of 1381

Between the twelfth and fourteenth centuries the European economy expanded and trade developed impressively. At first this expansion was contained within the limits of the feudal manor and the urban guild system, but in the fourteenth century tensions arose which caused the system to fissure and collapse. You can trace this change at the local level in Foxton and you can follow it on a national scale during the great peasant and artisan revolt of 1381.

Week VII

    Oct. 15 Pre-Columbian Caribbean and Meso-America (Professor Samuel Baily)

    Oct. 18 Pre-Columbian North America (Professor Calvin Martin)

    Readings: Wolf, Europe and the People Without History, 58-72

The Pre-Columbian Americas are often portrayed as a static world waiting to be "discovered." Nothing could be further from the truth, for there existed a variety of extremely dynamic civilizations, many of which were at least as sophisticated politically, economically, and culturally as the Euroean and West African civilizations. You will want to think about both their strengths and their potential weaknesses. What made American societies vulnerable to conquest in the 16th century? Consider the biological as well as the political and economic aspects of the question.

PART III   WORLDS IN COLLISION, 1500-1800

Week VIII European Expansion

    Oct. 22 Internal Causes

    Oct. 25 External Consequences

    Readings: Konig, Columbus: His Enterprise (entire)
                Wolf, Europe and the People Without History, 101-41
                Knight, The Caribbean, skim 23-49

The fourteenth and fifteenth centuries marked the beginning of the transition from feudalism to commercial capitalism in Western Europe. This constituted an internal crisis that was to have profound effects on both Europe itself and the rest of the Atlantic world. By focusing on Columbus the man rather than the legend, Konig shows how European expansion was the product of the breakup of the medieval world and the unleashing an unprecedented drive for profit and power exemplified by Columbus himself.

Week IX The Rise of the Atlantic System

    Oct. 29 Organization of the African Slave Trade
             SECOND PAPER DUE TODAY

    Nov. 1 Plantation Economies

Readings: Wolf, *Europe and the People Without History*, 149-57, 195-225
Tarikh, "Diaspora," 1-19 (compare with Wolf)
Knight, *The Caribbean*, 50-66, 81-120 (skim 67-81)

West Africa became the main supplies of slave labor for the American plantations. (Ask yourself what demographic, economic, and other factors explain why this happened.) African traders and political leaders successfully adapted to European commercial capitalism, and often gained from the contact, but overall the slave trade proved to be extremely harmful to Africa. The economy and society of the Caribbean were shaped by the plantation as a "total" institution which combined noncapitalist forms of labor with commercial dependency on the Atlantic capitalist system. European racism developed in the context of the slave trade and imperialism.

Week X Development of the Atlantic Societies in the 17th and 18th Centuries

Nov. 5 Europe and North America

Nov. 8 Afro-American Society and Culture

Readings: Hill, **From Reformation to Industrial Revolution**

Tarikh, "Diaspora," 41-46, 79-91, 56-68

In the course of the seventeenth and eighteenth centuries, the Atlantic world diversified. A division of labor, resources, and power developed that altered the previous relations between Europe, West Africa, and the Americas. Depending on their place in the Atlantic system, these regions evolved differently. And within each region economic and social structures reinforced inequalities of class, race, and gender that were to have fateful consequences for future development. While the Europeans dominated the plantation society, there nevertheless emerged a distinctive Afro-American culture, capable of resisting the most severe forms of oppression.

PART IV   REVOLUTION AND THE NEW IMPERIALISM, 1800-1945

Week XI The First Era of World Revolution

Nov. 12 The Industrial and Political Revolutions in Europe and North America
THIRD PAPER DUE TODAY

Nov. 15 Change in the Caribbean and West Africa

Readings: Wolf, **Europe and the People Without History**, 267-95
McKendrick, "The Making of the Wedgwood Factory"
Knight, *The Caribbean*, 131-39, 146-158
Tarikh, "Diaspora," 46-55, 92-116

510:114 -- page 7

The industrial revolution that began in Britain in the late eighteenth century was to transform not only Europe but the entire world. The effects of the political revolutions which were its accompaniment were no less profound. The old mercantile system was destroyed and replaced by a system of "free trade" dominated by Europeans; the slave trade was abolished; and a wave of rebellion swept the Atlantic world. We will be exploring the links between the industrial and political upheavals, and asking why the dual revolutions that occurred in Europe and North America did not take place in the same form in the Caribbean and West Africa.

Week XII   The Origins of Modern Imperialism

    Nov. 19   African Responses to European Imperialism
                DRAFT OF FINAL PAPER (LEVEL III STUDENTS) DUE TODAY

    Nov. 22   Thanksgiving

    Readings: Wolf, Europe and the People Without History, 296-313,
                313-18, 323-25, 330-43
                Knight, The Caribbean, 139-45, 167-77
                Webster and Boahen, West Africa Since 1800, 172-86,
                223-33

By the later 19th century the Atlantic system had entered a new phase. European domination through "free trade" was replaced by a New Imperialism of direct territorial acquisition. We will be exploring the reasons why this shift occurred. Some writers explain it in terms of the nature of industrial capitalism, while others stress either the new technologies or the ambitions of the modern nation state. We will also be looking at the African response to the New Imperialism, the ways its leaders both resisted and accomodated.

PART V   THE RISE OF THE CONTEMPORARY WORLD, 1945-PRESENT

Week XIII   The Second Era of World Revolution

    Nov. 26   The Eclipse of Europe and the Rise of the United States
                and the Soviet Union

    Nov. 29   Nationalism and Pan-Africanism

    Readings: Barraclough, An Introduction to Contemporary History,
                88-118
                Ajala, "The Rising Tide of Pan-Africanism," 35-45

                Denzer, "Constance A. Cummings-John of Sierra Leone,"
                20-32
                Webster and Boahen, West Africa Since 1800, 274-83, 313-25

                Tarikh, "Diaspora," 69-77

The twentieth century has seen remarkable shifts in the world
distribution of power and resources. While the basic pattern of
northern dominance remained intact, two world wars undermined the
dominance of Western Europe and opened the way for the rise of
two new powers, the United States and the Soviet Union. We will
see how the second great era of world revolution, beginning in
1917, destroyed the basis of the New Imperialism. Meanwhile, the
international economy facilitated huge transfers of crops,
products, and human labor during the course of the present
century. In response to European racism and economic/political
domination, African and Caribbean intellectuals and activists
developed the Pan-African and national movements. Most of the
former colonial world gained political independence through
bourgeois-led nationalist movements.

Week XIV   Contemporary Colonialism, Neocolonialism, and Socialist
           Revolution

Dec. 3   Southern Africa

Dec. 6   Revolution in Cuba and Elsewhere
           FINAL PAPER (LEVEL III STUDENTS) DUE TODAY

Readings: Wolf, Europe and the People Without History, 346-68, 379-83
           Bernstein, For Their Triumphs and For Their Tears,
           40-55
           Knight, The Caribbean, 177-212
           Rosberg and Callaghy, Socialism in Sub-Saharan Africa,
           122-29

In "settler" territories, the racial and economic situation meant
that Africans could not achieve independence through bourgeois
nationalist movements, but rather through revolution. We will
examine the reasons for this and also how intransigent whites in
South Africa have blocked democracy. We will also examine why
revolutions have taken place in many former plantation societies
and why the United States has taken a counter-revolutionary role.

Dec. 11 Overview of Main Themes; Discussion of Exam Question

PRINCETON UNIVERSITY
Department of History

History 402: Comparative Modernization

Professor C. E. Black

Spring Term 1982

We will be using the following books, which are on Closed Reserve (three copies each), and are also available at the University Store:

Dynamics of Modernization, Black (HM101.B5) Paperback.
Comparative Modernization, ed. Black (HN13.C64).
Political Development and Social Change, 2nd ed., Finkle and Gable
 (7543.349.1971) Paperback.
Modernization of Japan and Russia, Black and others (DS821.M3695).
Modernization of China, ed. by Gilbert Rozman.

The articles with one asterisk are also on Closed Reserve (five copies each); those with two asterisks will be distributed in class.

Feb. 2: Tuesday - Organization meeting, 230 Dickinson, 7:30 p.m.

Week of:

Feb. 8: Overview

    Dynamics of Modernization, 1-128.
    Comparative Modernization:
        "Introduction," 1-12.
        O'Connell, "The Concept of modernization," 13-24.
    *Avineri, "Marx and modernization."
    *Social Change (Marx, Weber, and Toennies), 30-62.

Feb. 15: Preconditions

    Comparative Modernization:
        Strayer, "The historical experience of nation-building in Europe," 109-115.
        Eisenstadt, "The influence of colonies and traditional political systems on the development of post-traditional social and political orders," 131-145.
    Political Development and Social Change:
        Sjoberg, "Folk and 'feudal' societies," 6-14.
        Gusfield, "Tradition and modernity: Misplaced polarities in the study of social change," 15-26.
        Smelser, "Mechanics of change and adjustments to change," 27-42.

Feb. 22: Preconditions

  Modernization of Japan and Russia, 1-123.
  Comparative Modernization:
      Biggerstaff, "Modernization - and early modern China,"
  *Modernization of China, "Eighteenth and Nineteenth Centuries," 203-216.

March 2: Transformation: Intellectual

  *Cooper, "Source and limits of human intellect," Daedalus, CIX (Spring 1980), 1-17.
  *Lewis, "Knowledge," Theory of Economic Growth, 164-200.
  *Bell, "The measurement of knowledge and technology," Indicators of Social Change, 145-246.

March 8: Transformation: Political

  *Almond and Coleman, "A Functional Approach to Comparative Politics," 3-64.
  Comparative Modernization: "Societal transformation," 161-164.
      Brown, "The French experience with modernization," 165-185.
  Modernization of Japan and Russia, 142-160.
  Political Development and Social Change:
      Olson, "Rapid growth as a destabilizing force," 557-568.
      Feierabend, "Social change and political violence," 569-604.

(Spring Recess, March 12-21)

March 22: Transformation: Economic

  Modernization of Japan and Russia, 161-197.
  Comparative Modernization:
      Kuznets, "Modern economic growth: findings and reflections," 186-200.
  Political Development and Social Change:
      Hagen, "How economic growth begins," 73-83.
      McClelland, "The achievement motive in economic growth," 83-100.
      Rostow, "The take-off into sustained growth," 141-161.
      Spengler, "Economic development: Political preconditions and political consequences," 161-176.

March 29: Transformation: Social and Individual

  Modernization of Japan and Russia, 198-243.
  Comparative Modernization:
      Jansen and Stone, "Education and modernization in Japan and England," 214-237.
      Inkeles, "A model of the modern man," 320-348.
      Coale, "The history of the human population," 201-213.

Political Development and Social Change:
Kilson, "The masses, the elite, and post-colonial politics in Africa," 379-383.
Deutsch, "Social mobilization and political participation," 384-405.

April 5: Advanced Modernization

*"China's Modernization in Historical Perspective," 482-516.
*Bell, The Coming of Post-Industrial Society, 3-45.
**Black, "Advanced modernization: Characteristics and problems,"
Comparative Modernization:
Heidenheimer, "The politics of public education, health and welfare in the USA and Western Europe," 278-304.
Blake, "The changing status of women in developed countries," 305-319

April 12: Advanced Modernization

Modernization of Japan and Russia, 246-354.
*Inkeles, "The emerging social structure of the world."
*Cooper, "The scientific and technological revolution in Soviet theory."

April 19: International Integration

Comparative Modernization:
Weinberg, "The problem of convergence of industrial societies," 353-36
Rosecrance and Stein, "Interdependence: Myth or reality?" 368-391.
Skolnikoff, "The international functional implications of future technology," 393-409.
Keohane and Nye, "Transgovernmental relations and international organizations," 410-431.
*Lasswell, "Future systems of identity in the world community."
*McNemar, "The future role of international institutions."

April 26: Critique

Comparative Modernization:
Tipps, "Modernization theory and the comparative study of societies,"
Desai, "Need for revaluation of the concept."
*Wallerstein, "The rise and future demise of the world capitalist system."
*Wallerstein, "Modernization: Requiescat in pace."

May 17: Term Papers Due

History 181 COMPARATIVE STUDIES IN HISTORICAL CULTURES II Winter 1983
John Broomfield, University of Michigan
"PROGRESS OR DECAY? CONFLICTING IDEAS ON THE DEVELOPMENT OF THE MODERN WORLD"

This course differs from the usual introductory course in two important ways. First, it stresses the value of comparison in understanding civilizations and cultures, including our own civilization. Unlike traditional American, Western or Asian civilization courses, it will not limit itself to a single historical culture but will try to draw on the experience of many cultures, classical and modern, Western and non-Western. Secondly, the course will be problem oriented, not survey oriented. It will not follow the "one damned thing after another" approach, by attempting to summarize the entire history of any of the cultures studied. Rather, it will emphasize the relevance of history as a tool for social analysis by examining the cross-cultural ramifications of major human problems.

The focus will be the question: "Progress or Decay? Conflicting Ideas on the Development of the Modern World." At the outset there will be consideration of the widespread belief in Western Civilization throughout the past 300 years that humans have progressed. Specific topics will then be chosen for more careful scrutiny. As each is examined it will be shown that there have been (and remain) schools of thought in the West that have denied that humans have progressed in such areas of activity. Similarly it will be shown that when there has been an intrusion into non-Western cultures, the fundamental differences of perception have resulted in even more radical disagreements.

The course will explore the nature of "history" itself, and its fundamental importance to Western Civilization. Students will be asked to consider some novel propositions: that there is not one history, but many histories; that a history is the perception in the present of the past; that in the study of history, uncontested fact is of relatively little significance compared with conflicting interpretations and varying perceptions of the past. History is a great debate. Students in this course will be asked to think for themselves. They will be offered challenging interpretations of the past and the present, and they will be invited to return the challenge to the instructors, and the books and articles they are asked to read.

"I do not think it matters much to the fortunes of man what abstract notions one may entertain concerning nature and the principles of things.... For my part I do not trouble myself with such speculative and unprofitable matters. My purpose, on the contrary, is to try whether I cannot in very fact lay more firmly the foundations, and extend more widely the limits, of the power and greatness of man."
  --Francis Bacon (1561-1626)

"It's sometimes argued that there's no real progress; that a civilization that kills multitudes in mass warfare, that pollutes the land and oceans with ever larger quantities of debris, that destroys the dignity of individuals by subjecting them to a forced mechanized existence can hardly be called an advance over the simpler hunting and gathering and agricultural existence of prehistoric times. But this argument, though romantically appealing, doesn't hold up. The primitive tribes permitted far less individual freedom than does modern society. Ancient wars were committed with far less moral justification than modern ones. A technology that produces debris can find, and is finding, ways of disposing of it without ecological upset. And the school-book pictures of primitive man sometimes omit some of the detractions of his primitive life--the pain, the disease, famine, the hard labor needed just to stay alive. From the agony of bare existence to modern life can be soberly described only as upward progress, and the sole agent for this progress is quite clearly reason itself."
  --Robert M. Pirsig: Zen and the Art of Motorcycle Maintenance (1974)

"The process of change in the modern era is of the same order of magnitude as that from prehuman to human life and from primitive to civilized societies; it is the most dynamic of the great revolutionary transformations in the conduct of human affairs. What is distinctive about the modern era is the phenomenal growth of knowledge since the scientific revolution and the unprecedented effort at adaptation to this knowledge that has come to be demanded of the whole of mankind."
  --C. E. Black: The Dynamics of Modernization (1966)

"Contemporary Western man in the overwhelming majority considers himself fundamentally different and distinct from the living world that gives him both substance and sustenance. This imagined separation between man and "nature' has provided the conceptual framework for a further doctrine, that of absolute human power and authority over the nonhuman. These ludicrous but terrifying notions have become solidified in our collective thought in a ridiculously brief period of human and Earth history.
  --John A. Livingston: One Cosmic Instant: Man's Fleeting Supremacy (1973)

Western civilization is dangerous "because in the interest of this growth it does not hesitate to destroy any other form of humanity whose difference from us consists in having discovered not merely other codes of existence but ways of achieving an end that still eludes us: the mastery by society of society's mastery over nature."
  --Marshall Sahlins: Culture and Practical Reason (1976)

"The reasonable man adapts himself to the world: the unreasonable one persists in trying to adapt the world to himself. Therefore all progress depends on the unreasonable man."
  --George Bernard Shaw: Man and Superman

History 181, Winter 1983	Page 3

TOPICS AND READINGS

*SELECTIONS AVAILABLE IN COURSE PACK (Albert's Copying, 535 E. Liberty Street)
+AVAILABLE IN BOOKSTORES FOR PURCHASE

1. THE IDEA OF PROGRESS

Carl Becker: "Progress," Encyclopedia of the Social Sciences, 1937 edition
+Herbert Butterfield: The Origins of Modern Science, 1300-1800 (Free Press paperback)
Larry Laudan: Progress and Its Problems: Towards a Theory of Scientific Growth (California paperback)
William Leiss: The Domination of Nature (Beacon paperback)
*John A. Livingston: One Cosmic Instant: Man's Fleeting Supremacy (Delta paperback)
*John T. Marcus: "Time and the Sense of History: West and East," Comparative Studies in Society and History, vol. III, no. 2, January 1961, pp. 123-139
*Sidney Pollard: The Idea of Progress: History and Society

2. SCIENCE

*Kenneth E. Boulding: "Science: Our Common Heritage," Science, vol. 207, no. 4433, February 22, 1980, pp. 831-836
+Herbert Butterfield: The Origins of Modern Science, 1300-1800 (Free Press paperback)
+Fritjof Capra: The Turning Point: Science, Society, and the Rising Culture (Simon & Schuster)
*Clifford Geertz: The Interpretation of Cultures (Basic Books paperback)
Sally Gregory Kohlstedt: "In From the Periphery: American Women in Science, 1830-1880," Signs, vol. 4, no. 1, Autumn 1978, pp. 81-96
+Thomas S. Kuhn: The Structure of Scientific Revolutions (Chicago paperback)
*Sara Ruddick & Pamela Daniels, eds.: Working It Out: 23 Women Writers, Artists, Scientists and Scholars Talk About Their Lives and Work (Pantheon paperback)
*James P. Spradley & David W. McCurdy, eds.: Conformity and Conflict: Readings in Cultural Anthropology
*Benjamin Lee Whorf: Language, Thought and Reality: Selected Writings (M.I.T. paperback)

3. MEDICINE

Vern L. Bullough & Bonnie Bullough: The Care of the Sick: The Emergence of Modern Nursing (Prodist paperback)
+Herbert Butterfield: The Origins of Modern Science, 1300-1800 (Free Press paperback)
+Fritjof Capra: The Turning Point: Science, Society, and the Rising Culture (Simon & Schuster)
Ralph C. Croizier: Traditional Medicine in Modern China
*Rene Dubos: Man Adapting (Yale paperback)
*John Ehrenreich, ed.: The Cultural Crisis of Modern Medicine
*Maureen A. Flannery: "Simple Living and Hard Choices," Hastings Center Report, vol. 12, no. 4, August 1982, pp. 9-12
Sally Guttmacher: "Whole in Body, Mind, and Spirit: Holistic Health and the Limits of Medicine," Hastings Center Report, vol. 9, no. 2, April 1979, pp. 15-21

+Ross Hume Hall: Food For Nought: The Decline in Nutrition (Harper paperback)
+Joshua S. Horn: Away With All Pests: An English Surgeon in People's China (Monthly Review paperback)
+Ivan Illich: Medical Nemesis: The Expropriation of Health (Bantam paperback)
+Michael Kidron & Ronald Segal: The State of the World Atlas (Simon & Schuster paperback)
Charles Leslie, ed.: Asian Medical Systems: A Comparative Study (California paperback)
Thomas McKeown: The Role of Medicine: Dream, Mirage, or Nemesis?
*Vincente Navarro: Medicine Under Capitalism (Prodist paperback)
*James P. Spradley & David W. McCurdy, eds.: Conformity and Conflict: Readings in Cultural Anthropology
Virgil J. Vogel: American Indian Medicine

4. FOOD

Richard J. Barnet: The Lean Years: Politics in an Age of Scarcity
Lester R. Brown: By Bread Alone (Praeger paperback)
+Fritjof Capra: The Turning Point: Science, Society, and the Rising Culture (Simon & Schuster)
Erik P. Eckholm: Losing Ground: Environmental Stress and World Food Prospects
*Wade Greene: "Triage: Who Shall Be Fed? Who Shall Starve?," New York Times Magazine, January 5, 1975, pp. 9-11, 44-45, & 51
+Ross Hume Hall: Food For Nought: The Decline in Nutrition (Harper paperback)
*Marvin Harris: Cows, Pigs, Wars, and Witches (Vintage paperback)
Jim Hightower: Eat Your Heart Out: Food Profiteering in America (Random House paperback)
*E.L. Jones & S.J. Woolf, eds.: Agrarian Change and Economic Development: The Historical Problems
+Michael Kidron & Ronald Segal: The State of the World Atlas (Simon & Schuster paperback)
Frances Moore Lappe, Joseph Collins, & David Kinley: Aid As Obstacle: Twenty Questions About Our Foreign Aid and the Hungry (I.F.D.P. paperback)

5. POPULATION

*Richard J. Barnet: "No Room in the Lifeboats," New York Times Magazine, April 16, 1978, pp. 32-38
*Robin Clarke, ed.: Notes for the Future: An Alternative History of the Past Decade
*Wade Greene: "Triage: Who Shall Be Fed? Who Shall Starve?," New York Times Magazine, January 5, 1975, pp. 9-11, 44-45, & 51
+Michael Kidron & Ronald Segal: The State of the World Atlas (Simon & Schuster paperback)
*Mahmood Mamdani: The Myth of Population Control: Family, Caste and Class in an Indian Village
*Thomas McKeown: The Modern Rise of Population
+Louise A. Tilly & Joan W. Scott: Women, Work and Family (Holt, Rinehart & Winston paperback)
E.A. Wrigley: Population and History (World University Library paperback)

6. TECHNOLOGY

Richard J. Barnet: The Lean Years: Politics in an Age of Scarcity
John Broomfield: "High Technology: The Construction of Disaster," Alternative Futures, vol. 3, no. 2, Spring 1980, pp. 31-44
+Fritjof Capra: The Turning Point: Science, Society, and the Rising Culture (Simon & Schuster)
Robin Clarke, ed.: Notes for the Future: An Alternative History of the Past Decade
*Robin Clarke: "The Pressing Need for Alternative Technology," Impact of Science on Society, vol. 23, no. 4, 1973, pp. 257-271
+Ross Hume Hall: Food For Nought: The Decline in Nutrition (Harper paperback)
+Ivan Illich: Medical Nemesis: The Expropriation of Health (Bantam paperback)
*Hans Jonas: "Toward a Philosophy of Technology: Knowledge, Power, and the Biological Revolution," Hastings Center Report, vol. 9, no. 1, February 1979, pp. 34-43
+Michael Kidron & Ronald Segal: The State of the World Atlas (Simon & Schuster paperback)
*David S. Landes: The Unbound Prometheus: Technological Change and Industrial Development in Western Europe from 1750 to the Present
*Katherine Stone: "The Origin of Job Structures in the Steel Industry," Radical America, vol. 7, no. 6, November-December 1973, pp. 19-64
E.P. Thompson: "Time, Work-Discipline, and Industrial Capitalism," Past and Present, no. 38, December 1967, pp. 56-97
*Peter Harper: "In Search of Allies for the Soft Technologies," Impact of Science on Society, vol. 23, no. 4, 1973, pp. 287-305

History 181/ Winter 1983

READING ASSIGNMENTS

* Available in course pack

+ Available in bookstores for purchase

IT IS RECOMMENDED THAT THE ASSIGNMENTS BE READ IN THE ORDER LISTED.

FOR WEEK BEGINNING:

1. January 10
    *Pollard, pp. 9-30 and 185-205
    *Livingston, pp. 16-23 and 148-182
    *Marcus

2. January 17
    +Butterfield, Chap. V
    +Capra, Chaps. II and IV
    *Boulding
    +Kuhn, Chaps. II-IV

3. January 24
    +Kuhn, Chaps. V-IX, XI, and XIII

4. January 31
    *Evelyn Keller in Ruddick & Daniels, pp. 77-91
    *Naomi Weisstein in Ruddick & Daniels, pp. 241-250
    +Capra, Chap. III
    *Dorothy Lee in Spradley & McCurdy, pp. 81-95
    *Geertz
    *Whorf

5. February 7
    +Butterfield, Chap. III
    +Capra, Chap. V
    *Barbara Ehrenreich & Deidre English in Ehrenreich, pp. 123-143
    *Leonard Stein in Spradley & McCurdy, pp. 185-193

6. February 14
    +Illich, parts I & II
    *Navarro

7. February 28
    *Flannery
    +Horn, pp. 53-65, 70-80, and 129-146
    +Capra, Chap. X
    *Dubos
    +Kidron & Segal, maps 36, 45

8. March 7
    *Jones & Woolf
    +Hall, pp. 129-171
    +Capra, pp. 252-260
    *Harris
    +Kidron & Segal, maps 18, 21, 40, 44

9. March 14
    +Hall, pp. 83-128 and 7-52
    +Kidron & Segal, maps 53, 54

10. March 21   *McKeown: Population, pp. 1-6, 18-43, and 152-163
               +Tilly & Scott, pp. 24-30, 89-103, 167-175, 216-225

11. March 28   *Linda Gordon in Ehrenreich, pp. 144-184
               *Mamdani
               *Greene
               *Barnet: "No Room in the Lifeboats"
               +Kidron & Segal, maps 32, 38, 49, 52, 63

12. April 4   *Landes
               *Stone
               *Jonas
               +Kidron & Segal, maps 19, 20

13. April 11   +Capra, Chap. XII
               +Illich, Chap. VIII
               *Clarke: "The Pressing Need for Alternative Technology"
               *Harper

History 181/ Winter 1983

LECTURES

Week #			
	January	5	Course introduction
		7	Idea of progress
1		10	Linear & cyclical time
		12	Idea of progress: Bacon & Descartes
		14	Idea of progress: Bentham & Marx
2		17	Idea of progress: Darwin & Wollstonecraft
		19	Science: the clockwork universe
		21	Normal science & scientific revolutions
3		24	Science as a field of power
		26	Social construction of scientific facts
		28	Linear & non-linear perception
4		31	Quantum mechanics & the participatory universe
	February	2	In reserve
		4	Traditional history of modern medicine
5		7	Presuppositions of scientific medicine
		9	History of U.S. medical profession
		11	Medical nemesis
6		14	Movie: "Are You Doing This For Me Doctor, Or Am I Doing It For You?"
		16	Movie: "Daughters of Time"
		18	In reserve
7		28	Medicine as a field of power
	March	2	Holistic health care: China & India
		4	Movie: "Eduardo the Healer"
8		7	What is disease?
		9	Technology, Food, Population
		11	Modern agricultural revolutions
9		14	Modern agricultural revolutions
		16	The shrewd peasant
		18	Real food or "fun food"?
10		21	Population & resources
		23	Population & resources
		25	Tape: "Population Control: the new fascism" - Germaine Greer
11		28	Population planning: discussion
		30	Populations & fossil fuel depletion
	April	1	Good Friday: no lecture
12		4	Humans & their technologies
		6	Movie: "Energy & Morality"
		8	High technology: the construction of disaster
13		11	Progress or decay? EXTRA MOVIE (evening this week to
		13	Progress or decay? be arranged): "Life & Times of
		15	Progress or decay? Rosie the Riveter"
		18	In reserve

UNIVERSITY OF PENNSYLVANIA

Fall, 1982　　　　　　　　　　　　　　　　　　Michael Zuckerman
　　　　　　　　　　　HISTORY 700
September 8　　　　Tradition and Modernity
　　　　　　　　　　　　　　　　　　　　　　Introductory Seminar
Introduction　　　　　　　　　　　　　　　for Graduate Students in History

September 15

　　Ruth Benedict, "Continuities and Discontinuities in Cultural
　　　　Conditioning," Psychiatry 1 (1938), 161-7
　　Pierre Bourdieu, "The Attitude of the Algerian Peasant toward
　　　　Time," in J. A. Pitt-Rivers, ed., Mediterranean Countrymen,
　　　　pp. 55-72
　　George Foster, "Peasant Society and the Image of Limited Good,"
　　　　American Anthropologist 67 (1965), 293-315
　　Clifford Geertz, "Person, Time, and Conduct in Bali," in The
　　　　Interpretation of Cultures, pp. 360-411
　　Clifford Geertz, "Deep Play: Notes on the Balinese Cockfight,"
　　　　in The Interpretation of Cultures, pp. 412-53
　　A. Irving Hallowell, "Ojibwa Ontology, Behavior, and World-View,"
　　　　in Stanley Diamond, ed., Primitive Views of the World, pp.
　　　　49-82
　　June Nash, "The Logic of Behavior: Curing in a Maya Indian Town,"
　　　　Human Organization 26 (1967), 132-9
　　Robert Redfield, "The Social Organization of Tradition," in
　　　　Peasant Society and Culture, pp. 40-59
　　Victor Turner, "A Ndembu Doctor in Practice," in The Forest of
　　　　Symbols, pp. 359-93
　　Eric Wolf, "Closed Corporate Peasant Communities in MesoAmerica
　　　　and Central Java," Southwestern Journal of Anthropology 13
　　　　(1957), 1-18

September 22
　　Talcott Parsons, et al., eds., Theories of Society, pp. 191-201
　　　　(Tonnies), pp. 208-13 and 436-43 (Durkheim), pp. 315-8 (Cooley),
　　　　and pp. 331-47 (Schmalenbach)
　　Robert Merton, "Patterns of Influence: Local and Cosmopolitan
　　　　Influentials," in Social Theory and Social Structure
　　C. E. Black, The Dynamics of Modernization, pp. 1-34
　　Samuel Huntington, "The Change to Change: Modernization, Develop-
　　　　ment, and Politics," Comparative Politics 3 (1971), 283-98
　　W. W. Rostow, The Stages of Economic Growth, pp. 1-35

September 29

　　Emmanuel LeRoy Ladurie, Montaillou
　　Emmanuel LeRoy Ladurie, "Motionless History," Social Science
　　　　History 1 (1977), 115-36

October 6

　　Fernand Braudel, The Mediterranean and the Mediterranean World
　　　　in the Age of Philip II, pp. 13-102, 138-67, 231-67, 276-95,
　　　　312-461, 657-756, 892-903, 1238-44

October 13
> Max Weber, *The Protestant Ethic and the Spirit of Capitalism*
> Keith Thomas, *Religion and the Decline of Magic*, ch. 1, 21, 22

October 20
> E. P. Thompson, "Time, Work-Discipline, and Industrial Capitalism," *Past and Present* 38 (1967), 56-97
> E. P. Thompson, "The Moral Economy of the English Crowd in the Eighteenth Century," *Past and Present* 50 (1971), 76-136
> Edmund Morgan, "The Labor Problem at Jamestown, 1607-1618," *American Historical Review* 76 (1971), 596-611
> Herbert Gutman, "Work, Culture, and Society in Industrializing America," *American Historical Review* 78 (1973), 531-88
> Christopher Hill, *The World Turned Upside Down*, ch. 1-2, 16-18
> Marcus Rediker, "'Under the Banner of King Death': The Social World of Anglo-American Pirates, 1716-1726," *William and Mary Quarterly* 38 (1981), 203-27

October 27
> Philippe Aries, *Centuries of Childhood*

November 3
> David Landes, *The Unbound Prometheus*, pp. 1-358

November 10
> Karl Marx, "Preface" to *The Critique of Political Economy*
> Karl Marx, *Pre-Capitalist Economic Formations*
> Karl Marx, *Manifesto of the Communist Party*
> Karl Marx, *The Eighteenth Brumaire of Louis Bonaparte*
> Karl Marx, "The British Rule in India" (on reserve)
> Andre Gunder Frank, *Latin America: Underdevelopment or Revolution?*, ch. 1

November 17
> Reinhard Bendix, "Tradition and Modernity Reconsidered," *Comparative Studies in Society and History* 9 (1967), 292-346
> Daniel Calhoun, "Participation versus Coping" (on reserve)
> Raymond Grew, "Modernization and its Discontents," *American Behavioral Scientist* 12 (1977), 289-312
> Alan Macfarlane, *The Origins of English Individualism*
> Lloyd and Susanne Rudolph, *The Modernity of Tradition*, pp. 3-14
> Dean Tipps, "Modernization Theory and the Comparative Study of Societies: A Critical Perspective," *Comparative Studies in Society and History* 15 (1973)
> E. A. Wrigley, "The Process of Modernization and the Industrial Revolution in England," *Journal of Interdisciplinary History* 3 (1972), 225-59
> Michael Zuckerman, "Dreams that Men Dare to Dream: The Role of Ideas in Western Modernization," *Social Science History* 2 (1978), 332-45

December 1
- David McClelland, *The Achieving Society*, ch. 1-4, 10
- Alex Inkeles and David Smith, *Becoming Modern*, ch. 1-3, 6-8, 9-12, 18-21
- Stanley Bailis, "Individuals Coping: Modernization and Habitual Change," in Harold Sharlin, ed., *The Freedoms of Enterprise* (forthcoming) (on reserve)

December 8
- Frederick Jackson Turner, "The Significance of the Frontier in American History," in *The Frontier in American History*
- Louis Hartz, *The Founding of New Societies*, ch. 1
- Bernard Bailyn, *Education in the Forming of American Society*, pp. 3-49
- James Henretta, *The Evolution of American Society, 1700-1815*
- James Henretta, "Families and Farms: Mentalite in Pre-Industrial America," *William and Mary Quarterly* 35 (1978), 3-32
- Michael Zuckerman, "The Fabrication of Identity in Early America," *William and Mary Quarterly* 34 (1977), 183-214

Harold Garrett-Goodyear
Mount Holyoke College

Women's Studies 102 (History 114/Anthro 102)
Spring Semester, 1982-83

Women, Spirituality and Power:
Cross-Cultural Comparisons

How are the changing and varied experiences of women related to notions of the sacred? How are the very distinctions between "women" and "men" affected by such notions? In what ways is spirituality a source of power for women, or a limit to their power? Can we develop a vocabulary for understanding women's experience in worlds which know no distinction between sacred and profane? Case studies from several cultures, and from several periods, will be used to address these questions. The critical and self-reflective use of analytical and interpretative approaches of anthropology and History will be central to this inquiry into the rleationships between women's experiences and the boundaries between sacred and profane in various cultures.

Joan Cocks, Politics (603 Library,x2334: Thurs, 3-5)
Anne Edmonds, Librarian
Harold Garrett-Goodyear,History (205 Lib,x2377: Thurs,1:30-3:30)
Eugenia Herbert,History (616 Lib, x2094: Mon & Wed, 4-6)
Andrew Lass, Anthropology/Sociology (204 Merrill,Mon & Wed, 1-3)

Books recommended for purchase are available from the College Bookstore. In each unit of the syllabus, some, perhaps most, reading assignments will be found in packets of multilithed materials, also available for puchase from the bookstore. One copy of each packet will also be found on Library Reserve.

Classes will ordinarily meet Tuesday and Thursday mornings from 10:00 a.m. until 12:15, in Skinner 214. In addition, hour sections will meet Tuesday afternoons at 2:00 and 3:00 in Library 203 and Thursday afternoons, also at 2:00 and 3:00, in places to be announced. During the first week, you will choose one section to which you will belong for the remainder of the semester.

Each section will divide itself further into four cells, of 2 or 3 students apiece, for collective projects important to class meetings and section discussions. Such projects will include finding and supplying your colleagues with background information on people, events, or issues, and also framing questions or theses for analysis and debate in sections.

Schedule of Classes and Assignments:

Feb. 1. An Introduction to people, sources, and approaches.

Feb. 3. An Introduction to topics, issues, and the course format.

Garrett-Goodyear

I. Christianity and Women in Late Medieval Europe

In late medieval Europe, Christianity offered both men and women a source of meaning and purpose to their lives; indeed, it was perhaps the principal source of meaning. But Christian women did not find the same meaning and purpose in the worship of the Christian God that men found there, and their experiences as Christains were by means identical to those of Christian men. By examining the teachings and institutions of the Christian Church in the 14th and 15th centuries, we shall try to understand ways in which women were offered different choices and subjected to different restraints than those offered, or imposed upon, men; and by examining evidence from or about several women prominent in the history of late medieval Christianity, we shall try to understand te distinctive features of women's experiences within the observance of Christianity and discover the distinctive contributions that women made to the shaping of Christian faith and practice. On the one hand, we shall be looking at the ways in which Christianity, as a central, even dominant institution and ideology within medieval society, assigned different roles and possibilities for women as opposed to men; on the other hand, we shll attempt to discover how differences between men and women in medieval society shaped Christianity, and the way in which Christianity interpreted for human beings the meaning of their lives.

(Please note that Library Reserve holds not only one copy of the two books recommended for purchase and one copy of the packet of multilithed materials for this unit, but also, for many of the selections assigned below, a copy of the full work from which passages were taken. Should you wish to read further in any of the works mentioned below, you may find it or related works on Reserve. Remember, however, that these works are only a fraction of those to be found in our library and other libraries in the Valley.

Feb. 8. Guest Lecture: Caroline Walker Bynum (History, University of Washington, and author of _Jesus as Mother_
"The Importance of Perspective: A Medievalist Looks at Gender and Religion"
New York Room, 10:00 a.m. Following her lecture on "Perspective", Prof. Bynum will give an informal introduction to Christianity and mysticism in the high and late middle ages for students and faculty in WS-102.

Reading: Julian of Norwich, _Revelations of Divine Love_
Richard Rolle, _The Fire of Love_
"From the _Sarum Missal_" and other readings from _Chaucer:Sources and Backgrounds_*

Prepare for February 10 a 2-3 page essay in which you analyse the language of a passage which you choose from Julian of Norwich's _Revelations_. Julian is not "typical," and we cannot generalize from her experience to that of all medieval mystics, nor can we generalize about all medieval women on the basis of her

meditations on a series of visions. If, however, we work with
care but imagination from her language, from the terms and images
that she used, to her (often unarticluated) convictions and
assumptions about reality, we can begin to understand the
distinctive features of her experience and the world of conduct
and consciousness in which such experience occurred. Your essay
should lay out for a reader at least one feature or aspect of
Julian's world that, once understood or grasped, would give us a
fuller understanding of what she said, how she said it, and why
she said it; but you should also rely on what she said, and how,
to support your point about Julian's world. (This is not, let us
emphasize, a research paper; use Julian herself to understand
Julian.)

Feb.10. Late Medieval Society and Women's Choices.

> Reading: David Herlihy,"The Natural History of Medieval
> III Women" and "Women in Medieval Society." *
> "Life of St. Umilta"*
> Selections from The Book of Margery Kempe*

During class on Feb. 10, Anne Edmonds will introduce us to
some of the strategies and tactics of research on women,
spirituality, and power, and give us some pointers on using the
Library to teach ourselves about medieval people -- or any other
people, for that matter. After her introduction, cell groups in
each section should divide up responsibility for finding and
sharing information on the individual mystics or other persons
whom we are reading, and for identifying good books or articles o;
people or issues pertinent to our present discussions. As soon as
possible, each section should have someone able to tell her
colleagues what scholars know or have surmised about the women and
men whose lives we are trying to understand.

Feb.15. Women's Responsibilities and Men's Dependence

> Reading: Selections from Letters of St.Catherine of Siena*
> Selections from The book of the Knight of La Tour Landry*
> Selections from The Paston Letters*
> R.H.Hilton, "Women in the Village"*

Feb.16.(Optional) Film: Robert Bresson,"The Trail of Jeanne d'Arc"
at 4:00 and 7:00 p.m., Library 210.

Feb.17. Warfare and Visions, Holiness and Witchcraft

> Reading: Joan of Arc by Herself and Her Witnesses*
> Christine de Pisan, "Ditie de Jehanne D'Arc"*
> "The Confession of Prous Boneta"*
> "The Inquisition of Toulouse"*
> "Trial of Giovanna Monduro of Salussola"*

Feb.22. The Meaning of Power

Garrett-Goodyear

Reading: Eleanor McLaughlin, "Women,Power and the Pursuit
of Holiness"*
Elizabeth Petroff,"Seven Stages to Power"*

Written Assignment: Relying on readings and classes to
date, write a short essay (max: 5 pages) in which you explain the
meaning of "power" for women in the late middle ages. You should
read McLaughlin and Petroff before writing this essay, but base
your own explanation on the sources that we have read and
discussed during the past three weeks.

****
II. Women, Spirituality and Power.
Spirituality and the Idea of Women's Culture:
Radical Feminism in the Contemporary Period

Our purpose in this section of the course is to explore the con-
nection between women, spirituality and power as they have taken
form within the feminist movement in the United States. We will
trace the path that has led some women beyond the boundaries of
traditional religions into women centered religious experience.
We will give special attention, however, to the current prominence
of spiritual motifs in the "secular" radical feminist movement. We
will then take a critical look at the notion of a separate women's
culture, the radical feminist celebration of organic nature, and
the feminist attempt to fuse spirituality and sensuousness.Finally
we will compare the concerns of a spiritual feminism with those of
its more single-mindedly political counterparts and predecessors,
and with other forms of critical attack on science, technology and
militarism in advanced industrial society.

Schedule of Readings and Lectures

Feb.24. "The Radical Feminist Critique of Patriarchy and the
Route out of Traditional Religion": Mary Daly, Beyond God
The Father

Mar. 1. "The Radical Feminist Critique Continued": Naomi
Goldenberg, Changing of the Gods

Mar.3. "Curious Comrades: Critical Social Theory, The New Age
Movement, and Cultural/Spiritual Feminism": Charlene
Spretnak, ed., The Politics of Women's Spirituality.
Spretnak, "Introduction";
Starhawk, "Witchcraft as Goddess Religion," p.49
Sojourner, "From the House of Yemanja...",p.57
Christ, "Why Women Need the Goddess," p. 71
Starrett,"The Metaphors of Power," p.187
Inglehart, "Expanding Personal Power...",p.294
Antonelli, "Feminist Spirituality...", p.399
Appendix, "Two Debates," p.530

Mar.8. "Spiritual Feminism Standing Alone": Susan Griffin,
Woman and Nature

Mar.10. "Antimonies, Unities and Contradictions": Carolyn Merchant
        The Death of Nature: Women, Ecology and the Scientific
        Revolution
Written Assignments:

III. Deconstructing Gender

   The degree to which sexual identity and genderization are
primarily cultural constructs rather than natural objects provides
the key problem around which this part of the course will be organized. What "male" and "female" means in different societies
requires that one first explore how a particular culture arti-
culates various domains of experience; the distinction between
culture and nature, the concept of the human body as well as the
related conceptualizations and expressions of morality and power,
sickness and ehalth, ghost and spirit, sacred and profane, all of
which exist in concrete, culturally specific ways.
   By looking at how some of the cultures of Papua New Guinea
construct their world through social and symbolic action, you will
be introduced to the basics of the anthropological analysis of
kinship, social and political organization, to some of the methods
involved in the cross-cultural understanding of symbolic systems,
and finally--and most importantly--to some of the controversies
that the anthropological enterprise leads to as we, in the process
of trying to understand others, confront ourselves (e.g. the
'straw men' of feminist anthropology).
   Lectures and discussion will incorporate the assigned reading
material (the READER containing all the articles will be available
at the college bookstore). There are also books of interest on
library reserve, including introductory textbooks to cultural
anthropology.

BOOKS ON LIBRARY RESERVE:

Foucault, M.: The History of Sexuality
Herdt, G. H.: Guardians of the Flutes
MacCormack & Strathern: Nature, Culture and Gender
Ortner & Whitehead: Sexual Meanings
Reiter, R. R.: Toward an Anthropology of Women
Rosaldo & Lamphere: Women, Culture & Society
Nanda: Cultural Anthropology; Introductory textbook

            Schedule of Classes and assignments:

Mar.15. Discussion.
            Reading: P.Webster,"Matriarchy: A Vision of Power"
         Lecture on Basic Concepts of Anthropology.

Mar.17. Continuation of Lecture on Basic Concepts: Anthropology
                  in the Highlands of Paua New Guinea.
         Discussion.

Reading: S. Ortner, "Is Female to Male as Nature is to Culture?"

Mar.29. Lecture: Self, Body and Society in Mt. Hagen.
Reading: Strathern, M.&A., "Popokl: The Question of Morality"; "The Female and Male Spirit Cults in Mount Hagen"; and " Sickness and Frustration in Two New Guinea Highland Societies."

Mar.31. Continuation of Lecture on Self, Body and Society.
Discussion.
Reading: M. Strathern, "No Nature, No Culture: The Hagen Case"
Assignment no. 1 due: An essay in which you apply Anthropological conceptualizations and approaches from readings and discussions of the past two weeks to any topic addressed earlier in this course. 3-5pp

Apr. 5. Discussion.
Reading: J.S. La Fontaine, "The Domestication of the Savage Male"; M. Strathern, "Culture in a Netbag: The Manufacture of a Subdiscipline in Anthropology"

April 7. Assignment no. 2 due: An essay in which you identify an issue, concept, argument, or theme in one of the articles read during this unit, and then use the library to find another article or further material relevant to that issue, etc. References in footnotes may be used to lead you to further material. With the additional material in hand, write a critical essay on the issue, etc. 5-7 pp.

****

IV. **Women, Spirituality and Power**
AFRICA AND AFRO-AMERICA

April 7. Introduction to women in African cultures.

Reading: Evans-Pritchard, "The Position of Women in Primitive Societies and in our own,"(1955)
Edwin Ardener, "Belief and the Problem of Women" (N.B., the Ardeners will speak at Mount Holyoke in early April, inshallah.)
The class on April 7 will include an introduction to research on Women in Africa by Anne Edmond. A Case Study: Women and Power among the Senufe. A model of equilibrium?

April 11 Monday   **Lecture**: Anita J. Glaze: "Women, Creativity
8.00 p.m . Gamble   and Power in Africa"

April 12   **Discussion with Anita Glaze**
Reading: Glaze, A. **Art and death in a Senufo Village** as much as you can but concentrate on Ch 2 and 3.

201

Glaze, A. "Women Power and Art in a Senufo Village," *African Arts.* VIII: 3 (Spring, 1975) on reserve

April 14 **Cults of Possession, Affliction and Healing in Africa.**
Readings: Iris, Berger, "Rebels or Status Seekers? Women as Spirit Mediums in East Africa
Martha, Binford, "Julia: An East African Diviner"
Anita, Spring, "Epidemology of Spirit possession among the Luvale of Zambia"
Susan, Middleton Keurn, "Convivial Sisterhood: Spirit Mediumship and Client-Core Networks among Black South African Women."

April 19 **Cults of Possession, Affliction and Healing in Afro-America.**
Guest Lecturer, Monica Gorden.
Readings: Leonard Barret, "Healing and Medicine in Jamaica," and "Witchcraft and Psychic Phenomena in Jamaica" (*From the Sun and Drum. African Roots in Jamaica*)
Monica, Schuler, "Central Africans in St. Thomas-in-the East" (from *Alas Alas Kongo.*)
Maureen Warner Lewis, "The Nkuyu: Spirit Messengers of the Kumina"
Yvonne Daniel, "The Potency of Dance: A Haitian Examination"
W.P. Bradford, "Puerto Rican Spiritism: Contrasts in the Sacred and the Profane"
Film: "To Serve the Gods"

April 21 **Change in African and Afro-American Religions**

Reading: John Q. Anderson," The New Orleans Voodoo Ritual Dance and its Twentieth-Century Survivals" (1960)
Molly Dougherty, "Southern Lay Midwives as Ritual Specialists" (1978)
Toni Cade Bambara, *The Salt Eaters* (excerpt)

Written Assignment: A 5-6 page paper on a specific cult or religious movement and the position of women in it.
Use bibliographies and refence librarians to find material.

V. Final Reflections and Generalizations

April 26 and 28. How are we to analyze and explain what appears to be the universal phenomenon of women's subordination to men? For most of this semester, our readings and discussions have emphasized those ways in which women have enjoyed access to power. But is Ortner perhaps correct, in thinking that it is necessary to account for universal occurrence of men's dominance of women?

As a starting point, we should identify the constraints under which women live in our own world; from there, we can turn to late medieval, AFrican, and Melpa people, to ask what patterns of dominance and subordination appear in the evidence and readings that we have examined earlier this semester.

May 3 and 5. We have been asking questions about women, power and spirituality -- but central to all of our discussions have been the distinctive experience and vision of women themselves. Why are we and others asking questions about women today, and why have people not asked such questions before?

Is it indeed appropriate to ask questions of this sort within the academy? What difference will it, or should it make to the academy, when we ask them. Finally, is there yet, or can there be, a feminist history? a feminist anthropology? (Marilyn STrathern's work may be usefully reconsidered at this point, along with Edwin Ardener's essay; so also might we look back at Caroline Bynum's lecture.)

University of Cincinnati
WOMEN IN ASIA: INDIA, CHINA, JAPAN   Autumn Quarter, 1984-85
Barbara N. Ramusack   History 15-075-531
Office Hours: MWF 11:00-11:50 a.m. and by appointment
Office: 353B McMicken. Office telephones: 475-6887 and 475-2144

Required texts: Cyril Birch (trans.), Stories from a Ming Collection.
                 Karen Brazell (trans.), Confessions of Lady Nijo
                 R. K. Narayan (trans.), The Ramayana
                 Jonathan D. Spence, The Death of Woman Wang.

*indicates that material is on reserve in the Central Library
#indicates that material will be distributed in class.

Sept. 19   Introduction. Studying Women in Cross-Cultural Perspective.

Sept. 21   WOMEN AS DAUGHTERS, WIVES AND MOTHERS - Social Roles and Legal Rights
            India: The Historical Context. Begin to read The Ramayana.

Sept. 24   India: Women as Wives - Marriage, Divorce, Widowhood
                The Ideal: Discussion of The Ramayana
                    Extracts from the Qur'an#
                    (Optional) Extracts from the Laws of Manu#
                Reality: David G. Mandelbaum, Society in India, I, chap. 5*.

Sept. 26   India: Women as Mothers

Sept. 28   China: The Historical Context.
            Begin to read The Death of Woman Wang.

Oct. 1   China: Women as Wives - Marriage, Divorce, Widowhood.
                The Ideal: Extracts from the Analects#
                    Pan Chao, "Lessons for Women," in Nancy Lee Swann*
                    Pan Chao, Foremost Woman Scholar of China, chap. 7
                Reality: Spence, The Death of Woman Wang.

Oct. 3   China: Women as Mothers

Oct. 5   Japan: The Historical Context
            Begin to read The Confessions of Lady Nijo.

Oct. 8   Japan: Women as Wives - Marriage, Divorce, Widowhood
                The Ideal: Kaibara Ekken, Onna Daigaku (The Women and Wisdom of Japan)*
                Reality: (Optional) Richard K. Beardsley, John W. Hall and Robert E. Ward,
                    Village Japan, chaps. 9 and 11.

Oct. 10   Japan: Women as Mothers

Oct. 12   Film: "Dadi's Family." Two to three page commentary on the film is due
                on October 17.

Oct. 15   WOMEN'S SEXUALITY: AS LOVERS AND AS COURTESANS
                India: Read from Van Buitenen, Tales of Ancient India, "The Tale of
                Two Bawds" and "The Red Lotus of Chastity." (Optional) "The Man Who
                Impersonated Vishnu."*

Oct. 17   China: Read from Birch, Stories from a Ming Collection, "The Pearl
                Sewn Shirt."

WOMEN IN ASIA
Fall 1984
page 2

Oct. 19 Japan: Discussion of Confessions of Lady Nijo, books 1-3.

Oct. 22 WOMEN IN POLITICS
         India. Review the Ramayana.

Oct. 24 China. (Optional) Priscilla Ching Chung, "Power and Prestige: Palace Women in the Northern Sung," in Guisso and Johannesson, eds., Women in China*; or skim her Palace Women in the Northern Sung.

Oct. 26 Japan. Review Confessions of Lady Nijo.

Oct. 29 WOMEN IN RELIGION: AS DIVINITIES AND AS DEVOTEES
         India: Heinrich R. Zimmer, Myths and Symbols in Indian Art and Civilization, chap. 5, "The Goddess."*

Oct. 31 Film: "Wedding of the Goddess," Two to three page commentary on film is due on November 5th.

Nov. 2   MID-QUARTER EXAMINATION. WILL COVER MATERIAL THROUGH "WOMEN IN POLITICS."

Nov. 5   China. Edward Schafer, The Divine Woman, chap. 1*. (Optional) Kathryn Tsai, "The Chinese Buddhist Monastic Order for Women: The First Two Centuries," in Guisso and Johannesson, eds., Women in China*.

Nov. 7   Japan. The Confessions of Lady Nijo, books 4 and 5.

Nov. 9   WOMEN IN LITERATURE: AS DOERS AND AS PORTRAYED
         India: Review the Ramayana. Poetry of Mirabai*. (Optional) Kalidasa, "Sakuntala and the Ring of Recollection," in Barbara Stoler Miller, ed., Theater of Memory*.

Nov. 12 VETERAN'S DAY. A HOLIDAY.

Nov. 14 China: Read from Stories from a Ming Collection, "The Lady Who Was a Beggar" and "The Fairy's Rescue." Adopt a poet who lived before 1800 from The Orchid Boat: Women Poets of China, translated and edited by Kenneth Rexroth and Ling Chung*.

Nov. 16 Japan: Review Confessions of Lady Nijo. Adopt a poet from the classic or Tokugawa periods in The Burning Heart: Women Poets of Japan, trans. and ed. by Kenneth Rexroth and Ikuko Atsumi*. (Optional) Murasaki Shikibu, Tale of Genji.

Nov. 19 WOMEN IN THE VISUAL ARTS
         India

Nov. 21 China and Japan

Nov. 23 THANKSGIVING HOLIDAY

Nov. 26 Individual Presentations.

WOMEN IN ASIA
Fall 1984
page 3

Nov. 28   Individual Presentations

Nov. 30   Review Session

This course will focus on the roles and activities of women in India, China and Japan prior to 1800. It will be a combination of lectures and discussions. The reading assignments are heaviest during the first four weeks of the course, and during the latter half of the course we will use the required texts as reference material and examine them from different perspectives. Class participation is encouraged and reading assignments should be done according to the schedule. There will be a mid-quarter and a final examination and the latter will be a take home examination. There will be an individual oral presentation of no more than fifteen minutes on a topic of the student's choice. Graduate students are expected to do the optional reading including one book in the Tale of Genji.

	Grade composition.	
	Class participation	10%
	Two papers on films, @5%	10%
	Mid-quarter examination	25%
	Individual presentation	15%
	Final Examination	40%
	TOTAL	100%

WOMEN IN PREMODERN ASIA: INDIA, CHINA AND JAPAN   1984-85
AN INTRODUCTORY BIBLIOGRAPHY - Barbara N. Ramusack

HISTORY TEXTS FOR GENERAL BACKGROUND
John K. Fairbank, Edwin O. Reischauer, and Albert M. Craig. EAST ASIA: TRADITION
    AND TRANSFORMATION
Stanley A. Wolpert. A NEW HISTORY OF INDIA
Romila Thapar. A HISTORY OF INDIA. Volume I.

BIBLIOGRAPHIES
Carol Sakala. WOMEN OF SOUTH ASIA: A GUIDE TO RESOURCES.

WOMEN AS DAUGHTERS, WIVES AND MOTHERS - Social Roles and Legal Rights
India
THE MAHABHARATA. Translated by J. A. B. Van Buitenen.
Doranne Jacobson and Susan S. Wadley. WOMEN IN INDIA: TWO PERSPECTIVES.
Shakambari Jayal. THE STATUS OF WOMEN IN THE EPICS.
Professor Indra. THE STATUS OF WOMEN IN ANCIENT INDIA.
THE LAWS OF MANU.
THE QUR'AN.

China
Albert O'Hara. THE POSITION OF WOMEN IN EARLY CHINA.
Nancy Lee Swann. PAN CHAO: FOREMOST WOMAN SCHOLAR OF CHINA.
Florence Ayscough. CHINESE WOMEN: YESTERDAY AND TODAY.
Jonathan D. Spence. THE DEATH OF WOMAN WANG.
Ann Waltner, "Widows and Remarriage in Ming and Ch'ing China," in Guisso and
    Johanesson, eds., WOMEN IN CHINA.

Japan
Kaibara Ekken, ONNA DAIGAKU (The Women and Wisdom of Japan).
William McCullough, "Heian Marriage Patterns," in HARVARD JOURNAL OF ASIATIC STUDIES,
    XXVII (1967), pp. 103-167.

WOMEN'S SEXUALITY: AS LOVERS AND AS COURTESANS
India
KAMASUTRA OF VATSYAYANA. Translated by Richard F. Burton.
TALES OF ANCIENT INDIA. Translated by J. A. B. Van Buitenen.
Mirza Ruswa. THE COURTESAN OF LUCKNOW.

China
Robert Van Gulick. SEXUAL LIFE IN ANCIENT CHINA.
Howard Levy. CHINESE FOOTBINDING: THE HISTORY OF A CURIOUS EROTIC CUSTOM.

Japan
Murasaki Shikuku. TALE OF GENJI. In either Waley or Seidensticker translation.
CONFESSIONS OF LADY NIJO. Translated by Karen Brazell.
[Also see section on "Women in Literature" below]

Women in premodern Asia Bibliography
page 2

WOMEN IN POLITICS
India
Rekha Misra. WOMEN IN MUGHAL INDIA: 1526-1748 A.D.

China
Richard Guisso. THE EMPRESS WU TSE-T'IAN.
C. P. Fitzgerald. EMPRESS WU.
Priscilla Ching Chung. PALACE WOMEN IN THE NORTHERN SUNG.

Japan
THE CONFESSIONS OF LADY NIJO. Translated by Karen Brazell.
Murasaki Shikuku. TALE OF GENJI.
Conrad D. Totman. POLITICS IN THE TOKUGAWA BAKUFU. Chapter V.

WOMEN IN RELIGION: AS DIVINITIES AND AS DEVOTEES
India
N. N. Bhattacharyya. INDIAN MOTHER GODDESS.
Thomas B. Coburn. DEVI MAHATMYA: THE CRYSTALLIZATION OF THE GODDESS TRADITION.
I. B. Horner. WOMEN UNDER PRIMITIVE BUDDHISM: LAYWOMEN AND ALMSWOMEN.
Gerald James Larson, Pratapaditya Pal, and Rebecca P. Gowen. IN HER IMAGE:
    THE GREAT GODDESS IN INDIAN ASIA AND THE MADONNA IN CHRISTIAN CULTURE.
Curt Maury. FOLK ORIGINS OF INDIAN ART.
James J. Preston (ed.). MOTHER WORSHIP: THEME AND VARIATIONS (BL325/.M6M67).

China
Diana Paul. WOMEN IN BUDDHISM.
Edward Schaefer. THE DIVINE WOMAN.
Kathryn Tsai. "The Chinese Buddhist Monastic Order for Women: The First Two
    Centuries," in WOMEN IN CHINA, edited by Guisso and Johanesson.

Japan

WOMEN IN LITERATURE
India
THE MAHABHARATA.
THE RAMAYANA.
Mira Bai. MIRABAI VERSIONS. Translated by Robert Bly.
Kalidasa. "Sakuntala and the Ring of Recollection," in THE THEATER OF MEMORY:
    THE PLAYS OF KALIDASA, edited by Barbara Stoler Miller.
Sudrasha. "Little Clay Cart," in TWO PLAYS OF ANCIENT INDIA. Translated by
    J. A. B. Van Buitenen.

China
STORIES FROM A MING COLLECTION. Translated by Cyril Birch.
THE ORCHID BOAT: WOMEN POETS OF CHINA. Translated and edited by Kenneth Rexroth
    and Ling Chung (PL2658/.E3R43/1972).
Wang Shih-chen. CHIN P'ING MEI (The Golden Lotus). Translated by Clement Egerton.
Hans H. Frankel. THE FLOWERING PLUM AND THE PALACE LADY. "Lonely Women," chap. 6.

Women in Premodern Asia Bibliography

WOMEN IN LITERATURE continued
Japan
Murasaki Shikubu. TALE OF GENJI. Translated by both Arthur Waley and Edward G. Seidensticker.
CONFESSIONS OF LADY NIJO. Translated by Karen Brazell.
Sei Shonagon. THE PILLOW BOOK OF SEI SHONAGON. Translated by Ivan Morris.
Kenreimon. THE POETIC MEMORIES OF LADY DAIBU. Translated by Phillip Tudor Harries.
Sugawara Taskasue no musume. AS I CROSSED A BRIDGE OF DREAMS: RECOLLECTIONS OF A WOMAN IN ELEVENTH-CENTURY JAPAN. Translated by Ivan Morris.
THE BURNING HEART: THE WOMEN POETS OF JAPAN. Translated and edited by Kenneth Rexroth and Ikuko Atsumi (PL782/.E3B84).
Ihara Saikaku. THE LIFE OF AN AMOROUS WOMAN AND OTHER STORIES. Translated and edited by Ivan Morris.

RUTGERS UNIVERSITY

510:366
The Emergence of the Third World

Spring 1984
Professor M. Adas
Jose Moya, T.A.

pbk = available in paperback in the bookstore
R = on Reserve

Jan. 23 Introduction to Most of the World.

I. <u>Poets, Prophets and Holymen: Third World Responses to European Global Dominance</u>

A. <u>China</u>

Jan. 25	The Crisis and Collapse of Chinese Civilization
Jan. 30	Confucian Catalepsy and the Taiping Rebellion
Feb. 1	"Liberal" Hopes and Marxist Solutions

Required: W. Franke, China: <u>A Century of Revolution,</u> chs. 1 & 2 (R)
L. Bianco, <u>Origins of the Chinese Revolution,</u> chs. (1-3) (pbk)

B. <u>India</u>

Feb. 6 The Road To Underdevelopment: Political Stability, Economic Dislocation, Population Explosion

Feb. 8 The Great "Mutiny" and the Hindu Renaissance
Required: W.N. Brown, <u>The United States and India, Pakistan, Bangladesh,</u> chs 1-3 (pbk-R)
T.R. Metcalf, <u>The Aftermath of Revolt, India,</u> 1857-1870 ch. 2 (R)

C. <u>The Islamic World</u>

Feb. 13 Western Penetration and the Crisis of Islam

Feb. 15 Religion and Islamic Revival - The Mahdi of the Sudan
Required: C. Brown, "The Sudanese Mahdiya," in R. Rothberg and A Mazrui, eds., <u>Protest and Power in Black Africa</u> (R)
M. Adas, <u>Prophets of Rebellion,</u> chs 4 & 6 (R)

D. <u>Africa</u>

Feb. 20 Edward Blyden and the Slow Disintegration of the Africans' World

Feb. 22 Up from Servitude and Humiliation: The Meaning and Impact of Negritude
Required: P. Bohanan & P. Curtin, <u>Africa and the Africans,</u> chs. 15, 18, 19, (R)

A. Irele, "Negritude and Black Cultural Nationalism,"
Journal of Modern African Studies (1965), pt. 1 and 2

II. NATIONALISM, COMMUNISM, REVOLUTION

A. Bourgeois Nationalism

Feb. 27 The Indian Prototype: From Debating Societies to Mahatma Gandhi
Required: W. Brown, The U.S. and India, etc., chs. 4-6

Feb. 29 The Rise and Role of Gandhi
Required: L. Fisher, Gandhi, entire (pbk)

Mar. 5 Egypt: From Arabi Pasha to Independence

Mar. 7 Nasser - Revolutionary Promise; Elite Retrenchment The Limits of Bourgeois Nationalism
Required: E. Wallerstein, The Road to Independence, chapters A-D

B. Violent Rebellion and Communal Struggle

Mar. 12 Imperalism, Settler Colonization & Resistance in Algeria

Mar. 14 Terrorism & Revolution: FILM "The Battle of Algiers"
Required: Eric Wolf, Peasant Wars of the Twentieth Century Chapter 5 (R)
Franz Fanon, A Dying Colonialism, chapter 3 (R)

SPRING BREAK

Mar. 26 Conflicting Nationalisms: The Roots of the Arab-Israeli Struggle.

Mar. 28 DEBATE: Solutions to the Palestinian "Problem"
Required: Fawaz Turki, The Disinherited, chs. 1, 4, 5 (R)
Articles by Syrkin, Stone & Gershman in Israel, the Arabs and the Middle East

C. Communist Nationalism

Apr. 4 China, the Basis of the Communist Mandate to Rule
Required: Bianco, Origins of the Chinese Revolution chapters 3-7

III. After Independence: The Struggle to Build Viable States and Societies in the Third World.

Apr. 9 The Crisis of Independence: Artificial States and Alien Elites

Apr. 11 Freedom without Revolution: Poverty, Overpopulation, Barriers to Change

	Required: Robert Heilbroner, *The Great Ascent*, ch 1-4 (pbk)
Apr. 16	The Failure of Charisma and Gradualism in the Third World Required: C. Achebe, *No Longer at Ease*, entire
Apr. 18	A Nation for the Few: Afrikaner Nationalism and the Rise of Apartheid in South Africa
Apr. 23	The Failure of Black Nationalism in South Africa: Causes and Consequences Required: B. Magubane, *The Political Economy of Race and Class in South Africa*, chapters 10 & 11 (R)
Apr. 25	The Rejection of Modernization: Khomeini and the Iranian "Revolution" Required: Theda Skocpol, "Rentier State and Shi'a Islam in the Iranian Revolution"
Apr. 30	Mao's Way in China: A Model for the Third World? The Gains and Costs of Revolution: Women and Intellectuals in Red China Required: M. Gasster, China's *Struggle to Modernize*, chapter 5 (R) Selections from Revolutionary Drama in China
May 2	Perilous Transition: The U.S. and the Future of the Third World Required: R. Heilbroner, chapters 5-8 (pbk)

Assignments: In addition to the required reading, there will be two take-home exam essays: one at mid-term, the other a final

All of the following books will be used: they are available in paperback at the university bookstore:

Louis Fisher, *Gandhi*
L. Bianco, *The Origins of the Chinese Revolution*.
R. Heilbroner, *The Great Ascent*
C. Achebe, *No Longer at Ease*

All other readings are on Reserve (R) at Alexander Library

University of Wisconsin at Green Bay

Social Change and Development 270 Professor Craig Lockard
Spring, 1984   MW, 2:30-3:55, SE 221

THE THIRD WORLD: DEVELOPMENT OR DESPAIR?

Food for Thought

"Almost five hundred years ago . . . two bold voyages from Iberia resulted in a chain of events that made the world one, but have not yet ceased to widen the disparities between different areal groupings of mankind. Two types of European dominance, two types of dependence, were initiated by these voyages . . . exploitative colonization and . . . the more enduring commercial dominance/dependence relationship . . . the whole contemporary world problem that we call variously that of 'underdevelopment,' 'modernization' or the 'economic development of the Third World' is concerned at base with a dominance/dependence relationship that is expressed in many ways" --Harold Brookfield

"The development of the industrialized countries continues to imply the stagnation -- now, even the regression -- of the nonindustrialized. The strong continue to feed upon the weak; and the weak continue to grow weaker. And it is to this, far more to anything else, that one must refer the troubles and upheavals -- even, here and there, the down-right banditries and piracies -- of the newly independent regimes. Not until this system and relationship begin to be radically changed will there be, or can there be, any resolution of a crisis which threatens now to become catastrophe" --Basil Davidson

"Here we stand/infants overblown,/posed between two civilizations,/finding the balance irksome,/itching for something to happen,/to tip us one way or the other,/groping in the dark for a helping hand/and finding none./I'm tired, O my God, but where can I go?" --Mabel Segun (Nigerian poet)

"They separate us/with passports visas frontiers all names for barriers/they rob us with their laws/sending bullets wrapped in dollars/forcing us to choose/and choose we must/there is no other way" --Usman Awang (Malaysian poet)

Introduction

This course is concerned with the past, present, and future of the societies of the "Third World" (Asia, Africa, Latin America); more specifically, it analyzes the state and process of what is often termed "underdevelopment": how did it develop? What does it entail? What strategies have been mounted to overcome it? "Underdevelopment" has political, economic, social, cultural, ecological, technological, and historical manifestations. Hence, any meaningful analysis of this condition must perforce take an interdisciplinary perspective; to separate, for example, an understanding of social or cultural realities from political and economic concerns - or the reverse - is misleading and even dangerous. The topic is also fraught with controversy, as any careful perusal of the course readings will confirm; men and women of goodwill can and will disagree on the causes and nature of underdevelopment in the Third World, and dispute even more vehemently about the solutions to difficult, complex problems. For American students in this course, whose previous education may or may not have rendered a sophisticated and accurate understanding of the Third World, this course is designed as a preliminary introduction - a general mapping of the terrain so that students may learn enough to consider where to explore further and gain some idea of the potential rewards for the effort. The role of the United States and of Americans in the Third World will also be explored. For students from Third World countries, the approach will hopefully follow the spirit articulated by the late African patriot, Amilcar Cabral: "Hide nothing from the masses of our people. Tell no lies. Expose lies whenever they are told. Mask no difficulties, mistakes, failures. Claim no easy victories." Hopefully the course will provide a broader perspective in which to comprehend the situations in your own societies.

The course is roughly divided into three segments of 4-5 weeks each. The first segment lays the groundwork by looking at the nature of traditional Third World societies and the process by which the Third World became incorporated into the modern world economy; special emphasis will be placed on the nature and impact of imperialism and colonialism. The middle segment examines the variety of political, economic and social systems to be found in the Third World since World War II, including nationalist and social revolutionary societies. Finally, we will discuss some of the major aspects of underdevelopment. I have opinions on many of the subjects under discussion and will try to make my biases clear. You are invited to take issue with my opinions and will not be penalized for doing so. I offer this observation in the spirit of C. Wright Mills, the late sociologist, who once wrote: "I have tried to be objective, but I do not claim to be detached." The objectives of the course are knowledge, understanding, and an increased ability to think and analyze. All that is required is an open mind and a willingness to learn about other peoples: their beliefs, aspirations and problems.

Texts

There are two paperback texts, both available in the bookstore and on reserve:
   L.S. Stavrianos, <u>Global Rift: The Third World Comes of Age</u> (Morrow)
   Paul Harrison, <u>Inside the Third World</u>, 2nd ed. (Penguin)
The books are coded for reading as S and H. Both books are controversial and have a point of view. Stavrianos is not an easy book but if you can read it critically and attentively you will learn much about how the modern world came to be the way that it

is. The choice of Stavrianos as the major text reflects my view that contemporary problems can only be understood in an historical and global context. There is also a required atlas, The Comparative World Atlas, New Revised Edition (Hammond). During the first several weeks you should begin to familiarize yourself with the various countries of Asia, Africa, Latin America, and Oceania (see data about map quiz below) as well as the major physical features, religions, cities, economic products, language groupings, and natural environments, all of which are included in atlas maps. You will continually need this information throughout the course, indeed throughout life.

Supplementary Readings

During the second half of the course each student is required to read and critically consider one of the following paperback books, all available in the bookstore and on reserve:
  Gerard Chaliand, Revolution in the Third World (Penguin)
  Harry Gailey, Africa: Troubled Continent (Krieger)
  Clark Neher, Politics in Southeast Asia (Schenkman)
  Dennis Pirages, Global Ecopolitics (Harcourt Brace)
  Thomas Skidmore and Peter Smith, Modern Latin America (Oxford)

As part of the final exam you will be tested on the major thrust of the book which you selected (see below). You should pay particular attention to the conceptual and theoretical framework of the book (the author's point of view, conclusions, and definition of what is important) and how these concur or differ with the two main texts and the relevant films.

Media Materials

I have also chosen to make extensive use of media materials as a way to give you a better "feel" for Third World peoples and also provide the class with case studies. The films should also stimulate discussion and illustrate some of the major points of the reading. We will tentatively have 17 film or slide presentations and two programs of music. You are also encouraged to attend as many of the foreign films to be shown on campus as possible; occasionally some of these films come from Third World countries such as India, Cuba or Senegal.

Course Format

The format is primarily reading and discussion, although I may sometimes give a minilecture. Nonetheless, the course will live or die on your willingness to participate in discussion. I will suggest several discussion questions or topics for each forthcoming session and expect you to be prepared to discuss them. Discussions will proceed on the assumption that you have completed the reading assignment. It is obviously impossible in a course of one bare semester to do true justice to the material and to discuss the Third World and its problems in a reasonable comprehensive manner. Even with a limitation on the subject areas, we will not be able to devote as much attention to any one subject as many of us would like. We will be moving through the material very quickly and it is important for you to keep with the readings and discussions. Even so we will not have the time to discuss all the relevant points raised by the reading.

Tentative Class Schedule

Session	Date	Topic (Reading Assignment)
1	Feb. 6	Introductory remarks
2	Feb. 8	Images of the Third World (S:23-43)
3	Feb. 13	Some Traditional Societies I (S:100-105, 310-315); Film: "The Tiv of Nigeria"
4	Feb. 15	Some Traditional Societies II Film: "Three Worlds of Bali"
5	Feb. 20	Roots of Underdevelopment I (S:44-66, 74-98, 141-168); Film: "The History Book, Part 1"
6	Feb. 22	Roots of Underdevelopment II (S:99-140, 169-176); Film: "The History Book, Part 2"
7	Feb. 27	Roots of Underdevelopment III (S:177-252) Quiz: Map Knowledge
8	Feb. 29	Colonialism and Imperialism I (S:256-308) Film: "White Man's Africa"
9	Mar. 5	Colonialism and Imperialism II (S:309-332, 349-427); Film: "The Turtle People"
10	Mar. 7	Colonialism and Decolonization (S:484-588)
11	Mar. 12	Decolonization and Revolution (S:433-483) Film: "The History Book; Part 3"
12	Mar. 14	The Heritage of the Past
13	Mar. 19	Midterm Examination
14	Mar. 21	Nationalist Societies I (S:623-632, 680-708) Film: "Mexico: The Frozen Revolution"
15	Mar. 26	Nationalist Societies II (S:632-664) Slides: "Malaysia"
16	Mar. 28	Nationalist Societies III (S:665-679) Film: "West Africa: Two Life Styles"

Session	Date	Topic (Reading Assignment)
		SPRING VACATION (March 31-April 8)
17	Apr. 9	Reformist Societies Program: "Chilean New Song"
18	Apr. 11	White Settler Societies (S:755-790)
19	Apr. 16	Social Revolutionary Societies I (S:709-711, 589-622) Film: "China: The Other Half of the Sky"
20	Apr. 18	Social Revolutionary Societies II (S:730-755); Film: "Cuba"
21	Apr. 23	The United States in Vietnam (S:711-730) Film: "The Village of My Ann"
22	Apr. 25	Aspects of Underdevelopment I (H:9-136) Film: "North India Village"
23	Apr. 30	Aspects of Underdevelopment II (H:139-208) Film: "Tauw"
24	May 2	Aspects of Underdevelopment III (H:211-327) Film: "Wet Earth, Warm People"
25	May 7	Aspects of Underdevelopment IV (H:333-448) Film: "Sky Chief"
26	May 9	Aspects of Underdevelopment V Program: "Contemporary African Music"
27	May 14	Development or Despair? I (S:791-814; H:449-462)
28	May 16	Development or Despair? II
	May 21	Final Examination (3:30-5:30)

Afterthoughts

"'Would you tell me, please, which way I ought to go from here?' (asked Alice)." That depends a good deal on where you want to get to', said the cat." - Lewis Carroll, Through the Looking Glass.

Course Requirements

Grading will be based on a combination of factors which include two essay examinations, class participation, a map quiz and an optional term project.

Course Requirements

1. Class participation: Since this course primarily relies upon reading and discussion, class participation is critical to its success. Satisfactory class participation as measured by reasonably regular attendance, completion of assigned readings, and contributions to discussion can help your grade in cases where "benefit of doubt" comes into play. On the other hand, poor class participation can easily threaten otherwise satisfactory exam and project results. Students who are frequently absent without reasonable excuses can expect to be dropped a grade or more. While class participation does not merit a stated percentage of the grade, I reserve the right to add or subtract points from the final grade based on class participation.

2. Map Quiz: There will be a short (10 minute) map quiz, tentatively scheduled for February 27. You will be asked to locate 25 countries from a list of 50 or so to be distributed a week before the quiz. The quiz will not count toward the final grade but students who fail to correctly locate at least 80% of the countries must continue taking the quiz weekly until they do pass.

3. Two Essay Examinations: The midterm is tentatively scheduled for March 19, and the final for May 21. For the 90 minute midterm you must write on two questions out of three alternatives; a list of six or seven questions will be distributed on March 14, of which three will be used for the exam. The questions will involve thought and analysis rather than regurgitation of factual information; you should demonstrate that you have mastered and thought about the course material as represented by the class discussion, films, assigned readings, and any relevant outside reading, or other sources which you have utilized. The final will follow the same pattern with two differences. First, several of the six questions may involve integration of material from both halves of the course. The questions will be distributed on the last class session (May 6). In addition, you will be asked to write on a third question based on the supplementary book you selected. The question will be broadly defined and concern the whole of the book - the main thrust - rather than of individual sections or chapters. Hence, the two hour final will require you to choose two out of three alternatives plus a question on the book. On both exams each questions will count equally toward the exam grade. The final will contribute 60% to your final grade and the midterm 40%.

In the interest of flexibility you can also satisfy the written course requirements by combining the two exams with one of the following individualized projects. The project grade will only be counted toward your final grade if it helps your final grade (raises your exam average); in this case the two exams will count one half of your grade and the project will count one half. Thus, you have an incentive to complete the project since it may improve your grade; at the same time you lose time and energy but no points if your project falls short and also gain experience in preparing and writing academic projects. There is absolutely no penalty for declining to undertake or complete a project. A wide choice of projects is open, such as:

1) A research paper (8-15 pages, typed, double-spaced) on any topic of relevance to the course and analyzing some aspect of the Third World development dilemma. A great many possibilities exist depending on your background and interests, but you must write about a country or region other than your own (e.g., Malaysians cannot choose a Malaysian topic, but they can prepare a paper on Singapore or Indonesia or treat Malaysia comparatively). One possibility would be to pick a particular country, such as Kenya or Bolivia or Thailand, and look at its developmental prospects in the context of its history, political economy, culture, resources and environmental setting. Or you could select a more specific or broader topic; some examples might include: Environmental policies in India; North Korean communism; Tanzanian socialism; the changing role of women in China; United States aid programs in the Third World (or to particular countries or regions); the activities of the C.I.A.; the conflict in El Salvador; the problem of refugees; hunger in the Sahel region of Africa; the English language literature of protest in West Africa; pollution problems in Argentina; the art of Diego Rivera and Mexican underdevelopment; Victor Jara and the Chilean "New Song" Movement: sociopolitical implications; Indonesian political development since 1950; French colonial economic structure in West Africa in the 1940's and the 1950's; critiques of dependency theory; activities of multinational corporations in the Third World; heritage of British colonialism in Guyana; the role of the mass media in African development; education in contemporary Mexico; health care delivery systems in India and Pakistan; Japan's economic role in Southeast Asia; Algerian politics and social change. Papers of a comparative nature are especially welcome; some sample topics might include: environmental policies in the United States and China; medicine and health care in China, Cuba, and Philippines; development strategies in Kenya and Tanzania; the structure of capitalism in Brazil and Malaysia; fiction as a vehicle for social commentary in the Third World: China Achebe (Nigeria) and Khamsing Srinawk (Thailand).

Whatever the topic, the papers should be in a standard academic form, including the following: an introduction and conclusion; a conceptual framework or thesis (a research paper is not an encyclopedia article or mere compilation of information); footnoting and documentation of factual information, quotations, and paraphrasing (see below); complete footnotes, with author, title, publisher, and pages cited (footnotes may be grouped at end of paper); correct grammar, spelling and punctuation; numbered pages; bibliography (with complete bibliographic information); and use of sophisticated sources (academic books and periodicals rather than popular magazines or encyclopedias). You are advised to take these guidelines seriously. The Stavrianos text contains good bibliographical information.

2) A Journal (20-50 pages) reflecting your impressions, criticisms, and evaluations of the assigned readings, relevant outside reading

and experiences, relevant media presentations (TV documentaries and newscasts, radio programs, films, newspaper and magazine articles, etc.), class films and discussions. It should reflect the scope, direction, and depth of your involvement and growth with the subject matter during the semester; what have been the most interesting, challenging, upsetting, revealing, stimulating, relevant ideas and impressions that have emerged? A journal should document what you have learned, how you react to what you are learning, what you would like to explore further, and how you feel you can apply the knowledge gained in this course. A journal is also a useful framework for mini-research papers and essays or for short reports on extra reading without the restrictions of more formal academic writing (as in options 1 and 3). An outstanding journal will normally include such material. A journal is not a one-shot affair but a growing record over the course of the term. It may be typed or handwritten legibly. Illustrations, poems, and other creative materials may be included, as well as any quotations or sayings you find revealing and helpful. The first half of the journal should be submitted to me by the midterm exam; this will not be graded at that time but my feedback will give you an indication of how you are doing.

3) A comparative and analytical review of books (8-15 pages in length, typed, doublespaced), dealing critically with 2-4 books. Reviews could focus on a particular theme (such as Chinese communism, industrialism in Latin America, socialism in Africa, Nigerian novelists and recent political change, revolutionary movements in Southeast Asia, feminism in the Third World, or contemporary Indonesia), or on several themes. Works of fiction (especially by Third World writers) are acceptable. I will be glad to suggest books for the review and to illustrate how an analytical book review differs from the traditional book report. Separate reviews of 2 or 3 books on different subjects will also be acceptable, providing that I am consulted on all of them. Reviews should be in standard academic form, with quotations and paraphrasing footnoted.

A work of imaginative/creative interpretation dealing with some aspect of Third World development and underdevelopment. You might submit a short story, or a play, or a group of poems, or several paintings, or a musical composition, or a photographic essay, or a series of political cartoons, or a collage or collage book -- any creative product demonstrating conscious relationship with the subject matter of the course.

This is a suggestive, not an exclusive list of project options. In the interest of flexibility you can (through consultation with me) work out some combination of projects, do a more extensive project, or suggest alternatives to the above list of options. The concept of the "project" is to link your aptitude and inclination to the subject. Advisement will be available to insure that conceptual rigor can be combined with personal virtuosity. The UWGB faculty has recommended strong penalties for plagiarism in papers; you must footnote or otherwise cite the sources from which you quote, paraphrase, or utilize factual or interpretative data. Submission of work prepared by others is a serious offense. I have prepared short hand-outs on how to prepare research papers, journals, and book reviews; these are available from me upon request. You must get my approval for your project and your topics, and should have selected your particular project by the end of the fourth week of class, earlier for those writing journals. A one-page (hand-written) outline of the project should be submitted by the end of the eighth week. Indeed, you are strongly encouraged to let me see some of your work at various stages during the semester (rough drafts, journals in progress, etc.). Projects must be handed in no later than the last class session (earlier submissions are welcome). Except in the most exceptional circumstances late projects will not be accepted; on the other hand, failure to complete your project won't count against you either -- your grade will be based on the two exams.

Grades

For those who choose not to do a project, the two exams count for 100% of your final grade. Only under extraordinary circumstances will a grade of incomplete be given; students should request incompletes in writing by the last class session.

Office Hours

My office is in the Community Sciences building (CS), room 350 (tel. 2714). My regular office hours are MWF 9:30-10:00, W 1:30-2:30; I am often there at other times as well, and am available by appointment. Please call me at home (468-0623) in a dire emergency; however, people who call me at home early in the morning, during the evening news or "Prairie Home Companion;" on weekends, or after 10 at night are subject to the "death of a thousand slices," an old Chinese favorite. Messages can be left for me with the CCS secretaries (2355).

Yale University Robin W. Winks
HISTORY 265a

The British Empire and Commonwealth: From the American Revolution to the "New Imperialism." Meetings Tu and Th, 9:00-10:15 a.m. R. W. Winks, office hours Tuesday, 11-12:30 and by appointment, in The Master's Study, Berkeley College. Messages may be left with secretary, and appointments made, by calling 436-8580. The Teaching Assistant is Ms. Jill Felzan.

The purposes of this course are two: a) to introduce students to certain continuous themes in British imperial history from 1783 to the present, and b) to make possible comparative explorations between the British and other imperial experiences. "Imperial experience" is interpreted to mean both the experience of the British (and other European) settlers overseas, and the responses of the indigenous societies to the presence of the European. The lectures will not constitute a "survey course," as such, for they will dwell upon certain themes at some length, to the exclusion of others. We will move well beyond 1870--the date usually associated with the "New Imperialism"--when appropriate to a theme, or to a particular national history.

The principal themes we will pursue are three: a) the notion of nationalism, and how a particular fragment of European settlers comes to see itself constituting a separate national identity; b) the variables which arise in interracial contacts, which led to divergent patterns of race relations in different colonies, empires, and areas of the world; and c) the problem of "the collaborator," or how elements within an indigenous society chose, for reasons of their own, to cooperate with the encroaching European society. On the whole, emphasis will be on intellectual and social history, rather than the diplomatic or administrative history of imperialism. There will be assigned readings specifically designed to fill the gaps which will result from concentrating the lectures in this manner.

Since it is quite impossible to deal with forty or more cultures in any depth, we will select certain national histories for purposes of narrative interpretation and the application of case studies. In the first semester, these will largely be the histories of the "fragment society" areas: Canada, Australia, New Zealand, South Africa, and to a lesser extent the West Indies, Ireland, and Sierra Leone. The "Colonies of exploitation"--largely Africa, India, and Malaysia, and the Pacific--will be studied more closely in History 265b.

There will be a mid-term and a final examination.

The following are the books which will be read in History 265a. Copies may be purchased in the Yale Co-op; copies are on reserve in the Cross Campus Library; and at least one copy remains for circulation in Sterling. The books will be read approximately in the order given here, unless publishers fail to supply a particular title, in which case substitutions will be made. Those marked * are available in paperback editions.

*Carlo M. Cipolla, <u>Guns</u>, <u>Sails</u> <u>and</u> <u>Empires</u>: <u>Technological</u> <u>Innovation</u> <u>and</u> <u>the</u> <u>Early</u> <u>Phases</u> <u>of</u> <u>European</u> <u>Expansion</u>. <u>1400-1700</u> (New York: Minerva, 1965).

*David K. Fieldhouse, <u>The</u> <u>Colonial</u> <u>Empires</u> <u>from</u> <u>the</u> <u>Eighteenth</u> <u>Century</u>: <u>A</u> <u>Comparative</u> <u>Survey</u> (New York: Delacourte, 1966).

*Robin W. Winks, ed., <u>Slavery</u>: <u>A</u> <u>Comparative</u> <u>Perspective</u> (New York: New York University Press, 1972).

*Barry Gough, <u>Canada</u> (Englewood Cliffs, N. J.: Prentice-Hall, 1975).

*Hugh Maclennan, <u>Barometer</u> <u>Rising</u> (Toronto: McClelland & Stewart); reprint of 1941 edition.

*D. A. G. Waddell, <u>The</u> <u>West</u> <u>Indies</u> <u>&</u> <u>the</u> <u>Guianas</u> (Englewood Cliffs, N. J.: Prentice-Hall, 1967).

*A. G. L. Shaw, <u>The</u> <u>Story</u> <u>of</u> <u>Australia</u> (London: Faber & Faber, 1969).

*W. H. Oliver, <u>The</u> <u>Story</u> <u>of</u> <u>New</u> <u>Zealand</u> (London: Faber & Faber, 1963).

*C. W. de Kiewiet, <u>A</u> <u>History</u> <u>of</u> <u>South</u> <u>Africa</u> (London: Oxford University Press, 1966).

*Robin W. Winks, <u>British</u> <u>Imperialism</u>: <u>Gold</u>, <u>God</u>, <u>Glory</u> (New York: Holt, Rinehart, Winston, 1963).

*Roger Owen and Bob Sutcliffe, <u>Studies</u> <u>in</u> <u>the</u> <u>Theory</u> <u>of</u> <u>Imperialism</u> (London: Longman, 1972).

Oliver MacDonagh, <u>Ireland</u> (Englewood Cliffs, N. J.: Prentice-Hall, 1967).

Recommended books: Many other titles have been placed in the Cross Campus Library, some on reserve, where a list of them may be consulted. The Yale Co-op has been asked to stock a few copies of four standard histories which those without any previous background in British, African, or other imperially-related histories might wish to consult. These are Nicholas Mansergh, <u>The</u> <u>Commonwealth</u> <u>Experience</u>; *James Morris, <u>Pax</u> <u>Britannica</u>: <u>The</u> <u>Climax</u> <u>of</u> <u>an</u> <u>Empire</u>; H. Duncan Hall, <u>Commonwealth</u>; and Robin W. Winks, <u>Historiography</u> <u>of</u> <u>the</u> <u>British</u> <u>Empire-Commonwealth</u>.

The following is an approximate sequence of lectures and subjects. Material on South Africa will be presented <u>seriatim</u> throughout the term by David Jones.

        Renaissance Man as Explorer
        Inventing the <u>beau</u> <u>sauvage</u>
        Race-thinking and racism
        The economics of slavery
        Variables in race relations
        Mercantilism and Colbertism

The American Revolution breaks an empire
The Anglican Tie
The Structure of the Canadian experience
The problem of "fragment societies" and "garrison states"
Anglo-French relations and the plural society
The Durham Report, from Canada to Kenya
"Economic independence" and "imperial federation"
Federation and the first decolonization
Theories of Nationalism: What is a Nation?
Nationalism and social communication: Introducing the "collaborator"
The Problem of a colonial foreign policy: Canada and the United States
Literature and cultural nationalism
Precedents for devolution of Empire
The Rise of the Colonial Office
Who Ruled the Empire? Whitehall to 1870
The Structure of the Australian experience
Race relations and ricochet empire: Australia as a case study
Missionary Activities and the Colonies
Maori and pakeha in the South Seas
Maori and missionary: A case study in cultural adaptation
Maoritanga and "ethnic nationalism" in New Zealand
Social laboratory for the Empire: Socialism abroad
Dependent economies: New Zealand and Uruguay compared
Black and White Settlers: Three Historiographies for Africa
Empire at Home: Institutions of Reinforcement (The Reader)
Empire at Home: Institutions of Reinforcement (The School)
Empire at Home: Institutions of Reinforcement (The Church)
Empire at Home: Institutions of Reinforcement (The Scholar)

YALE UNIVERSITY

Fall 1983　　　　　　　　　　　　　　　　　　　　　　　Prof. Ivo Banac
History 246a

HISTORY OF THE INTERNATIONAL COMMUNIST MOVEMENT

Reading List:

Franz Borkenau, World Communism.
Nikolai Bukharin, The ABC of Communism.
Santiago Carillo, Eurocommunism and the State.
Milovan Djilas, Conversations with Stalin.
Maurice Halperin, The Rise and Decline of Fidel Castro.
Enver Hoxha, The Khrushchevites.
Jakub Karpinski, Homage to Catalonia.
Edgar Snow, Red Star over China.

Copies of these books are available at the Yale Co-op. A limited number is also on reserve at the Cross Campus Library.

Course Requirements:
 a. Regular attendance and participation at section meetings;
 b. One paper of approximately seven pages to be written in conjunction with one of the volumes on the reading list or on a subject approved by the instructor.
 c. A mid-term examination covering the assigned reading lectures through Oct. 20.
 d. A final examination covering the assigned reading and lectures from Oct. 25 through the close of the course.

Films:
Arrangements will be made for the screening of "Lenin in October". a Soviet film directed in 1937 by Mikhail Romm, and Angi Vera, a Hungarian film directed in 1979 by Pal Gabor.

Week 1
Sept. 8　　Introduction: The Origins of Marxist Socialism
No section meetings.

Week 2
Sept. 13　　Leninism: The Continuation and Development of Marxism?
Sept. 15　　"The Workers' and Peasants' Revoluation Has Been Acomplished."
Sections:　　Nikolai Bukharin, The ABC of Communism (complete)

Week 3
Sept. 20　　"The International of Open Mass Struggle": The Comintern in the Period of the biennio rosso (1919-1920)
Sept. 22　　The Splits in European Socialism and the Rise of the "United Front" (1921-1923)
Sections:　　Borkenau, pp. 9-256.

225

Week 4.
    Sept. 27   The Years of "Relative Stabilization" and the Trotskyist Challange (1924-1928)
    Sept. 29   Bypassing Capitalism in the Colonial World: The "National and Colonial Question" (1917-1927)
    Sections: Borkenau, pp. 257-331.

Week 5
    Oct. 4   "Class Against Class": The Stalinization of the Comintern and the Rise of Fascism (1929-1933)
    Oct. 6   The "Popular Front" and the Spanish Civil War (1934-1939)
    Sections: Borkenau, pp. 332-429; George Orwell, Homage to Catalonia (complete)

Week 6
    Oct. 11   The Apogee of Stalinism and the Naze-Soviet Alliance
    Oct. 13   The "Grand Alliance" Against Hitler and the Dissolution of the Comintern

    Sections: Milovan Djilas, Conversations with Stalin (Complete)

Week 7
    Oct. 18   Communist Resistance in Hitler's Festung Europa
    Oct. 20   The "People's Democracies" of Eastern Europe" (1944-1948)

    Sections: MID-TERM EXAMINATION

Week 8
    Oct 25   The Chinese Revolution
    Oct. 27   The Legend of Nguyen Ai Quoc

    Sections: Edgar Snow, Red Star over China

Week 9
    Nov. 1   "....And They Are Slaughtering Communists Over There": De Stalinization and the Storm in Eastern Europe
    Nov. 3   The Sino-Soviet Split

    Sections: Enver Hoxha, The Khruschevites (complete)

Week 10
    Nov. 8   "Revolution in the Revolution": The Long March of Fidel Castro
    Nov. 10   "Long Live the Victory of the People's War!": Vietnam, the Cultural Revolution, and International Maoism

    Sections: Maurice Halperin, The Rise and Decline of Fidel Castro (complete)

Week 11
    Nov. 15   The Course of Reform in Eastern Europe: The Prague Spring and the "Mass Movement" in Croatia
    Nov. 17   Eurocommunism vs. Soviet "Real Socialism"
    Sections: Santiago Carillo, Eurocommunism and the State (complete)

Week 12
    Nov. 29   The Theory of the "Three Worlds" and the Decline of Maoism
and *gauchisme*
    Dec. 1   The Polish Revival
    Sections: Jakub Karpinski, *Countdown* (complete)

Week 13
    Dec. 6   Whither Communism and a Gloss on the Communist Movement in the United States
    Dec. 8   The Communist Style
NO SECTION MEETINGS

HY. 381, 382, 592, BOISE STATE UNIVERSITY
481, 482   CROSS-CULTURAL HISTORY   FALL 1984
HP. 492   L. 231
Instructor Tim Shin   Office Ph. 385-3427
Office 1-229   Ofice Hr. W. 11:30-12:00
                                                         1:30- 3:00
                                                      and by Appt.

I. Course Description

        This course is a historical survey of Cross-cultural relations between the
    West and the East. It deals with an introduction of Eastern Culture and its
    influence on the West as well as the introduction of Western culture and its
    influence on the East.

II. Course Readings

    (A) Required Textbooks

        Ward, The Interplay of East and West
        Franke, China and the West
        Teng/Fairbank, China's Response to the West
        Fukuzawa, The Autobiography

    (B) Reserved Books

        Bodde, Chinese Ideas in the West
        _____, China's Gift to the West

    (C) Recommended Books.

        Cameron, N., Barbarians and Mandarins: The Thirteen Centuries of Western
                Travellers in China.
        Chěn, J., China and the West
        Christy, A., The Orient in American Transcendentalism
                _____, The Asian Legacy and American Life
        Clyde L. Beers, The Far East: A History of the Western Impact and the
                Eastern Response 1830-1965
        Curtin, P., Cross-culture Trade in World History
        Danton, G., The Culture Contacts of the United States and China
        Dean and Harootunian, West and Non-West
        Edwardes, M., The West in Asia 1850-1914
        Fairbank,J., Chinese American Interactions
        Hudson, G., Europe and China: A Survey of Their Relations From the Earliest
                Times to 1800
        Komroff,M., The Travels of Marco Polo
        Lataurette, K.S., A History of Christian Mission in China
        McNeill, W., The Rise of the West
        Murphey, R., The Outsiders: The Western Experience in China and India
        Needham, J., Science and Civilization in China
        Northrop, F.S.C., The Meeting of East and West
        Panikkar, K.M., Asia and Western Dominance
        Parkinson, C.N., East and West
        Radhakrishnan, S., Eastern Religion and Western Thought
        Reichwein, A., China and Europe: Intellectual and Artistic Contacts in the
                Eighteenth Century
        Sansom, G., The Western World and Japan

Cross-Cultural History
Page 2

        Spence, J., *To Change China: The Western Advisors in China 1620-1960*
        Schwartz, W.L., *The Far East in Modern French Literature*
        Toynbee, A., *The World and the West*
        Treadgold, D., *The West in Russia and China*
        Ward, B., *India and the West*

III. Course Requirements and Evaluation

        You must read all the required textbooks as well as reserved books, attend class and participate in class discussions. You are required to present oral reports and to submit one term paper. Course grade will be based on the oral reports and class discussions (50%) and the term paper (50%).

VI. Course Schedule

    Sept. 4   Introduction: Agents, Ideas, changes.
         11   Part I: Comparisons between Eastern and Western Culture and History
                   Required Reading: Ward, *The Interplay of East and West*

                Part II: An Intorduction of Eastern Culture and its Influence on the West
                Required Teading: Bodde, *Chinese Ideas* pp. 1-42
                                  Bodde, *Chinese Gift* pp. 1-40
                                  Franke, China and the West pp. 1-33 & pp. 140-151

         18   Asia and Europe (1)
         25   Asia and Europe (11)
    Oct. 2   Asia and America

                Part III: An Introduction of Western Culture and its Influence on the East
         9   The West and Japan and Korea
                Required Reading: Fukuzawa, *The Autobiography* entire book
         16   The West and India and Vietnam
         23   The West and China (I: up to the 17c)
                Required Reading: Franke, *China and the West* pp. 1-65
                                  Teng/Fairbank, *China's Response* pp. 1-21
         30   The West and China (II: 19c)
                Required Reading: Franke, *China and the West* pp. 66-119
                                  Teng/Fairbank, *China's Response* pp. 23-131

    Nov. 6   The West and China (III: 20c. Republican period)
                Required Reading: Franke, *China and the West* pp. 119-139
                                  Teng/Fairbank, *China's Response* pp. 133-246
                                              pp. 251-276
         13   The West and China (IV: 20c. Communist period)
                Required Reading: Teng/Fairbanks, *China's Response* pp. 246-251
                Part IV: Oral Presentations
         20   1st group
         27   2nd group
    Dec. 4   3rd group
         11   4th group

COLUMBIA UNIVERSITY

HISTORY-MIDDLE EAST W3901y
INDIA IN THE WESTERN HISTORICAL IMAGINATION
Profs. Ainslie Embree & Robin Lewis
4 points

Wednesday 4:10-6
1134 IAB

PRIMARY READINGS

I. THE EIGHTEENTH CENTURY: THE EUROPEAN DISCOVERY OF INDIA

Rev. J.Z. Holwell- "A genuine narrative of the deplorable deaths of the English gentlemen and others who were suffocated in the Black Hole in Fort William, at Calcutta, in the kingdom of Bengal, in the night succeeding 20 June, 1756" (1757)

*Robert Orme- A history of the military transactions of the British nation in Indostan (1763): Volume 2, Section the First, pp. 147-185.

Sir William Jones- "On the Hindus" (1784)

Charles Grant- "Observations on the State of Society among the Asiatic Subjects of Great Britain, particularly with respect to Morals, and on the means of Improving It" (1792)

*William Hickey- Memoirs, 1749-1809 [1913]: pp. 117-134 (Madras), 237-254 (Calcutta).

*Eliza Fay- Original Letters from India, 1779-1815 (1817): pp. 17-25, 114-168.

II. THE EARLY NINETEENTH CENTURY: DESCRIPTION AND ANALYSIS

*James Mill- A History of British India (1818): Volume 1, pp. 376-423.

*Reginald Heber- Narrative of a journey through the Upper Provinces of India, from Calcutta to Bombay, 1824-25 (1828): pp. 25-54 (Benares), 166-191 (Oudh), 224-249 (Delhi and Agra).

*G.W.F. Hegel- "The Oriental World: India" in The Philosophy of History (1830-31).

*Victor Jacquemont- Letters from India (1835): Volume I, pp. 305-405.

*William Henry Sleeman- Rambles and Recollections of an Indian Official (1844): pp. 1-91.

C. Grey & H.L.O. Garrett- European Adventurers of Northern India, 1785-1849 [1929]: pp. 117-147 (Paolo di Avitable), 265-291 (Alexander Gardiner).

*Fanny Parks- Wanderings of a Pilgrim, in search of the Picturesque, during four-and-twenty years in the East (1850): Volume 1, pp. 20-57 (Calcutta), 87-97 (Life in the Zenana), 173-227 (Oudh), 321-359 (the Taj Mahal).

Major Herbert B. Edwardes- A Year on the Punjab Frontier in 1848-49 (1851): Volume 1, pp. 3-87, 421-432.

*Karl Marx- "The British Rule in India" and "The Future Results of British Rule in India" in The Marx-Engels Reader (1853)

III. 1857: MUTINY NARRATIVES AND INTERPRETATIONS

*Ainslie Embree (ed.)- 1857 in India: Mutiny or War of Independence? [1963]

*W.H. Russell- My Indian Mutiny Diary (1860): pp. 3-16, 67-77, 129-181, 280-288.

IV. 1858-1910: "THE ILLUSION OF PERMANENCE"

Andrew Wilson- The Abode of Snow: Observations on a Tour from Chinese Tibet to the Indian Caucasus, Through the Upper Valleys of the Himalaya (1875): pp. ix-xvi (Preface), 1-35 ("To the Heights"), 278-339 (Kashmir).

Dr. F.R. Hogg- Indian Notes (1880): pp. 1-23.

Max Muller- "India- What Can It Teach Us?" in The Collected Works of T. Max Muller (Volume XIII) (1882)

George Alfred Henty- With Clive in India, or The Beginnings of an Empire (1884): pp. 277-299 (The Battle of Plassey).

Rudyard Kipling- Selected Poetry (1888-98)

*Sir Alfred Lyall- The Rise and Expansion of the British Dominion in India (1893): pp. 351-356 ("The Future of Our Indian Empire"), 376-390 ("Internal Administration").

Mark Twain- Following the Equator (1897): Chapters II-III (Bombay), XII-XIV and XVI (Allahabad and Benares), XVII (the Taj Mahal), XVIII-XIX (the Black Hole of Calcutta, Darjeeling), XXI ("The Snake and Tiger Death-Roll"), XXIII ("Exaggerating the Taj").

G.N. Curzon- "The True Imperialism" (1907)

*Max Weber- "India: The Brahman and the Castes" in From Max Weber: Essays in Sociology (1916-17): pp. 396-415.

*Lt.-Gen. Sir George F. MacMunn- The Romance of the Indian Frontiers (1931): pp. 106-131 (the North-west Frontier), 132-154 ("Clans and Tribes on the Frontier").

V. THE TWENTIETH CENTURY: REINTERPRETING INDIA

*C.E. Tyndale Biscoe- Kashmir in Sunlight and Shade (1922): Chapters I-IV ("My First Journey into Kashmir"), VI ("Character of the Kashmiris"), XXI-XXIV ("A Kashmir Mission School").

*Katherine Mayo- Mother India (1927): Introduction, Chapters I-IV, VII-VIII, XVIII.

*E.M. Forster- The Hill of Devi (1953): pp. 7-9 (Preface), 25-52 ("Letters of 1912-13"), 79-237 ("Letters of 1921").

*Louis Fischer- Gandhi: His Life and Message for the World (1954): pp. 56-145.

Allen Ginsberg- Indian Journals:March 1962-May 1963 (1970): pp. 20-45, 63-68, 116-126, 141-144.

*V.S. Naipaul- India: A Wounded Civilization (1976): Foreword, Part One ("A Wounded Civilization"), Part Three ("Not Ideas, But Obsessions").

*Jan Morris- "Mrs. Gupta Never Rang-Delhi, 1975" in Destinations (1980)

*Christopher Isherwood- My Guru and His Disciple (1982): pp. 3-53.

David Selbourne- Through the Indian Looking-Glass (1982): pp. 20-33 ("Through the Indian Looking-Glass"), 66-71 ("On the Condition of the People"), 143-153 ("State and Ideology in India"), 171-173 ("The Big White Chief Across the Waters: An Obituary"), 189-193 ("India on its Knees"), 205-216 ("The Return of Mrs. Gandhi").

SECONDARY READINGS

*K.K. Dyson- A Various Universe: A Study of the Journals and Memoirs of British Men and Women in the Indian Subcontinent, 1765-1856 (1978)

*H.K. Kaul (ed.)- Travellers' India: An Anthology (1979)

*Partha Mitter- Much Maligned Monsters: A History of European Reactions to Indian Art (1977)

*Philip Woodruff- The Men Who Ruled India (1954)

*Clark Worswick & Ainslie Embree- The Last Empire: Photography in British India, 1855-1911 (1976)

UNIVERSITY OF PENNSYLVANIA

SOCIOLOGY 410   HISTORY 422

"The Family in England and China: Continuity and Change"

Susan Watkins   Susan Naquin
Sociology   History
228 McNeil   304B College Hall
x4258   x4958
387-6041   382-5782

I   Introduction

    Week 1:   Sociological perspectives on the family

    Week 2:   Survey of recent history: China

    Week 3:   Survey of recent history: England

II The Pre-Modern Family

    Week 4:   The traditional family in fiction

    Week 5:   Family and household: formation and dissolution

    Week 6:   Relationships within the family

    Week 7:   The family in society

III The Family in Transition

    Week 8:   Fictional attacks on the family

    Week 9:   Criticisms of the family from within

    Week 10: Pressures on the family from without

IV The Contemporary Family

    Week 11: The family today

    Week 12: Trends and uniformities

This course will compare the evolution of the family in England and China from the 16th century to the present. Drawing on materials from history and from sociology, it will emphasize elements of continuity in the structure of the family and the interactions between the family and the broader society in both countries during a period of tumultuous social change.

Sociology 410   History 422

The class will meet on Wednesdays from 3:00 to 5:00 p.m. in the Lounge on the 5th floor of Ware College House.

Attendance in class is expected.

The reading assignments are listed below. All readings are on reserve in Rosengarten. Books marked with asterisks** are for sale at the Penn Book Center (3721 Walnut).

The primary emphasis in the course will be on reading and class discussion. During the semester, each student will also prepare four short (5 page) reports on the readings, summaries of which will be presented in class.

READING ASSIGNMENTS

Week 1:   Sociological Perspectives on the Family

William J. Goode, The Family (1982, 2nd edition), pp. 1-14, 33-35, 50-127, 180-95
E.A. Wrigley, Population and History (1969), pp. 1-61, 90-143

Questions for discussion:
What functions must any society perform to assure societal continuity?
Which of these are usually performed by the family?
How is membership in the family defined?
What benefits do families provide for members?

Week 2:   Recent History: China

Gilbert Rozman, "Social Integration" in The Modernization of China (1981), pp. 141-182, 203-216, 352-400, 443-454
Ramon Myers, "Economic Structures and Growth" in The Modernization of China, pp. 107-140, 318-329

Questions for discussion:
What have been the major changes in Chinese society in the last three centuries
What are the major changes and continuities in the Chinese family?
How are class differences reflected in the family?
What other social organizations were important in China? what was their effect on the family?
How did the family system in China inhibit its modernization, according to Rozman?

234

Sociology 410   History 422

Week 3: Recent History: England

E.J. Hobsbawm, Industry and Empire (1968), pp. 13-133, 154-171, 273-93
Keith Wrightson, English Society, 1580-1680 (1982) 17-36

Questions for discussion:

    What have been the major changes in English society in the last three
        centuries?
    What are the major changes and continuities in the English family?
    How are class differences reflected in the family?
    What other social organizations were important? What was their effect on
        the family?
    On the basis of Hobsbawm, did the English family system contribute to or
        inhibit modernization?

Week 4: The Traditional Family in Fiction

    CHINA.   Cao Xue-qin, The Story of the Stone (ca. 1754).**
            Translated by David Hawkes. Volume 1, pp. 47-500.

    ENGLAND. Jane Austen, Pride and Prejudice (1813). **
            Any edition. All. (ca. 350 pages)

Questions for discussion:

    What is the picture of the ideal family that we get from these novels?
    What are the characteristics of a good wife? husband? son? daughter?
        grandmother, etc.
    Characterize the relationships between family members.
    When an individual makes an important decision, who is consulted and why?
    What benefits do family members provide for one another?
    What are the grounds for association beyond the family?

Sociology 410   History 422

Week 5: Family and Household: Formation and Dissolution

CHINA.   Maurice Freedman, Chinese Lineage and Society: Fukien and
               Kwangtung (1966), pp. 43-67
            Arthur P. Wolf & Chieh-shan Huang, Marriage and Adoption in
               China, 1845-1945 (1980), pp. 57-69, 108-117, 133-142

ENGLAND.   John Hajnal. "Two Kinds of Pre-Industrial Household Formation
               System," Population and Development Review 3:8 (1982)
               449-494
            Keith Wrightson, English Society, "Family Formation" pp. 66-88

Questions for discussion:

    What is the correspondence between the family and household?
    How are families formed and dissolved?
    How does the composition of the household change over the family cycle?
    What happens to family fragments?
    Compare the marriage systems in China and England.
    How much flexibility was there in each of these traditional systems?

Week 6: Relationships Within the Family

CHINA.   Ida Pruitt, The Daughter of Han: The Autobiography of a Chinese
               Working Woman (1945), "The Family," pp.11-54 **
            Jonathan Spence, The Death of Woman Wang (1978), "The Woman
               Who Ran Away," pp. 99-132 **

ENGLAND.   Alan Macfarlane, The Family of Richard Josselin: A Seventeenth
               Century Clergyman (1970), pp. 81-160
            Lawrence Stone, The Family, Sex and Marriage in England, 1500-
               1800 (paperback edition 1979), "Plebian Sexual Behavior
               pp. 382-404
            Keith Wrightson, English Society, "Affective Relations"
               pp. 89-118

Questions for discussion:

    Who did what within the family economy?
    How was power distributed within the family?
    Where were the strongest ties of affection within the family?
    How were children socialized?

Sociology 410   History 422

Week 7: The Family in Traditional Society

CHINA.   Maurice Freedman, Chinese Lineage and Society (1966), "Village,
            Lineage, and Clan," pp. 1-42
         M. Freedman, "The Politics of an Old State: A View from the Chinese
            Lineage, " in The Study of Chinese Society (1979), ed.
            G.W. Skinner, pp. 334-350
         Martin Yang, A Chinese Village: Taitou, Shantung (1945), "The
            Rise and Fall of a Family," pp. 132-142

ENGLAND. Alan Macfarlane, The Origins of English Individualism (1978),
            pp. 62-79
         Keith Wrightson, English Society, "Social Relations in the Local
            Community," pp. 39-65
         Richard Smith, "Three Centuries of Fertility, Economy, and Household
            Formation in England," Population and Development Review
            (1982) 595-622
         Lawrence Stone, The Family, Sex, and Marriage in England, "The
            Growth of Affective Individualism," pp. 149-180

Questions for discussion:

    Beyond the family, what other social institutions performed competing
        functions?
    How relevant were kinship ties outside the household?
    Compare English "individualism" with Chinese "familism."

Week 8: Fictional Attacks on the Family

CHINA.   Pa Chin. Family (1931). All. (ca. 330 pages) **

ENGLAND. Samuel Butler. The Way of All Flesh (1903). All.
            (ca. 550 pages)

Questions for discussion:

    On what grounds does the author attack the traditional family system?
    What are the points of greatest tension and conflict within these families?
    Compare these families with those in the novels of week 4. What changes
        do you see?

237

Sociology 410   History 422

Week 9: Criticisms of the Family from Within

    CHINA.   Olga Lang, Chinese Family and Society (1946), "Old Men and
                Old Women," pp. 227-237
            Mary Rankin, "The Emergence of Women at the End of the Ch'ing:
                The Case of Ch'iu Chin," in Women in Chinese Society
                (1975), ed. Margery Wolf & Roxanne Witke, pp. 39-66
            Roxanne Witke, "Chiang Ch'ing's Coming of Age," in Wolf and Witke,
                Women in Chinese Society, pp. 227-237
            Edgar Snow, Red Star Over China (1937), "Mao Tse-tung's
                Autobiography" pp. 129-55

    ENGLAND. J. A. and Olive Banks. Feminism and Family Planning in Victorian
                England (1964), pp. 15-129

Questions for discussion:

    What were the various grounds for criticism of the traditional family?
    Who did they come from?
    What were the effects of these criticisms on the family?
    Compare feminist ideas in China and England.

Week 10: Pressures on the Family From Without

    CHINA.   Marion Levy, The Family Revolution in Modern China (1949),
                "Transitional Kinship Structure," pp. 313-349
            William Hinton, Fanshen: A Documentary of Revolution in a
                Chinese Village (1966), pp. 128-160 **
            Olga Lang, Chinese Family and Society, pp. 134-146, 203-214,
                259-282

    ENGLAND. Louise Tilly & Joan Scott, Women, Work and Family (1978)
                pp. 89-145
            Flora Thompson, Lark Rise to Candleford (1945) pp. ??

Questions for discussion:

    What were the sources of pressure on the family for change in the 20th
        century?
    What aspects of these family systems seem most resistant to change?
    What kinds of changes in the family does industrialization encourage?

Sociology 410   History 422

Week 11: The Family Today

   CHINA.   B. Michael Frolic, Mao's People (1980), "Little Brother's
            Wedding""My Neighborhood," pp. 87-99, 224-241
            William Parish & Martin Whyte, Village and Family in
               Contemporary China (1978) 131-199, 235-247, 301-337 **
            "The Marriage Law," Peking Review 11 (March 16, 1981) 24-27

   ENGLAND. Michael Young & Peter Willmott, Family and Kinship in
               East London (1957), pp. 17-169 **
            Lawrence Stone, The Family, Sex and Marriage in England,
               "Conclusions" pp. 407-428

   Questions for discussion:

       How does the contemporary family differ from the traditional one?
       Which roles and relationships have changed the most?
       What are the points of tension within the contemporary family?

Week 12: Trends and Uniformities

   E.A. Wrigley, Population and History, pp. 164-202
   William Goode, World Revolution and Family Patterns (1970), pp. 1-86
   Leo Goodstadt, "China's One Child Family: Policy and Public Response"
       Population and Development Review 8:1 (1982) 37-58
   A.J. Coale, "The Demographic Transition Reconsidered," International
       Population Conference, Liege, 1973, pp. 57-71

   Questions for discussion:

       Compare long-term demographic trends in England and China.
       What were the causes of the demographic transition?
       Are the Chinese and English families becoming more similar?
          If so, why?
       What are the current agents of change?

239

Anthropology-History V3910y

Columbia University

Spring 1984
Tuesday 11-12:50

Myron Cohen, Professor of Anthropology, 932 S.I.A. & 466 Scherm

Isser Woloch, Professor of History, 520 Fayerwenther

COLLOQUIUM ON PEASANT SOCIETIES AND THEIR TRANSFORMATION: FRANCE AND CHINA Anthropological and historical perspectives on the peasant societies of France and China. The characteristics of the traditional peasant societies of both countries; patterns of peasant protest; and the transformation of these societies in modern times.

Assignments: Three essays of a comparative nature, based on the assigned readings (6 to 8 pages each, typewritten, double-spaced, with adequate margins). The papers are due on February 21, March 20, and April 24.

Jan. 24 I. INTRODUCTION: THE ANALYSIS OF PEASANT SOCIETY

  Suggested reading: Eric Wolf, Peasants (Prentice-Hall)

Jan. 31 II. TRADITIONAL RURAL SOCIETY IN FRANCE

  Marc Bloch, French Rural History: An Essay on its Basic Characteristics (U. of California), chs. 2-6

  Pierre Goubert, "The Seventeenth-Century Peasantry: a regional example" reprinted in I. Woloch, ed., The Peasantry in the Old Regime: Conditions and Protests.

Feb. 7 III. TRADITIONAL RURAL SOCIETY IN CHINA

  Myron Cohen, "Introduction" to Arthur Smith, Village Life in China.

  Albert Feuerwerker, State and Society in Eighteenth-Century China (Michigan Papers in Chinese Studies, 1970)

  Laurence Thompson, Chinese Religion: An Introduction (Wadsworth, 3rd ed.), pp. 34-83, 121-33

  Arthur Wolf, "Gods, Ghosts and Ancestors," in A. Wolf, ed., Religion and Ritual in Chinese Society.

Feb. 14 IV. THE PEASANT COMMUNITY IN PRE-REVOLUTIONARY FRANCE

  Thomas Sheppard, Lourmarin in the Eighteenth Century (John Hopkins), chs 1-7

Jean-Louis Flandrin, Families in Former Times: Kinship, Household, and Sexuality (Cambridge), pp. 34-65, 92-145

Feb. 21 V. THE PEASANT COMMUNITY IN TRADITIONAL CHINA

Hsiao-t'ung Fei, Peasant Life in China (1938)

(First Essay Due. Topic: The Peasant Community in Traditional Society.)

Feb. 28 VI. PEASANT DISAFFECTION AND REBELLION IN FRANCE.

E. LeRoy Ladurie, "Rural Revolt and Protest Movements in France from 1675 to 1788," Studies in 18th Century Culture, Vol. V. (University of Wisconsin, 1976), 423-50

Georges Lefebvre, The Great Fear of 1789 (Princeton).

Woloch, ed., The Peasantry in the Old Regime, pp. 74-97

Mar. 6 VII. THE IMPACT OF THE FRENCH REVOLUTION

Georges Lefebvre, "The Place of the Revolution in the Agrarian History of France," In O. Ranum & R. Forster, eds., Rural Society in France: Selection from the Annales.

Albert Soboul, "The French Rural Community in the 18th and 19th Centuries," Past & Present, 1956, pp. 78-95. Reprinted in D. Johnson, ed., French Society and the Revolution.

Sheppard, Lourmarin in the Eighteenth Century, ch. 8

T.H. LeGoff and D. Sutherland, "Revolution and Rural Community in 18th Century Brittany," Past & Present, Feb., 1974, pp. 96-119. Reprinted in D. Johnson, ed., French Society and the Revolution.

Charles Tilly, "Civil Constitution and Counter-revolution in southern Anjou," French Historical Studies, 1959, 172-99.

Tilly, "Some Problems in the History of the Vendee," American Historical Review, LXVII (1961), 19-33.

Mar. 13   VACATION

Mar. 20 VIII. PEASANT DISAFFECTION AND REBELLION IN CHINA

Albert Feuerwerker, Rebellion in Nineteenth-Century China (Michigan Papers in Chinese Studies, 1975).

Susan Naquin, The Eight Trigrams Rebellion, pp. 1-60.

Elizabeth Perry, Rebels and Revolutionaries in North China (Stanford), chs. 1-5

(Second Essay Due. Topic: Peasant Uprisings)

Mar. 27 IX. DYNAMICS OF SOCIAL CHANGE IN CHINA

Maurice Meisner, Mao's China (Free Press), chs. 1-4

James Sheridan, China in Disintegration (Free Press), chs 1-4, 6.

Perry, Rebels and Revolutionaries, chs 6-7

Apr. 3 X. DYNAMICS OF SOCIAL CHANGE IN RURAL FRANCE

Eugen Weber, Peasants into Frenchman: The Modernization of Rural France, 1870-1914 (Stanford,) pages to be assigned.

Apr. 10 XI. VILLAGE LIFE IN REVOLUTIONARY CHINA

Meisner, Mao's China, chs. 8, 10, 14

C.K. Yang, A Chinese Village in Early Communist Transition. Reprinted in Yang, Chinese Communist Society: The Family and the Village (M.I.T.)

Apr. 17 XII VILLAGE LIFE IN MODERN FRANCE

Pierre-Jakez Helias, The Horse of Pride: Life in a Breton Village (Yale), chs. 1,3,4,6,7,8.

Weber, Peasants into Frenchmen, pp. 471-96

Apr. 24 XIII. RURAL SOCIETY IN CONTEMPORARY CHINA

William Parish and Martin Whyte, Village and Family in Contemporary China (Chicago,) chs. 4-6, 8-12

(Third Paper Due.) Topic: Social Change-Evolution and Revolution. The essay may be approached on a general or case-study basis, on a national or community level.

May 1 XIV CONCLUDING SESSION

Return of Essays; Recapitulation; Unanswered questions

The following texts should be purchased at the Columbia University Bookstore:

China:
    A. Feuerwerker, *State and Society in Eighteenth-Century China* (U. of Michigan).

    A. Feuerwerker, *Rebellion in Nineteenth-Century China* (U of Michigan)

    W. Parish & M. Whyte, *Village and Family in Contemporary China* (U. of Chicago).

    F. Perry, *Rebels and Revolutionaries in North China* (Stanford)

    C.K. Yang, *Chinese Communist Society: the Family and the Village* (M.I.T.)--if available (may be out of print)

France: M. Bloch, *French Rural History* (U. of California)

    P-J Helias, *The Horse of Pride: Life in a Breton Village* (Yale)

    G. Lefebvre, *The Great Fear of 1789* (Princeton).

    T. Sheppard, *Lourmarin in the Eighteenth Century* (Johns Hopkins)

    E. Weber - *Peasants into Frenchmen: The Modernization of Rural France, 1870-1914* (Stanford).

All other material will be on reserve -- the material on France at Butler Library Reserve Desk, and the material on China in the East Asian Library (Kent Hall). Though they will be on reserve, the following texts have also been ordered at the C.U. Bookstore:

    J.L. Flandrin, *Families in Former Times: Kinship, Household and Sexuality* (Cambridge)

    M. Meisner, *Mao's China* Free Press)

    J. Sheridan, *China in Disintegration* (Wadsworth)

    L.A. Thompson, *Chinese Religion* (Wadsworth)

    E. Wolf, *Peasants* (Prentice-Hall)

    I. Woloch, ed., *The Peasantry in the Old Regime* (Krieger)

About the Editor

Kevin Reilly is a founder of the World History Association and currently President-Elect. He is the author of <u>The West and the World: A Topical History of Civilization</u> (Harper & Row, 1980), a college text. He is also the editor of <u>The Introductory History Course: Six Models</u> (American Historical Association, 1984). He teaches at Somerset County College (N.J.) and lives in New York City.